D0375390

DANISH-ENGLISH
ENGLISH-DANISH

Dictionary & Phrasebook

Dictionary & Phrasebooks

Albanian
Arabic (Eastern)
Australian
Azerbaijani
Basque
Bosnian
Breton
British
Cajun
Chechen
Croatian
Danish
Esperanto
French
Georgian
German
Greek
Hebrew *romanized & script*
Igbo
Ilocano
Irish
Italian

Japanese *romanized*
Lao *romanized*
Lingala
Malagasy
Maltese
Pilipino (Tagalog)
Polish
Québécois
Romanian
Romansch
Russian
Shona
Slovak
Somali
Spanish (Latin American)
Swahili
Swedish
Tajik
Thai *romanized*
Turkish
Ukrainian

DANISH-ENGLISH
ENGLISH-DANISH
Dictionary & Phrasebook

ERNA MAJ

HIPPOCRENE BOOKS, INC.
New York

ISBN 0-7818-0917-7

For information, address:
Hippocrene Books, Inc.
171 Madison Avenue
New York, NY 10016

Cataloging-in-Publication data available from the Library of Congress.

Printed in the United States of America.

CONTENTS

INTRODUCTION TO DENMARK

With its main peninsula projecting into the North Sea from northern Germany and 400 islands scattered in its waters, this small democracy (constitutional monarchy) covers 16,630 square miles of flat land and is home to about 5.3 million people. Greenland and the Faeroe Islands are Danish territories with home rule. Denmark is a member of both NATO and the EU. Copenhagen is the capital and by far the largest urban area. The countryside primarily consists of farmland, and beautiful beaches stretch along the coasts. The climate is temperate with mild winters, cool summers, and a fair amount of precipitation. Given its northern location, midsummer daylight lasts until midnight, but around the winter solstice, daylight is limited to about seven hours, and the Danes scatter the darkness by lighting an abundance of candles. The Danes enjoy a very high standard of living, including free higher education and national health care, and they are well educated with a strong command of English. Denmark is known for its comprehensive welfare system, financed through high taxes. As a result of an influx of immigrant workers and refugees, Denmark has become a multiethnic society. Denmark is renown for its dairy, meat, and fish products, metal manufacturing, design, and significant export of machinery and furniture. Other Danish trademarks are a deep joy in the small pleasures of everyday existence and a very strong emphasis on *hygge*—domestic coziness and closeness in relationships, be they with friends or family.

THE DANISH LANGUAGE

Compared to English, with its 400 million native speakers, the Danish language is obviously a very small one. Danish, Icelandic, Norwegian, and Swedish comprise the North Germanic side of the Indo-European language family; Dutch, English, Flemish, Frisian, German, and Yiddish comprise the West Germanic side. Consequently, Danish and English have many similarities with respect to sounds, semantics, syntax, etc. These similarities will become obvious as you explore this book and visit Denmark, but as you will see in the grammar section below, Danish has remained a much more inflected language than English, and there are some significant differences in pronunciation. While visiting Denmark you may also discover that the Danes speak several 'languages' among themselves—the dialects can be very strong. The guidelines for pronunciation listed below refer to *rigsdansk* (standard pronunciation).

DANISH ALPHABET AND PRONUNCIATION

The Danish alphabet has 29 letters: a, b, c, d, e, f, g, h, i, j, k, l, m, n, o, p, q, r, s, t, u, v, w, x, y, z, æ, ø, å. The three letters unfamiliar to English speakers are vowels. Like English, Danish is not a phonetic language, and only a few words are onomatopoeic. A particular letter can have different pronunciations or be silent, and it is worth remembering that in many words the number of letters does not correspond with the number of sounds. For example, the English word *six* has three letters but four sounds (phonemes) /siks/.

All the languages of the world together consist of a limited set of speech sounds that are combined to represent meaning. When learning a foreign language, it is essential to examine how its smallest units of sound, *the phonemes*, are articulated when air passes through the vocal tract. Many phonemes are identical in English and Danish, but differences exist. Phonemes distinguish meaning. All native speakers of English intuitively know that 'pill' and 'bill' mean different things because their initial sounds differ. In Danish, /p/ and /b/ distinguish meaning as well—'pande' means 'forehead' whereas 'bande' means 'to swear'. However, Danish has distinguishing factors that are unfamiliar to a speaker of English. *Vowel length* distinguishes meaning. For example, 'vilde' /vilə/ with a short first vowel means 'wild', but 'hvile' /viːlə/ with a long first vowel means 'rest'. *The glottal stop*, during which the vocal cords are tightly closed, also distinguishes meaning. For example, 'men' /mæn/ without a glottal stop means 'but', whereas 'mænd' /mænʔ/ with a glottal stop means 'men'.

Various sets of phonetic symbols have been developed as an efficient tool for describing speech sounds. The symbols used below are primarily based on *Danias*

Lydskrift (the phonetic notation system usually used to transcribe Danish), developed years ago by the Danish linguist Otto Jespersen.

Consonants

Most of the consonants in Danish are very similar, if not identical, to their English counterparts.

/b/	As in **b**ottle, **b**u**bb**le	**b**ad (bath), **b**o**b**le (bubble)
/d/	As in **d**og, sen**d**, **d**oo**d**le	**d**reng (boy), me**d**alje (medal), sol**d**at (soldier)
/ð/	Similar to the 'th' in **th**e, brea**th**e, but the tip/blade of the tongue stays a bit farther back. Also, this sound does not occur as syllable-initial in Danish.	sø**d** (sweet), blø**d**e (bleed), bå**d** (boat)
/f/	As in **f**ish, cou**gh**, co**ff**ee	**f**isk (fish), gira**f** (giraffe), ka**ff**e (coffee)
/g/	As in **g**et, le**g**, a**g**riculture	**g**iftig (poisonous), **g**ik (went), **g**ul (yellow)
/g/	Semivowel similar to /j/, but articulated slightly farther back in the mouth. This sound does not occur in English, but it is similar to Spanish 'luego'.	ka**g**e (cake), fla**g** (flag), sæl**g**e (sell)

/h/	As in hat, who, rehabilitation. The letter 'h' is silent in Danish before 'v' and 'j' (except in certain dialects).	have (garden), hage (chin), halvvejs (halfway)
/j/	As in you, yellow	ja (yes), jeg (I)
/ʝ/	Similar to /j/, but whereas /ʝ/ has a relatively restricted airflow, /j/ is a semivowel.	hej (hi)
/k/	As in cat, kitchen, mechanic. Unlike in English, the letter 'k' is not silent before 'n'.	kat (cat), mælk (milk), kniv (knife)
/l/	Standard Danish only has the alveolar /l/ as in leaf and laugh. Some dialects also have the so-called velarized /ɫ/ as in feel and ball (also called 'dark l').	lyst (light), hul (hole), hals (neck)
/m/	As in man, stream, summer	mand (man), tom (empty), sommer (summer)
/n/	As in no, can, manners	nej (no), morgen (morning), eventyr (fairy tale)
/ŋ/	As in sing, finger, ankle	konge (king), dronning (queen), ting (thing)
/p/	As in pet, top, apple	pære (pear), pakke (parcel)

/r/	One type of Danish 'r' is produced by raising the back/root of the tongue and pulling it back toward the uvula. The tip of the tongue is curled downwards below the bottom teeth. The degree of lip rounding and the amount of friction vary, depending on the neighboring sounds.	rime (rhyme), rose (rose)
/ɹ/	Similar to 'r' in 'car'. This 'r' is a semivowel. The vocal tract is narrowed, but not to the extent that the airstream is obstructed. During /ɹ/ the greatest narrowing takes place in the pharynx. Also occurs with glottal stop.	mor (mother), færge (ferry), kirke (church), mord (murder ['d' is silent])
/s/	As in sunshine, grass, fasten	solskin (sunshine), græs (grass), cirkus (circus)
/t/	As in two, night	to (two), tag (roof)
/v/	As in valley, shove, gravel	vand (water), svinekød (pork)

/w/	As in **w**ater, **w**e. The sound /w/ is found in loanwords and in some Danish dialects. In loanwords, 'w' is most often pronounced /v/. The sound /w/ also occurs in diphthongs as an off-glide.	**w**eekend (weekend), **w**ebsted (web site)
/ʃ/	Similar to the sound in **sh**oe, fa**sh**ion, fi**sh**, but the airflow is less forceful, and the lips are not as rounded.	**sj**ælden (rare), **sh**ampo (shampoo), na**ti**on (nation)
/dʒ/	As in **j**u**dg**e, re**gi**on, **j**ello. The sound /dʒ/ occurs only in loanwords.	**j**azz, **j**eep
/r/	The so-called flap as the 'dd' in la**dd**er or the 'tt' in bo**tt**le. This consonant is characterized by a single rapid contact of the tongue against another point in the mouth.	sle**tt**e (delete), slu**dd**er (nonsense)

| /ʔ/ | Glottal stop. As described above, the glottal stop is a tight closure of the vocal cords. The glottal stop can occur with the vowel sounds, diphthongs and some consonants such as /gʔ, jʔ, lʔ, mʔ, nʔ, ŋʔ, ɹʔ, wʔ/. | sø (lake), løget (the onion), hund (dog ['d' is silent]) |

Vowels

Danish has more vowel sounds than English. As mentioned above, Danish vowels can have glottal stops or length as distinguishing features in addition to the ones used to describe the characteristics of English vowels: degree of backness in the mouth, height, and degree of lip rounding.

Front Vowels

/i/	As in English **see**, **eel**, **feet** (long). The sound occurs *long, short*, and with *glottal stop* with the exact same quality. /iː/ long: ile (hurry) /i/ short: ildebrand (fire) /iʔ/ with glottal stop: fil (file)
/y/	An /i/ with rounded lips as in German 'über' (long version). The sound does not occur in English. It occurs *long, short*, and with *glottal stop* with the exact same quality. /yː/ long: nyse (sneeze) /y/ short: drysse (sprinkle) /yʔ/ with glottal stop: bly (lead [metal])
/e/	Almost as in English **sin**, **mitt** (short version), but slightly lower. This sound occurs *long, short*, and with *glottal stop* with the exact same quality.

/e:/ long: mene (be of the opinion)
/e/ short: mindes (remember)
/eʔ/ with glottal stop: tre (three)

/ø/   An /e/ with rounded lips as in German 'hören' (long version). The sound does not occur in English. It occurs *long*, *short*, and with *glottal stop* with the exact same quality.
/ø:/ long: høre (hear)
/ø/ short: høste (harvest)
/øʔ/ with glottal stop: sø (lake)

/æ/   Almost as in English get, best. It occurs *long*, *short*, and with *glottal stop* with the exact same quality.
/æ:/ long: æble (apple)
/æ/ short: hælde (pour)
/æʔ/ with glottal stop: hæl (heel)

/ö/   An /æ/ with rounded lips. The sound does not occur in English. It occurs *long*, *short* and with *glottal stop* with the exact same quality.
/ö:/ long: høne (hen)
/ö/ short: søndag (Sunday)
/öʔ/ with glottal stop: frø (frog)

/ä/   Somewhat like English sand. In between /æ/ and /a/. Occurs only before or after 'r'. *Short* only.
/ä/ short: træffe (meet)

/ö̈/   An /ä/ with rounded lips. The sound does not occur in English. Occurs only before or after 'r'. It occurs *long*, *short* and with *glottal stop* with the exact same quality.
/ö̈:/ long: røre (touch)
/ö̈/ short: tør (dry)
/ö̈ʔ/ with glottal stop: påsmøre (smear on)

The Central Vowel

/ə/   As in English again, melody, danger. Neutral, always short vowel used in unstressed syllables.
/ə/ short: huse (houses)

The Back Vowels

/u/   As in English **roof**, **glue**, **too**. The sound occurs *long*, *short*, and with *glottal stop* with the exact same quality.
/u:/ long: p**u**de (pillow)
/u/ short: k**u**lde (cold)
/uʔ/ with glottal stop: j**u**l (Christmas)

/o/   Similar to the 'u' in p**u**ll or p**u**t, but slightly lower and with very rounded lips—the same lip position as in the end of saying the English word **go**. The sound occurs *long*, *short*, and with *glottal stop* with the exact same quality.
/o:/ long: k**o**ne (wife)
/o/ short: f**o**tografere (photograph)
/oʔ/ with glottal stop: s**o**l (sun)

/å/   Tongue and jaw position the same as in the sound of 'a' in **all** and 'l**a**w', but with rounded lips.
/å:/ long: m**å**ne (moon)
/å/ short: **o**nd (evil)
/åʔ/ with glottal stop: bl**å** (blue)

/ɔ/   The quality of this sound is between the sounds in English h**o**t and h**u**t. The sound occurs *long*, *short*, and with *glottal stop* with the exact same quality.
/ɔ:/ long: t**å**re (tear)
/ɔ/ short: d**o**ktor (doctor)
/ɔʔ/ with glottal stop: t**å**rn (steeple)

/á/   Similar to the 'a' in c**a**n, m**a**d, but a little lower. The sound occurs *long*, *short*, and with *glottal stop* with the exact same quality.
/á:/ long: h**a**ne (rooster)
/á/ short: k**a**nde (jar)
/áʔ/ with glottal stop: pl**a**n (plan)

/a/   The so-called Continental 'a' sound as often used in for example **man** in British accents. In between /á/ and /ɑ/. Usually only occurs *short* and with *glottal stop*.
/a/ short: k**a**ffe (coffee)
/aʔ/ with glottal stop: n**e**gl (nail)

/ɑ/   Like the 'a' in rather, marble, disaster. The sound occurs *long*, *short*, and with *glottal stop* with the exact same quality. Only occurs before or after 'r'.

/ɑ:/ long: rasende (furious)
/ɑ/ short: amme (breast-feed)
/ɑʔ/ with glottal stop: arm (arm)

Diphthongs

A diphthong uses the movement from a vowel to a semi-vowel within the same syllable as in boy (/ɔj/), tie (/aj/) and brown (/aw/). In Danish, the semivowels /j/, /w/ and /ɹ/ serve as off-glides, and /j/ serves as an on-glide. As the list below shows, Danish encompasses numerous diphthongs.

/uj/	huje (hoot, yell)
/ɔj/	tøj (clothes)
/aj/	mig (me)
/iw/	livlig (lively)
/aw/	sav (saw [tool])
/aw/	navn (name)
/åw/	låg (lid)
/ɔw/	ovn (oven)
/ew/	peber (pepper)
/äw/	revne (crack)
/æw/	evne (ability)
/öw/	støvle (boot)
/ȫw/	vrøvl (nonsense)
/øw/	døv (deaf)
/yw/	tyv (thief)
/iɹ/	spir (steeple)
/eɹ/	ser (see [present tense])
/uɹ/	sur (sour)
/oɹ/	sort (black)
/já/	ja (yes)
/jæ/	hjem (home)
/jo/	jord (soil)
/jɔ/	jomfru (virgin)
/ju/	jul (Christmas)

/jy/   **J**ylland (Jutland)
/jø/   **j**øde (Jew)

Spelling and Sound Values

Note! In this section, no distinction has been made between long, short, and with glottal stop.

A   This letter is pronounced as:
/á?/   /á/ as in apple [g**a**de/street]
         /a/ see description of sound above [k**a**ffe/coffee]
         /ɑ/ as in marble before and after 'r' [v**a**rm/warm]

B   This letter is pronounced as:
/be?/   /b/ as in **b**oy in most words [**b**old/ball]
         /w/ as in **w**ater in a few words (as part of the diphthong /ew/) [pe**b**er/pepper]

C   This letter only occurs in word of foreign
/se?/   origin and is pronounced as:
         /s/ as in **c**igarette [**c**igar/cigar]
         /ʃ/ as in **sh**oe in combinations such as 'ch' and 'tion' [**ch**okolade/chocolate]

D   This letter is pronounced as:
/de?/   /d/ as in **d**og in initial position, before a stressed
         vowel, and sometimes when doubled.
         [**d**reng/boy; i**d**e/idea; bre**dd**e/width]
         /ð/ almost as in **th**e (see description of sound
         above) in front of an unstressed vowel or in
         final position. [si**dd**e/sit; blø**d**/soft]
         /r/ as in la**dd**er sometimes when doubled
         [slu**dd**er/nonsense]
         Sometimes *silent*: before 't' [li**d**t/a little],
         before 's' [pla**d**s/space], after 'n' [hun**d**/dog],
         after 'l' [luneful**d**/capricious], after 'r'
         [fjer**d**e/fourth], before 'k' [sne**d**ker/fine trim
         carpenter], colloquially in a number of words,
         and always in *sagde* (said) and *lagde* (laid).

E   This letter is pronounced as:
/e?/   /e/ see description of sound above [s**e**n/late]
         /æ/ almost as in g**e**t (see description of sound
         above) [b**e**dst/best]

/ɑ/ before or after 'r' (see description of sound above) [stjerne/star]

/ə/ as in melody in unstressed positions only [huse/houses]

/a/ in many combinations with 'j' and 'g' (as part of the diphthong /aj/) [nej/no]

/i/ in the two personal pronouns *de* and *De* and the plural definite article *de* (short sound)

F
/æf/

This letter is pronounced as:

/f/ as in fine [fisk/fish]

/w/ as in water in the prefix *af-* (as part of the diphthong /aw/) [afinstallere/uninstall]

Silent in the preposition *af*

G
/geʔ/

This letter is pronounced as:

/g/ as in goose [gå/walk]

/g/ see description of sound above [bage/bake]

/j/ in some combinations 'eg', 'øg', and 'ig' (as part of the diphthongs /aj/ and /ɔj/) [løg/onion]

/ʃ/ almost as in shoe (see description of sound above) in some French loanwords [bagage/luggage]

Silent in a great number of words [spurgte/asked]

H
/hɑʔ/

This letter is pronounced as:

/h/ as in hat [hoved/head]

Silent before 'j' and 'v' [hjem/home; hvem/who]

I
/iʔ/

This letter is pronounced as:

/i/ as in seat [time/hour]

/e/ see description of sound above [kvinde/woman]

/a/ in the words 'mig', 'dig', and 'sig' (as part of the diphthongs /aj/)—see description of sound above [mig/me]

J
/jɔð/

This letter is pronounced as:

/j/ as in yellow [ja/yes]

/ʃ/ almost as in shoe in the combination 'sj' and in French loanwords [sjælden/rare]

/j/ as part of the diphthong /aj/ [maj/May]

Silent in some words [vejr/weather]

K
/kå?/ This letter is pronounced as:
/k/ as in **k**ey [**k**age/cake]
/g/ as in **g**o after 's' [s**k**ole/school; medially
before a consonant [fa**k**tum/fact]; before /ə/,
/əɹ/, and /ən/ [tæn**k**e/think]
/ɟ/ in the word 'se**k**sten' (as part of the
diphthong /aɟ/)
*This letter is NOT silent in the combination
'kn'. [**k**niv/knife]

L
/æl/ This letter is pronounced as:
/l/ as in **l**eaf [**l**ivlig/lively] – see description above
Silent colloquially in some words and always in
the word 'nog**l**e'

M
/æm/ This letter is pronounced as:
/m/ as in **m**an [**m**ulig/possible]

N
/æn/ This letter is pronounced as:
/n/ as in **n**ose [**n**æse/nose]
/ŋ/ as in ki**n**g when occurring before 'g' or 'k'
[ko**n**ge/king; læ**n**ke/chain]
Silent colloquially in some words

O
/o?/ This letter is pronounced as:
/o/ see description of sound above [p**o**se/bag]
/ɔ/ as in c**au**se [k**o**mme/come]
/å/ see description of sound above [t**o**g/train]

P
/pe?/ This letter is pronounced as:
/p/ as in **p**lay [**p**åskeæg/Easter egg]
/b/ as in **b**oy after 's' [s**p**ille/play]; medially
before a consonant [ka**p**sel/bottle cap];
before /ə/, /əɹ/, and /ən/ [gru**pp**e/group]

Q
/ku?/ This letter is pronounced as:
/k/ as in **k**ey (only occurs in loanwords)
[**q**uilte/quilt]

R
/är/ This letter is pronounced as:
/r/ see description of sound above [**r**is/rice]
/ɹ/ see description of sound above
[bje**r**g/mountain]

S
/æs/ This letter is pronounced as:
/s/ as in **s**un [**s**ol/sun]
/ʃ/ as in **sh**oe in the combination 'sj' [**sj**æl/soul]

T
/te?/   This letter is pronounced as:
         /t/ as in took when syllable initial or in final
            position after a vowel [tag/roof]
         /d/ as in dog after 's' [stige/ladder]; medially
            before /ə/, /ən/, and /əɹ/ [katten/the cat];
            medially before /s/ and /ʃ/ [dets/its]; and
            before the ending -ig [uartig/naughty]
         /ð/ almost as in the (see description of sound
            above) in the ending -et [huset/the house]
         /ʃ/ as in shoe in the ending -tion
            [operation/operation]
         Silent in some words [det/it]

U
/u?/   This letter is pronounced as:
         /u/ as in boot [hus/house]
         /å/ see description of sound above [dukke/doll]
         /y/ in French loanwords – see description of
            sound above [parfume/perfume]

V
/ve?/   This letter is pronounced as:
         /v/ as in very [vente/wait]
         /w/ as in water as part of several diphthongs –
            see list above [syv/seven]
         Silent: always in the word 'havde' [havde/had];
         frequently after 'l' [gulv/floor]; often in the
         colloquial pronunciation of a number of words
         [givet/given]

W
/dɔbəl   /v/ as in very and only occurs in words of
ve?/   foreign origin [watt/watt]
         /w/ as in water by many Danes as more and
            more English words enter the Danish
            language [websted/web site]

X
/æks/   This letter is pronounced as:
         /ks/ as in extra [Tampax/Tampax]
         /s/ as in xerox [xylofon/xylophone]

Y
/y?/   This letter is pronounced as:
         /y/ see description of sound above [nyde/enjoy]
         /ø/ see description of sound above [kysse/kiss]
         /ö/ after 'r' [tryk/push]
         /ɔ/ in the word 'fyrre' [fyrre/forty]

| Z | This letter is pronounced as: |
| /sæt/ | /s/ as in sun and only occurs in words of foreign origin [zoologisk have/zoo] |

Æ	This letter is pronounced as:
/æ?/	/æ/ almost as in bet [æble/apple]
	/ɑ/ before or after 'r' – see description of sound above [præstegård/vicarage]

Ø	This letter is pronounced as:
/ø?/	/ø/ see description of sound above [kød/meat]
	/ö/ see description of sound above [skrøbelig/fragile]
	/ɔ/ before or after 'r' – see description of sound above [grøn/green]
	/ɔ/ as in cause in most, but not all instances of the combinations 'øj' [tøj/clothes] and 'øg' [løg/onion] (as part of the diphthong /ɔj/)

Å	This letter is pronounced as:
/å?/	/å/ see description of sound above [råbe/shout]
	/ɔ/ as in cause [tårn/tower]
	Note! This letter used to be written 'aa', and this old-fashioned orthographic presentation can still be found in geographical and personal names.

Stress and Intonation

In most Danish words, the stress is on the first syllable (in compounds, too). The main exceptions are: loanwords, especially of Greek, Latin, or French origin; words with feminine endings *(-esse, -inde)*, all words beginning with the prefixes *be-*, *er-*, *ge-*, and *for-* (except when *for-* means 'front' or 'fore', or 'before'), and several Danish geographical names. Stress can distinguish meaning in Danish. For example, the words *'billigst* (cheapest) and *bi'list* (motorist) contain the exact same sounds, but in *billigst* the first syllable is stressed, in *bilist* the second syllable carries the main stress. Stress on a syllable can also be used for emphasis or contrast. The stress may change when prefixes or suffixes are added to a word. As in English, when a word is pronounced in isolation, at least one syllable is fully stressed with no reduction in vowel quality (strong form). In connected speech, however, many changes take place. Vowels may be reduced or disappear, consonants may be altered or disappear (weak form). In other words, a given word is not always pronounced exactly the same way. For example, *mig* (me) would be /maj/ in its strong form and only /ma/ in its weak form. English and Danish intonation patterns are similar, and like in English, changes in intonation can change the meaning of a sentence.

BASIC DANISH GRAMMAR

Word Formation

The following two sections provide a rudimentary description of the main word classes and the inflectional and derivational rules that apply to them. Inflectional markers are affixes that never change a word's class, but convey grammatical information such as case, number, gender, tense, person, voice, etc. In English, for example, the past tense inflectional marker is -ed for regular verbs. Derivational markers purvey semantic information and often alter the word class. In English, for example, adding the derivational morpheme -dom to the adjective *free* results in the noun *freedom*.

Inflectional Rules

Nouns

Nouns are either common or neuter in gender and singular or plural in number. Gender is extremely important as it is reflected in, for example, the indefinite article, the definite form, demonstrative pronouns, and adjective endings. Gender must be memorized along with each individual noun.

Indefinite form

Common nouns have the indefinite article *en*, and neuter nouns have the indefinite article *et*.

en dreng (a boy)
en pige (a girl)
et hus (a house)
et træ (a tree)

Definite form

Sometimes the definite form is created by moving the article to the end of the noun.

en dreng   drengen (the boy)
en pige   pigen (the girl)
et hus   huset (the house)
et træ   træet (the tree)

Sometimes a definite article precedes an adjective/noun combination. In this case, the definite article *den* is used for common gender, singular nouns; the definite article *det* is used for neuter gender, singular nouns; and the definite article *de* is used for plural nouns. Regardless of gender and number the adjective ending is then *-e*, and no ending is added to the noun (except possibly a plural marker).

en dreng	**Den** store dreng er ...	(The big boy is ...)
en pige	**Den** store pige er ...	(The big girl is ...)
et hus	**Det** store hus er ...	(The big house is ...)
et træ	**Det** store træ er ...	(The big tree is ...)
træer	**De** store træer er ...	(The big trees are ...)

Number (singular and plural)

The indefinite plural is formed by adding an inflectional suffix to the singular, indefinite noun.
If the noun ends with a consonant, the ending is usually *-e*.
If the noun ends with a vowel, the ending is usually *-r* or *-er*.

The definite plural is formed by adding *-ne* to the indefinite plural.

Singular/ Indefinite	*Singular/ Definite*	*Plural/ Indefinite*	*Plural/ Definite*
en dreng	drengen	drenge	drengene
et hus	huset	huse	husene
en pige	pigen	piger	pigerne
et træ	træet	træer	træerne

Small irregularities exist, and the same is true for a number of totally irregular nouns.

Compound nouns

The Danish language contains a tremendous number of compound nouns, and they are often very long words.

The gender follows the last part of a compound noun. For example, the word *ultralydsundersøgelsesapparatur* consists of *ultralyd* (ultrasound), *undersøgelse* (examination), *s* (a so-called *fuge-s* is often added to the compound nouns to facilitate easier pronunciation), and *apparatur* (equipment).

Possessive/Genitive

In general, the possessive is formed by adding *-s* to a noun (or by using a possessive adjective or pronoun).

Pigens hår var brunt.	The girl's hair was brown.
Drengens cykel var blå.	The boy's bicycle was blue.
Husets øverste etage ...	The top floor of the house ...

As in English, specific rules for forming the possessive apply if a noun ends with the sound /s/, or if we are dealing with abbreviations or acronyms. Without going into detail, the following examples illustrate some of the rules.

Jens' (Jens's) cykel er grøn.	Jens' bicycle is green.
Karl Marx' (Marx's) skrifter er interessante.	Karl Marx's writings are interesting.
USA's præsident	the president of the United States
NATOs omdømme/ NATO's omdømme	NATO's reputation

Adjectives

Adjectives describe nouns, and adjective endings in Danish must match the gender and number of the noun.

Adjective endings

If a singular noun is common gender (*en*), no ending is added to the adjective.

en stor dreng (a big boy)	Drengen er stor. (The boy is big.)
en ung pige (a young girl)	Pigen er ung. (The girl is young.)

If a singular noun is neuter gender (*et*), *-t* is added to the adjective. However, the *-t* is not normally added to adjectives that end in *-sk*.

et stort hus (a big house)	Huset er stort. (The house is big.)
et ungt træ (a young tree)	Træet er ungt. (The tree is young.)

If a noun is plural, or a word indicates a number other than one, *-e* is added to the adjective.

to store huse (two big houses)	Husene er store. (The houses are big.)
to unge drenge (two young boys)	Drengene er unge. (The boys are young.)

ingen store huse (no big houses)
mange unge drenge (many young boys)
Store sky**er** kom. (Big clouds came.)

If an adjective is placed between a definite article and a noun, the adjective ending is always *-e* regardless of gender and number.

Den unge pige er ...	(The young girl is ...)
Det store træ er ...	(The big tree is ...)
De store huse er ...	(The big houses are ...)

Comparison

As in English, you compare Danish adjectives by using endings, or for longer words by using *mere/mest* (more/most). As in English, a few adjectives are irregular.

Positive	Comparative (*-ere*)	Superlative (*-est*)
smuk (beautiful)	smuk**kere**	smuk**kest**
kold (cold)	kold**ere**	kold**est**
varm (warm)	varm**ere**	varm**est**
fantasifuld (imaginative)	**mere** fantasifuld	**mest** fantasifuld
interesseret (interested)	**mere** interesseret	**mest** interesseret
kompliceret (complicated)	**mere** kompliceret	**mest** kompliceret

god (good)	**bedre**	**bedst**
ung (young)	**yngre**	**yngst**
gammel (old)	**ældre**	**ældst**

Adverbs

Adverbs can describe verbs, adjectives or other adverbs. Some adverbs, such as *aldrig* (never) and *naturligvis* (of course), are "pure" and do not normally change form. Others are formed by adding *-t* to an adjective.

Hun var smuk. (She was beautiful.)
Hun var smukt klædt på. (She was beautifully dressed.)

A distinction is made between *mådesbiord* (manner adverbs) and *gradsbiord* (degree adverbs). If an adverb is a manner adverb, *-t* is added; if an adverb is a degree adverb, *-t* is optional. The ending *-t* is optional on adverbs that come from adjectives ending in *-vis*. The *-t* is optional on many adverbs of time. The *-t* is not normally added to adjectives that end in *-sk*.

Han kørte frygteligt. (He drove awfully.) – manner
    adverb
Han kørte frygtelig(t) dårligt. (He drove awfully badly.)
    – degree adverb/manner adverb
Det skal gøres gradvis(t). (It must be done gradually.)
    – adverb formed from an adjective ending in *-vis*
Du skal stå tidlig(t) op. (You must get up early.)
    – adverb of time

Comparison

Adverbs follow the same rules for comparison as adjectives do.

Han gik stærkt. (He walked quickly.)
Han gik stærkere end konen. (He walked **more** quickly
    than his wife.)
Han var den i gruppen, der gik stærkest. (He was the
    one in the group who walked **most** quickly.)

Verbs

Just like their English counterparts, Danish verbs appear
in various tenses that are based on the infinitive/stem, but
unlike English verbs they do not reflect number.

Infinitive/Stem

at spise (to eat); stem: spis
at arbejde (to work); stem: arbejd
at sige (to say); stem: sig

Imperative

The imperative is identical with the stem of a verb.
Occasionally, this creates an awkward word, in which
case the sentence must be restructured (usually by using
the passive voice).

spis (eat)
arbejd (work)
sig (say)

Present tense

The present tense is formed by adding *-er* to the stem.

jeg spis**er** (I eat)	jeg arbejd**er** (I work)	jeg sig**er** (I say)
du spis**er** (you eat)	du arbejd**er**	du sig**er**
han etc. spis**er** (he etc. eats)	han etc. arbejd**er**	han etc. sig**er**
vi spis**er** (we eat)	vi arbejd**er**	vi sig**er**
I spis**er** (you eat)	I arbejd**er**	I sig**er**
de spis**er** (they eat)	de arbejd**er**	de sig**er**

Past tense

Past tense endings for regular verbs fall into three categories:

I. In some cases, *-te* is added to the stem of the verb.

  jeg spis**te** (I ate)
  du spis**te**

han, hun, den, det spis**te**
vi spis**te**
I spis**te**
de spis**te**

II. In some cases, **-ede** is added to the stem of the verb.

jeg arbejd**ede** (I worked)
du arbejd**ede**
han, hun, den, det arbejd**ede**
vi arbejd**ede**
I arbejd**ede**
de arbejd**ede**

III. Some verbs are irregular. The past and perfect tenses have been listed with the individual irregular verbs in this book. With regular verbs, only the past tense ending has been listed.

jeg sagde (I said)
du sagde
han, hun, den, det sagde
vi sagde
I sagde
de sagde

Perfect and past perfect tenses

The auxiliary verbs *at være* (to be) and *at have* (to have) are used to create the perfect and past perfect tenses. The main verb generally has the ending *-t*, but exceptions do occur.

The Perfect

jeg **har** spist (I have eaten)	... **har** arbejdet (I have worked)	... **har** sagt (I have said)
du **har** spist	... **har** arbejdet	... **har** sagt
han, hun, den, det **har** spist	... **har** arbejdet	... **har** sagt
vi **har** spist	... **har** arbejdet	... **har** sagt
I **har** spist	... **har** arbejdet	... **har** sagt
de **har** spist	... **har** arbejdet	... **har** sagt

<u>The Past Perfect</u>

jeg **havde** spist	... **havde** arbejdet	... **havde** sagt
(I had eaten)	(I had worked)	(I had said)
du **havde** spist	... **havde** arbejdet	... **havde** sagt
han, hun, den,	... **havde** arbejdet	... **havde** sagt
det **havde** spist		
vi **havde** spist	... **havde** arbejdet	... **havde** sagt
I **havde** spist	... **havde** arbejdet	... **havde** sagt
de **havde** spist	... **havde** arbejdet	... **havde** sagt

Auxiliary verbs

Auxiliary verbs are used to form the various tenses and the passive voice. There is, however, no equivalent of the English auxiliary verb 'to do'. Questions and negations are formed through word order. (See section on syntax below.)

at være	at have	at blive
(to be)	(to have)	(to become)
jeg er (I am)	jeg har (I have)	jeg bliver (I become)
jeg var (I was)	jeg havde (I had)	jeg blev (I became)
jeg har været (I have been)	jeg har haft (I have had)	jeg er blevet (I have become)

Modal verbs

at ville (would)	at skulle (must)	at kunne (could)
jeg vil	jeg skal	jeg kan
jeg ville	jeg skulle	jeg kunne
jeg har villet	jeg har skullet	jeg har kunnet

at måtte (may)	at turde (dare)	at burde (should/ought to)
jeg må	jeg tør	jeg bør
jeg måtte	jeg turde	jeg burde
jeg har måttet	jeg har turdet	jeg har burdet

Future tense

The present tense is often used to express future tense, and so are some of the modal verbs as well as the verb *at blive* (to become).

Hvad tid spiser vi? (What time are we eating?)
Hvad tid skal vi spise? (What time will we be eating?)
Hvornår bliver det mørkt? (When does it get dark?)

Active and passive voice

As in English, it is possible to choose active or passive voice. There are two ways of making verbs passive in Danish:
• Analytic passive: by using *at blive* as an auxiliary verb in combination with the perfect.
• Synthetic passive: by adding the ending *-es* to the stem of a verb.

As in English, the direct object from the active sentence becomes subject in the passive sentence, and the subject from the active sentence is omitted or becomes part of a prepositional phrase at the end of the sentence.

Active: Jens kører Karen i skole. (Jens drives Karen to school.)
Passive I: Karen **bliver** kørt i skole **af** Jens. (Karen is driven to school by Jens.)
Passive II: Karen kø**res** i skole **af** Jens. (Karen is driven to school by Jens.)

Active: Drengen passer sin hund. (The boy looks after his dog.)
Passive I: Hunden **bliver** passet **af** drengen. (The dog is looked after by the boy.)
Passive II: Hunden pass**es af** drengen. (The dog is looked after by the boy.)

Danish also has types of passive voice unfamiliar to the speaker of English:
• Impersonal passive: Der må ikke klapp**es** i kirken. (*There must not be clapped in church/There is no clapping in church.)

- Deponent verbs: Træerne **grønnes** om foråret. (*The trees are greened in the spring/The trees turn green in the spring.)
- Middle voice: Hun fryder sig over det gode vejr. (She is delighted with the good weather.)

Subjunctive/Conditional mood

The conditional mood is formed by using auxiliary and modal verbs or the past tense.

Jeg **ville** komme, hvis jeg **havde** tid. (I would come if I had time.)

Jeg **kunne** gøre det, hvis jeg **havde** en skruetrækker. (I could do it if I had a screwdriver.)

Jeg **ville** ikke have gjort det, hvis jeg **havde** vidst bedre. (I would not have done it, had I known better.)

Hvis bare jeg **havde** 100 kr. (If only I had 100 kr.)

Hvis bare jeg **var** rask. (If only I were healthy.)

Tense and aspect

As in English, the different tenses are used to place an event or state in relation to the time of speaking; aspect is used to describe the type of event or state, for example whether the event is still going on or already finished. The use of tense and aspect differs slightly between English and Danish.

Present tense
- Used to describe future events: Hvornår ankommer gæsterne? (When will the guests arrive?)
- Used to describe general events: Han læser meget avis. (He reads the newspaper a lot.)
- Used to describe ongoing events: Han arbejder i haven. (He is working in the garden.)

Progressive
As mentioned above, Danish generally uses the present tense to describe ongoing events where English uses the progressive, but the progressive can be formed in Danish in two ways:
- By using 'sidder og' (sits and), 'ligger og' (lies and), 'går og' (walks and), 'står og' (stands and) + present tense: Hun sidder og læser avis. (She is sitting and

reading the newspaper.) Han går og arbejder i haven. (He is walking around and working in the yard.)

- By using 'ved at', 'i færd med', 'i gang med' + infinitive: Jeg er ved at skrive et brev til min moster. (I am writing a letter to my aunt.) Han er i gang med at reparere taget. (He is repairing the roof.) These expressions mean 'is in the middle of/in the process of'.

<u>Simple Past</u>
- Used to describe an event finished or a state terminated at a certain point in time prior to the time of speaking: Jeg betalte regningen i tirsdags. (I paid the bill last Tuesday.)
- Used to express surprise or caution: Det var altså en skam! (That really is a pity!)
- Used to be polite: Jeg ville høre, om bogen er kommet? (I wanted to ask if the book has come in?)

<u>Present/Past Perfect</u>
- Used to describe a finished event or a state terminated prior to the time of speaking, but the time is unknown: Hvor har du købt de sko? (Where have you bought those shoes?/Where did you buy those shoes?)
- Used to describe an event or a state initiated prior to the time of speaking but continuing into the present: Hun har arbejdet som sygeplejerske i næsten 20 år. (She has worked as a nurse for almost 20 years.)

Pronouns

Many of the pronouns clearly indicate the gender and number of the noun they modify or replace:

Pronoun ending in *-n* ~ common gender singular (noun has the indefinite article *en*)
Pronoun ending in *-t* ~ neuter gender singular (noun has the indefinite article *et*)
Pronoun ending in *-e* ~ plural

Personal pronouns

jeg (I)
du (you)

han/hun/den, det (he/she/it)*
vi (we)
I (you)
de (they)

*'It' has two forms: den (for common gender nouns) and det (for neuter gender nouns).

Possessive adjectives/pronouns

min, mit, mine (my/mine)
din, dit, dine (your/yours)
hans, hendes, dens, dets, sin, sit, sine (his/her(s)/its)
vores – more formal: vor, vort, vore (our/ours)
jeres (your/yours)
deres (their/theirs)

Hans/hendes/dens/dets/deres vs. sin/sit/sine

Sin, sit, sine are possessive adjectives that refer to a 3rd person singular subject. For referring to the 3rd person plural, *deres* is used regardless of the word's grammatical role. *Sin, sit, sine* do not function as possessive pronouns, i.e. they do not stand alone.

Han brækkede **sin** arm.	He broke **his** arm. (his own arm)
Han brækkede **hans** arm.	He broke **his** arm. (some other male's arm)
Hunden er **hendes**.	The dog is **hers**.
De tog **deres** børn med.	They brought **their** children.

Demonstrative pronouns

Den pige er stor.	That girl is big. (common gender singular)
Det hus er stort.	That house is big. (neuter gender singular)
De huse er store.	Those houses are big. (plural)
Denne pige er stor.	This girl is big. (common gender singular)
Dette hus er stort.	This house is big. (neuter gender singular)
Disse huse er store.	These houses are big. (plural)

Reflexive pronouns

Reflexive pronouns do not change according to person and number, but must be chosen according to context.

Selv
Han gjorde det **selv**. (He did it himself.)
Han vaskede **selv** bilen. (He washed the car himself.)

Sig
Hun klædte **sig** på. (She got dressed.)
Han vaskede **sig**. (He washed himself.)

*It can often be difficult for the non-native speaker to tell the difference between *sig* used as a reflexive pronoun versus as part of a middle voice construction. (See page 27.)

Sig selv
Han grinede ad **sig selv**. (He laughed at himself.)
Hun så på **sig selv** i spejlet. (She looked at herself in the mirror.)

Relative pronouns

Danish has two relative pronouns: *som* and *der*. If the relative pronoun is the subject in the sentence, it is equally correct to use *som* or *der*. If the pronoun is anything but the subject, only *som* can be used.

Manden, **der/som** (subject) boede i huset, var gammel.
(The man, who lived in the house, was old.)
Manden, **som** (object) jeg så på gaden, er min fætter.
(The man, whom I saw in the street, is my cousin.)

Interrogative pronouns

hvem (who)
hvad (what)
hvor (where)
hvordan (how)
hvorfor (why)
hvornår (when)

Derivational Rules

Some examples are:

- Antonyms can be formed by adding the prefix **u-**:

tålmodig (patient)	**u**tålmodig (impatient)
væsentlig (important)	**u**væsentlig (unimportant)
gunst (favor)	**u**gunst (disfavor)

- Nouns can be formed by adding the suffixes **-dom** or **-hed** or **-skab** to an adjective:

vis (wise)	vis**dom** (wisdom)
hellig (holy)	hellig**dom** (holiness)
fri (free)	fri**hed** (freedom)
dum (stupid)	dum**hed** (stupidity)
gal (mad)	gal**skab** (madness)
klog (wise)	klog**skab** (wisdom)

- Nouns can be formed by adding the suffix **-eri** to the stem of a verb:

male (paint)	mal**eri** (painting)
rode (make a mess)	rod**eri** (mess)

- Adjectives can be formed by adding the suffix **-elig** to another adjective, a noun or the stem of a verb:

ædru (sober)	ædru**elig** (sober)
jomfru (virgin)	jomfru**elig** (virginal)
påstå (state)	påstå**elig** (opinionated)

- Adjectives can be formed by adding the suffix **-agtig** to a noun:

barn (child)	barn**agtig** (childish)
nar (fool)	nar**agtig** (foolish)

- Adjectives can be formed by adding the suffix **-bar** to the stem of a verb:

bruge (use)	brug**bar** (useable)
justere (adjust)	juster**bar** (adjustable)

Syntax

Sentence structure

A Danish statement basically has the same structure as an English statement.

Jens gik i skole. (Jens went to school.)
Hun drikker kaffe. (She drinks coffee.)
Du er smuk. (You are beautiful.)

No auxiliary verb is used to form a negative statement. In a negative sentence, the word *ikke* is simply added.

Jens gik ikke i skole. (Jens did not go to school.)
Hun drikker ikke kaffe. (She does not drink coffee.)
Du er ikke smuk. (You are not beautiful.)

No auxiliary verb is used to form a question. To form a question the order of the subject and verb is simply reversed.

Gik Jens i skole? (Did Jens go to school?)
Drikker hun kaffe? (Does she drink coffee?)
Er du smuk? (Are you beautiful?)

Subordinate clauses are abundant in Danish as sentences are often very long. In a subordinate clause, the word *ikke* is placed between the subject and verb.

Jeg ved, at Jens ikke gik i skole. (I know that Jens did not go to school.)
Hun sagde, at hun ikke drikker kaffe. (She said that she does not drink coffee.)

Punctuation

Most Danish punctuation marks are used the same way as their English equivalents. The comma is the exception. There is now a new comma system (*nyt komma*) that is similar in usage to the English comma, but the traditional comma system (*grammatisk komma*) is still the most common one. In this system, a comma is used to separate subordinate clauses every time there is a subject and a verb.

Huset, der brændte, lå ved siden af skolen. (The house that burned was located next to the school.)

Den dame, jeg så i toget, var vores nabo, da jeg var barn. (The lady I saw on the train was our neighbor when I was growing up.)

ABBREVIATIONS

adj.	adjective
adv.	adverb
art.	article
conj.	conjunction
geog.	geographical
interj.	interjection
intr.	intransitive
n.	noun
num.	numeral
pl. same	indefinite, plural form same as the indefinite, singular form
pre.	present tense
pref.	prefix
prep.	preposition
pron.	pronoun
sing.	singular
tr.	transitive
v.	verb

DICTIONARY FORMAT

Nouns

majestæt *n.:* *-en, pl. -er* majesty; **Hendes Majestæt Dronning Margrethe II** Her Majesty Queen Margrethe II

majestæt = Danish word
n. = noun
-en = ending definite form, singular
pl. = plural
-er = ending indefinite form, plural
majesty = English translation
Hendes Majestæt Dronning Margrethe II = example of usage
Her Majesty Queen Margrethe II = translation of example

Verbs

marinere *v.:* *-ede* marinate, pickle; **marinerede sild** pickled herring

marinere = Danish word
v. = verb
-ede = past tense ending—gets added to the stem of the verb (in this case *mariner*)
marinate, pickle = English translation
marinerede sild = example of usage
pickled herring = translation of example

sige *v.:* *sagde, sagt* say

sige = Danish word
v. = verb
sagde = past tense (irregular verb)
sagt = perfect tense (irregular verb)
say = English translation

DANISH-ENGLISH DICTIONARY

A

abe *n.: -n, pl. -r* monkey

abort *n.: -en, pl. -er* abortion;
provokeret abort
(induced) abortion;
spontan abort
miscarriage; **fri abort**
legal abortion

abstrakt *adj.* abstract;
abstrakt kunst abstract art

adel *n.: -en* nobility;
adelsmand nobleman;
adelsdame noblewoman

adelig *adj.* noble; **af adelig
herkomst** of noble
descent

adgang *n.: -en, pl. -e*
admission, access

adgangsbillet *n.: -ten, pl. -ter*
admission ticket

adresse *n.: -n, pl. -r* address

adresseændring *n.: -en,
pl. -er* change of address

adskillige *adj.* several, many,
quite a few

advare *v.: -ede* warn, caution

advarsel *n.: -en* or *advarslen,
pl. advarsler* warning

advent *n.: -en, pl. -er* Advent;
adventskrans *n.: -en,
pl. -e* wreath with four
candles used for Advent

advokat *n.: -en, pl. -er*
lawyer, attorney;
advokatvirksomhed law
firm

afbestille *v.: -te* cancel;
afbestilling *n.: -en, pl. -er*
cancellation

afbryde *v.: afbrød, afbrudt*
interrupt, disconnect,
cut off

afbud *n.: -det, pl. same*
cancellation; **at sende
afbud** to cancel (meeting
or visit)

afdeling *n.: -en, pl. -er*
department; hospital ward

afdød *adj.* deceased

affald *n.: -et* trash

afgang *n.: -en, pl. -e* departure

afgift *n.: -en, pl. -er* fee, toll

afgrøde *n.: -n, pl. -r* crop

afgøre *v.: afgjorde, afgjort*
decide, determine

afgå *v.: afgik, afgået* depart

afhente *v.: -ede* pick up

afkølet *adj.* chilled

aflevere *v.: -ede* return, turn
in; pass (a ball);
afleveringsfrist deadline

aflyse *v.: -te* cancel

afløb *n.: -et, pl. same* drain

afsender *n.: -en, pl. -e* sender

afsidesliggende *adj.* remote

afstand *n.: -en, pl. -e* distance

aftage *v.: aftog, aftaget* abate

aftale *n.: -n, pl. -r* agreement;
appointment

aften *n.: -en, pl. -er* evening

aftenkaffe *n.: -n* evening
coffee

aftensmad *n.: -en* dinner

akavet *adj.* awkward

al/alt *adj.* all, everything

alder *n.: -en, pl. aldre* age

aldrig *adv.* never

alene *adj.* alone

alkohol *n.: -en* alcohol;
alkoholiker *n.: -en, pl. -e*
alcoholic

allerede *adv.* already

alligevel *adv.* anyway
almindelig *adj.* common, plain
alter *n.:* *-et, pl. altre* altar
altid *adv.* forever; all the time
alting *pron.* everything
ambassade *n.:* *-n, pl. -r* embassy
ambulance *n.:* *-n, pl. -r* ambulance
amme *v.:* *-ede* breast-feed
anbefale *v.:* *-ede* recommend
andelsbevægelse *n.:* *-n, pl. -r* cooperative movement (common type of ownership in Denmark)
anderledes *adj.* different
angribe *v.:* *angreb, angrebet* attack
anholde *v.:* *anholdt, anholdt* arrest, take into custody
anklage for *v.:* *-ede* accuse of
ankomme *v.:* *ankom, ankommet* arrive; **ankomst** *n.:* *-en, pl. -er* arrival
anlæg *n.:* *-get, pl. same* park, garden
anmeldelse *n.:* *-n, pl. -r* review
anstændig *adj.* decent, proper
ansvar *n.:* *-et* responsibility; **ansvarlig** *adj.* responsible
antal *n.:* *-let* number; **antal gæster** number of guests
antik *adj.* antique; **antikviteter** antiques
apotek *n.:* *-et, pl. -er* pharmacy
appetit *n.:* *-ten* appetite
april *n.* April
arbejde *v.:* *-ede* work
arbejdsløs *adj.* unemployed; **arbejdsløshedsunderstøttelse** unemployment benefits

arkitektur *n.:* *-en* architecture
arktisk *adj.* arctic
arrestere *v.:* *-ede* arrest
asfalteret *adj.* paved (with asphalt)
assistance *n.:* *-n* assistance, help
atten *num.* eighteen
attest *n.:* *-en, pl. -er* certificate; **fødselsattest** birth certificate; **vielsesattest** marriage license
automatisk *adj.* automatic; **automatgear** automatic transmission
automobil *n.:* *-en, pl. -er* car; **automobilværksted** *n.:* *-et, pl. -er* car repair shop
autoriseret *adj.* registered, authorized
avis *n.:* *-en, pl. -er* newspaper

B

bade *v.:* *-ede* swim, go in the water (ocean); bathe (shower, tub)
badedragt *n.:* *-en, pl. -er* bathing suit (women)
bag *prep.* behind
bagage *n.:* *-n* luggage
bageri *n.:* *-et, pl. -er* bakery
baggård *n.:* *-en, pl. -e* courtyard (often dark) enclosed by tall apartment buildings
baghus *n.:* *-et, pl. -e* rear building in apartment complex
bajer *n.:* *-en, pl. -e* bottle of beer
bakke *v.:* *-ede* go in reverse
bakke *n.:* *-n, pl. -r* tray
balkon *n.:* *-en, pl. -er* balcony
banegård *n.:* *-en, pl. -e* railroad station

bange *adj.* afraid
bank *n.: -en, pl. -er* bank;
 bankkonto *n.: -en, pl.*
 bankkonti bank account
bankospil *n.: -let* bingo
barbere *v.: -ede* shave
barfodet *adj.* barefoot
barn *n.: -et, pl. børn* child;
 barndom *n.: -men*
 childhood
barnebillet or **børnebillet** *n.:*
 -ten, pl. -ter half-price
 ticket (child)
barnepige *n.: -n, pl. -r*
 babysitter
batteri *n.: -et, pl. -er* battery
bede *v.: bad, bedt* pray; **bede**
 om ask for
bedømme *v.: -te* assess,
 judge
befolkning *n.: -en, pl. -er*
 population
begrave *v.: -ede* bury
begravelse *n.: -n, pl. -r* funeral
begynde *v.: -te* start
behandle *v.: -ede* treat;
 behandling *n.: -en, pl. -er*
 treatment
bekræfte *v.: -ede* confirm
bemærke *v.: -ede* notice;
 comment
benytte *v.: -ede* use
benzin *n.: -en* gasoline;
 benzinstation *n.: -en,*
 pl. -er gas station
beregne *v.: -ede* calculate
beruset *adj.* drunk
berømt *adj.* famous
besked *n.: -en, pl. -er*
 message; **lægge en**
 besked leave a message
beskytte *v.: -ede* protect
beslutte *v.: -ede* decide
bestille *v.: -te* order;
 bestilling *n.: -en, pl. -er*
 order

besvare *v.: -ede* reply, answer
besværlig *adj.* troublesome,
 difficult
besøge *v.: -te* visit
betale *v.: -te* pay
betjene *v.: -te* serve;
 betjening service
betjent *n.: -en, pl. -e* police
 officer
betyde *v.: betød, betydet*
 mean
bibliotek *n.: -et, pl. -er*
 library; **bibliotekar**
 librarian
bide *v.: bed, bidt* bite
bil *n.: -en, pl. -er* car; **bilferie**
 road trip
billede *n.: -t, pl. -r* picture
billet *n.: -ten, pl. -ter* ticket;
 billetkontor ticket office
billig *adj.* cheap, inexpensive
biltelefon *n.: -en, pl. -er* car
 phone
binde *v.: bandt, bundet* tie
bindingsværk *n.: -et* half-
 timbering
biograf *n.: -en, pl. -er* movie
 theater
bistand *n.: -en* aid,
 assistance; **bistandshjælp**
 welfare payments
bistik *n.: -ket, pl. same* bee
 sting
bivej *n.: -en, pl. -e* small
 country road
bivirkning *n.: -en, pl. -er* side
 effect
blad *n.: -et, pl. -e* magazine;
 leaf
blande *v.: -ede* mix
blank *adj.* shiny, glossy; blank
bleg *adj.* pale
blikstille *adj.* dead calm
 (especially about water or
 ocean)
blind *adj.* blind

blind vej *n.* dead end
blive *v.: blev, blevet* become; stay; **blive natten over** stay overnight
blod *n.: -et* blood
blomst *n.: -en, pl. -er* flower
blond *adj.* blond
blonde *n.: -n, pl. -r* lace
blufærdighed *n.: -en* modesty
bluse *n.: -n, pl. -r* blouse
blyant *n.: -en, pl. -er* pencil; **blyantspidser** *n.: -en, pl. -e* pencil sharpener
blækpatron *n.: -en, pl. -er* ink cartridge
blæksprutte *n.: -n, pl. -r* octopus, squid; **Blæksprutten** annual collection of political cartoons
blæsevejr *n.: -et* windy weather
blød *adj.* soft
bløde *v.: -te* bleed
blå *adj.* blue
bo *v.: -ede* live, reside
boardingkort *n.: -et, pl. same* boarding card
bog *n.: -en, pl. bøger* book; **boghandel** bookstore
bogstav *n.: -et, pl. -er* letter (in alphabet)
bold *n.: -en, pl. -e* ball; **fodbold** soccer
bolsje *n.: -t, pl. -r* piece of hard candy
bombe *n.: -n, pl. -r* bomb
bonde *n.: -n, pl. bønder* farmer
bondegård *n.: -en, pl. -e* farm; **bondegårdsferie** farm holiday (where guests experience Danish farming)
booke *v.: -ede* book, reserve

bopæl *n.: -en, pl. -e* address, place of residence; **fast bopæl** permanent address
bord *n.: -et, pl. -e* table
borddame *n.: -n, pl. -r* the lady a man is seated with at a dinner party
bordel *n.: -let, pl. -ler* brothel, bordello
bordmanerer *n. (pl.)* table manners; **at holde bordskik** to remain at the table until everybody has finished
borg *n.: -en, pl. -e* castle
borger *n.: -en, pl. -e* resident; **statsborger** citizen
borgmester *n.: -en, pl. borgmestre* mayor
bowle *v.: -ede* bowl
brailleskrift *n.: -en* braille
brand *n.: -en, pl. -e* fire
brandalarm *n.: -en, pl. -er* fire alarm; **brandbil** fire truck; **brandmand** firefighter
brandbar *adj.* flammable, combustible
brandsikker *adj.* fireproof
bred *adj.* wide
breddegrad *n.: -en, pl. -er* latitude
bremse *v.: -ede* brake
brev *n.: -et, pl. -e* letter
brevsprække *n.: -n, pl. -r* mail slot
briller *n. (pl.)* eyeglasses
bringe *v.: bragte, bragt* bring
bro *n.: -en, pl. -er* bridge; **broafgift** bridge toll
bronzealder *n.: -en* Bronze Age
bror *n.: -en, pl. brødre* brother
brosten *n.: -en, pl. same* cobblestone; **brolagt** *adj.* cobblestone

brud *n.: -en, pl. -e* bride

brudgom *n.: -men, pl. -me* groom

brudsikker *adj.* unbreakable

bruge *v.: -te* use

brugs *n.: -en, pl. -er* supermarket (also called *brugsforening*)

brugsanvisning *n.: -en, pl. -er* user manual

brugskunst *n.: -en* applied art, crafts

brusebad *n.: -et, pl. -e* shower; **karbad** bath (in tub)

brygge *v.: -ede* brew; **hjemmebryg** home brew

bryllup *n.: -pet, pl. -per* wedding

bryst *n.: -et, pl. -er* breast; *n.: -et, no plural* chest

brække *v.: -ede* break

brække sig *v.: -ede sig* vomit

brænde *v.: -te* burn

brændevin *n.: -en* schnapps

brød *n.: -et, pl. same* bread; **rugbrød** dark rye bread; **franskbrød** white bread

budskab *n.: -et, pl. -er* message

bue *n.: -n, pl. -r* bow; arch; **bue og pil** bow and arrow

buffet *n.: -en, pl. -er* buffet; **tagselvbord** buffet meal

bugt *n.: -en, pl. -er* bay

buket *n.: -ten, pl. -ter* bouquet

bukser *n. (pl.)* pants; **buksetrold** *n.: -en, pl. -e* cute toddler

buldre *v.: -ede* rumble (like thunder)

bums *n.: -en, pl. -er* pimple; bum, tramp

bund *n.: -en* bottom; **at kunne bunde** to be able to reach the bottom

bundt *n.: -et, pl. -er* bunch

burde *v.: burde, burdet (pre. bør)* ought to, should

bus *n.: -sen, pl. -ser* bus; **buschauffør** bus driver; **busstation** bus station

busk *n.: -en, pl. -e* bush

butik *n.: -ken, pl. -ker* store, shop

by *n.: -en, pl. -er* town; **bybus** city bus; **byfest** town festival

byde *v.: bød, budt* offer

bydel *n.: -en, pl. -e* section of town; **bymidte** downtown

byg *n.: -gen* barley

byge *n.: -n, pl. -r* rain shower; **enkelte byger** scattered showers

bygge *v.: -ede* build; **byggemester** builder, contractor

bygning *n.: -en, pl. -er* building

bygrænse *n.: -n, pl. -r* town limit

bytte *v.: -ede* exchange

bæk *n.: -ken, pl. -ke* creek

bænk *n.: -en, pl. -e* bench

bær *n.: -ret, pl. same* berry

bære *v.: bar, båret* carry; **bærbar computer** laptop computer

bøde *n.: -n, pl. -r* fine, ticket

bøg *n.: -en, pl. -e* beech

bøjle *n.: -n, pl. -r* coat hanger

bølge *n.: -n, pl. -r* wave, swell

bøn *n.: -nen, pl. -ner* prayer; **fadervor** Lord's Prayer

børnebillet *n.: -ten, pl. -ter* half-price ticket, child fare

børnebog *n.: -en, pl. børnebøger* children's book

børnebørn n. (pl.) grand-
children

børnedødelighed n.: -en
infant mortality

børnehave n.: -n, pl. -r
preschool, daycare

børnehaveklasse n.: -n, pl. -r
kindergarten

børnehjem n.: -met, pl. same
children's home

børnelokker n.: -en, pl. -e
child molester

børnesygdom n.: -men, pl.
-me childhood disease

børs n.: -en stock exchange

børste v.: -ede brush; n.: -n,
pl. -r brush (for hair,
teeth, & sweeping, etc.)

bøsse n.: -n, pl. -r rifle; salt or
pepper shaker;
homosexual male

båd n.: -en, pl. -e boat

både adv. both; **både ... og**
both ... and

bål n.: -et, pl. same bonfire;
sankthansbål bonfire cel-
ebrating midsummer

bånd n.: -et, pl. same tape;
ribbon

båndmål n.: -et, pl. same
measuring tape

båndoptager n.: -en, pl. -e
tape recorder

båre n.: -n, pl. -r stretcher

C

campere v.: -ede camp

campingplads n.: -en, pl. -er
campsite

campingvogn n.: -en, pl. -e
camper (RV)

centralvarme n.: -n central
heating (usually with hot
water)

chance n.: -n, pl. -r chance

chancebilist n.: -en, pl. -er
driver without a ferry
reservation

charmerende adj. charming

chauvinistisk adj.
chauvinistic

check n.: -en, pl. -e check
(money); **gummicheck**
rubber check

checke v.: -ede check, look
into

checket adj. cool and
together, stylish

chef n.: -en, pl. -er boss,
manager

centralt beliggende adj. cen-
trally located

chik adj. elegant, fashionable

chikane n.: -n, pl. -r
harassment; **seksuel
chikane** sexual
harassment

chip n.: -pen, pl. -s computer
chip

chok n.: -ket, pl. same shock

chokeret adj. shocked

chokolade n.: -n, pl. -r
chocolate; **varm kakao**
hot chocolate; **med
chokoladeovertræk**
chocolate-coated

cigar n.: -en, pl. -er cigar

cigaret n.: -ten, pl. -ter
cigarette

cirkel n.: cirklen, pl. cirkler
circle

cirkus n.: -et, pl. -er circus

citat n.: -et, pl. -er quotation

civil adj. civilian;
civilbefolkning civilian
population

civiliseret adj. civilized

clips n.: -en, pl. same paper
clip

CPR abbr. for **Det Centrale
Personregister** the
Central National Register

CPR-nummer (CPR-nr.) *n.:*
-et, pl. CPR-numre social
security number (date of
birth + four digits)

cykel *n.: cyklen, pl. cykler*
bicycle; **cyklist** cyclist

cykellås *n.: -en, pl. -e* bicycle
lock; **cykelpumpe**
bicycle pump;
cykelstativ bicycle rack

cykelsti *n.: -en, pl. -er* bike
path

D

da *adv.* when (referring to
something in the past); as
(referring to a reason)

dag *n.: -en, pl. -e* day

dagblad *n.: -et, pl. -e* daily
newspaper

dagbog *n.: -en, pl. dagbøger*
diary

daggry *n.: -et* dawn

daglig *adv.* daily

dagligstue *n.: -n, pl. -r* family
room, den

dagpleje *n.: -n* daycare;
dagplejemor daycare
mother (occupation)

dagslys *n.: -et* daylight

dagsorden *n.: -en, pl. -er*
agenda

dagvagt *n.: -en, pl. -er* day
shift

dal *n.: -en, pl. -e* valley

dambrug *n.: -et, pl. same* fish
farm

dame *n.: -n, pl. -r* woman,
lady; **damefrisør** ladies'
hairdresser, beauty parlor

damp *n.: -en, pl. -e* steam;
dampbad steam bath

dankort *n.: -et, pl. same* most
commonly used debit card
in Denmark

Dannebrog *n.: -et, pl. same*
the Danish flag

danse *v.: -ede* dance

dansk *adj.* Danish

danskfødt *adj.* born in
Denmark

dansksproget *adj.* Danish-
speaking

dase *v.: -ede* relax, loaf, laze;
ligge og dase i solen bask
in the sun

dato *n.: -en, pl. -er* date (for
example May 1, 2002)

datter *n.: -en, pl. døtre*
daughter; **datterselskab**
subsidiary company

de *pron.* they; **De** you *sing.*
(formal language)

debat *n.: -ten, pl. -ter* debate;
folketingsdebat
parliamentary debate

debut *n.: -en, pl. -er* debut

december *n.* December

defekt *adj.* defective

dej *n.: -en* dough, batter

dejlig *adj.* nice, wonderful

del *n.: -en, pl. -e* part, section;
bydel section of town

dele *v.: -te* share

deltage *v.: deltog, deltaget*
participate

dement *adj.* senile; **demens**
n. senile dementia

demokrati *n.: -et, pl. -er*
democracy; **demokratisk**
adj. democratic

den *pron.* it; *art.* the

dengang *adv.* when, at that
time

depositum *n.: -met, pl. -mer*
deposit

deprimeret *adj.* depressed;
deprimerende *adj.*
depressing

deres *pron.* theirs

Deres *pron.* yours *sing.*
(formal language)

desinficere *v.: -ede* disinfect

desperat *adj.* desperate

dessert *n.:* *-en, pl.* *-er* dessert; **dessertvin** dessert wine

desværre *adv.* unfortunately

det *pron.* it; *art.* the

detalje *n.:* *-n, pl.* *-r* detail

detektiv *n.:* *-en, pl.* *-er* detective; **detektivroman** detective novel

devaluere *v.:* *-ede* devalue

diabetisk *adj.* diabetic

diadem *n.:* *-et, pl.* *-er* tiara

diagnose *n.:* *-n, pl.* *-r* diagnosis

dige *n.:* *-t, pl.* *-r* dike

digt *n.:* *-et, pl.* *-e* poem; **digter** poet; **digtsamling** poetry collection

direkte *adj.* direct; **direkte forbindelse** direct connection

direktør *n.:* *-en, pl.* *-er* managing director, president

dis *n.:* *-en* haze, mist; **diset** *adj.* hazy

diskotek *n.:* *-et, pl.* *-er* discotheque, disco

diskret *adj.* discreet

diskrimination *n.:* *-en* discrimination

diskvalificere *v.:* *-ede* disqualify

distrahere *v.:* *-ede* distract

diæt *n.:* *-en, pl.* *-er* diet

dobbelt *adj.* double

dogmefilm *n.:* *-en, pl. same* current artistic style in Danish filmmaking

doktor *n.:* *-en, pl.* *-er* doctor

dokumentarfilm *n.:* *-en, pl. same* documentary movie

domkirke *n.:* *-n, pl.* *-r* cathedral

dommer *n.:* *-en, pl.* *-e* judge; **domstol** court

donkraft *n.:* *-en, pl.* *-e* jack (for changing tires)

doven *adj.* lazy

DR (Danmarks Radio) public radio and television channel

dr. *abbr. for* **doktor** doctor

drab *n.:* *-et, pl. same* homicide, killing; **uagtsomt drab** manslaughter

drager *n.:* *-en, pl.* *-e* porter

dramatisk *adj.* dramatic

dranker *n.:* *-en, pl.* *-e* alcoholic, drunk

dreng *n.:* *-en, pl.* *-e* boy

drikke *v.:* *drak, drukket* drink; **drikkevare** *n.:* *-n, pl.* *-r* drink (soft and alcoholic)

drikkepenge *n. (pl.)* tips, gratuity

drikkevand *n.:* *-et* drinking water

drikkevise *n.:* *-n, pl.* *-r* drinking song

drivhus *n.:* *-et, pl.* *-e* greenhouse; **drivhuseffekt** greenhouse effect

dronning *n.:* *-en, pl.* *-er* queen

drukne *v.:* *-ede* drown

dryppe *v.:* *-ede* drip

dræbe *v.:* *-te* kill

drømme *v.:* *-te* dream; **drøm** *n.:* *-men, pl.* *-me* dream; **drømmeferie** dream vacation

dråbe *n.:* *-n, pl.* *-r* drop; **regndråbe** raindrop

du *pron.* you *(sing.)*

dufte *v.:* *-ede* smell (for pleasant aromas)

dug *n.:* *-en, pl.* *-e* tablecloth

dug *n.:* *-gen* dew

dukke *n.:* *-n, pl.* *-r* doll

dum *adj.* stupid, dumb; **dumdristig** foolhardy, rash

dun *n.: -et, pl. same* down;
dundyne *n.: -n, pl. -r*
down comforter

dusin *n.: -et, pl. same* dozen

dusør *n.: -en, pl. -er* reward
(for finding something)

dyb *adj.* deep

dygtig *adj.* competent,
capable, talented, skilled

dykke *v.: -ede* dive; **dykker**
scuba diver

dyne *n.: -n, pl. -r* down
comforter

dynge *n.: -n, pl. -r* pile

dyr *n.: -et, pl. same* animal;
dyrerige animal kingdom

dyr *adj.* expensive

dyrlæge *n.: -n, pl. -r*
veterinarian

dytte *v.: -ede* honk

dæk *n.: -ket, pl. same* tire

dække *v.: -ede* cover; play
defense on

dække bord *v.: -ede bord* set
the table; **dækkeserviet**
place mat

dækningsløs *adj.* unsecured;
dækningsløs check bad
check

dø *v.: -de* die

døbe *v.: -te* baptize

dødfødt *adj.* stillborn

dødkedelig *adj.* extremely
boring; **dødlækker**
extremely wonderful

dødsattest *n.: -fen, pl. -fe*
death certificate

dødsfald *n.: -et, pl. same* death

dødshjælp *n.: -en* euthanasia

dødsstraf *n.: -fen, pl. -fe*
capital punishment, death
penalty (not used in
Denmark)

dødsårsag *n.: -en, pl. -er*
cause of death

døgn *n.: -et, pl. same* 24
hours; **hele døgnet,**
døgnet rundt 24 hours
per day

dømme *v.: -te* judge; referee

dør *n.: -en, pl. -e* door

døv *adj.* deaf

dåb *n.: -en* baptism,
christening; **dåbsattest**
certificate of baptism

dårlig *adj.* bad, of poor
quality

dåse *n.: -n, pl. -r* can, tin;
dåseøl canned beer

dåsemad *n.: -en* canned food;
dåseåbner *n.: -en, pl. -e*
can opener

E

ed *n.: -en, pl. -er* oath; swear-
word, obscenity

edb *abbr. for* **elektronisk**
databehandling
electronic data processing

efter *adv.* after

efterhånden *adv.* gradually,
little by little

efterlade *v.: efterlod,*
efterladt leave behind,
abandon

efterlyse *v.: -te* look for;
advertise for; **efterlyst af**
politiet wanted by the
police

efternavn *n.: -et, pl. -e* last
name

efterskole *n.: -n, pl. -r*
boarding school for
students in grades 8, 9,
or 10

eftersom *adv.* as, because

egen *adj.* own; **egen fejl** own
fault

egn *n.: -en, pl. -e* locality,
region; **egnshistorie**
history of a region

eje *v.:* *-ede* own
ejendel *n.:* *-en, pl. -e*
  belonging
ejendom *n.:* *-men, pl. -me*
  property;
  ejendomsmægler real
  estate broker
ejer *n.:* *-en, pl. -e* owner
eksklusive *conj.* not included
ekspedient *n.:* *-en, pl. -er*
  store salesperson (male);
  ekspeditrice *n.:* *-n, pl. -r*
  (female)
ekspert *n.:* *-en, pl. -er* expert
eksplodere *v.:* *-ede* explode
ekstra *adj.* extra
elastik *n.:* *-ken, pl. -ker*
  elastic, rubber band;
  elastikspring bungee
  jumping
elektricitet *n.:* *-en* electricity;
  elektrisk *adj.* electrical;
  elektriker *n.:* *-en, pl. -e*
  electrician
elendig *adj.* poor, pathetic,
  feeling terrible, miserable
elev *n.:* *-en, pl. -er* student
elevator *n.:* *-en, pl. -er*
  elevator
eller *conj.* or
ellers *adv.* otherwise
elleve *num.* eleven; **elvte**
  eleventh
elske *v.:* *-ede* love; **elsker**
  lover; **elskerinde** mistress
emballage *n.:* *-n, pl. -r*
  packaging
en *num., pron., art.* one, a/an
end *conj.* than; **mindre end**
  smaller than
ende *v.:* *-te* end; *n.:* *-n, pl. -r*
  end; rear end; **endefuld**
  spanking
endnu *adv.* still; additional,
  more

ene *adj.* alone, by oneself
enestue *n.:* *-n, pl. -r* private
  room in hospital;
  enkeltværelse single
  room (in hotel)
enfamilieshus *n.:* *-et, pl. -e*
  single family dwelling
engel *n.:* *englen, pl. engle*
  angel; **en engels**
  tålmodighed the patience
  of a saint
engelsk *adj.* English
enkeltbillet *n.:* *-ten, pl. -ter*
  one-way ticket
enlig *adj.* single (divorced,
  widowed or not married)
ens *adj.* identical, same,
  congruent
ensom *adj.* lonely
ensporet *adj.* single-track
  (railroad); one-track
  (mind)
ensrettet *adj.* one-way
  (street)
entré *n.:* *-en, pl. -er* entrance
  (in house); entry,
  appearance; **entrébillet**
  admission ticket
erhverv *n.:* *-et, pl. same*
  profession
erotisk *adj.* erotic
erstatning *n.:* *-en, pl. -er*
  replacement;
  compensation, damages
eskimo *n.:* *-en, pl. -er* Eskimo
et *num., art.* one, a/an
etage *n.:* *-n, pl. -r* floor, story;
  stueetage ground floor;
  første etage second floor
etiket *n.:* *-ten, pl. -ter* label
etisk *adj.* ethical
etnisk *adj.* ethnic
Europa *n.* Europe; **europæer**
  n. European; **europæisk**
  adj. European

evakuere *v.: -ede* evacuate
eventyr *n.: -et, pl. same* fairy tale
evig *adj.* eternal, everlasting, immortal

F

fabrik *n.: -ken, pl. -ker* factory; **fabriksarbejder** factory worker
fadervor *n.: -et* Lord's Prayer
fagforening *n.: -en, pl. -er* labor union
faktura *n.: -en, pl. -er* invoice, bill
falde *v.: faldt, faldet* fall
faldskærm *n.: -en, pl. -e* parachute; **faldskærmsudspring** parachuting
fallit *adj.* bankrupt
falsk *adj.* false, fake
familie *n.: -n, pl. -r* family
fan *n.: -en, pl. -s* fan (admirer)
fane *n.: -n, pl. -r* banner, flag
fange *v.: -ede* catch; *n.: -n, pl. -r* prisoner
farbar *adj.* navigable, passable
fare *n.: -n, pl. -r* danger
fare vild *v.: for vild, faret vild* get lost
farlig *adj.* dangerous
farmaceut *n.: -en, pl. -er* pharmacist
fart *n.: -en* speed; **fartgrænse** speed limit
farvand *n.: -et, pl. -e* waters, fairway, channel
farve *n.: -n, pl. -r* color; **farvefilm** color film; **farvefjernsyn** color television
farvel *interj., n.: -let* goodbye

fastboende *adj.* with permanent residence
fastelavn *n.: -en* Danish equivalent of Halloween
fattig *adj.* poor
feber *n.: -en* fever; **feberstillende** antipyretic
februar *n.* February
fed *adj.* fat
fedt *n.: -et* fat; **fedtholdig** *adj.* fatty; **fedtindhold** fat content
fejl *n.: -en, pl. same* error
f.eks. *abbr. for* **for eksempel** for example
fem *num.* five; **ved femtiden** about five o'clock
femogtyveøre *n.: -n, pl. -r* 25 øre (unit of currency)
femten *num.* fifteen
ferie *n.: -n, pl. -r* vacation, holiday; **på ferie** on vacation
fersk *adj.* fresh (not salty); **ferskvand** freshwater
fest *n.: -en, pl. -er* party
film *n.: -en, pl. same* film, movie; **filmstjerne** movie star
filter *n.: -et, pl. filtre* filter
finale *n.: -n, pl. -r* final; **finalist** finalist
finanslov *n.: -en, pl. -e* annual budget (government)
finansminister *n.: -en, pl. finansministre* secretary of the treasury
finansår *n.: -et, pl. same* fiscal year
finde *v.: fandt, fundet* find
finger *n.: -en, pl. fingre* finger; **fingeraftryk** fingerprint
fire *num.* four; **ved firetiden** about four o'clock

firepersoners *adj.* for four people

firkantet *adj.* square

firma *n.: -et, pl. -er* company

firs *num.* eighty

fisk *n.: -en, pl. same* fish

fjerkræ *n.: -et* poultry

fjern *adj.* remote, distant; **fjernbetjening** remote control

fjerne *v.: -ede* remove

fjernsyn *n.: -et, pl. same* television

fjorten *num.* fourteen

flad *adj.* flat; **fladfisk** flatfish

flag *n.: -et, pl. same* flag; **Dannebrog** the Danish flag

flamme *n.: -n, pl. -r* flame

flaske *n.: -n, pl. -r* bottle

fleksibel *adj.* flexible; **flekstid** flexible work hours

flere *adj.* more

flertal *n.: -let, pl. same* majority

flint *n.: -en* flint; **flyve i flint** get very angry

flue *n.: -n, pl. -r* fly; **fluesmækker** flyswatter

flugtbilist *n.: -en, pl. -er* hit-and-run driver

fly *n.: -et, pl. same* airplane

flydende *adj.* liquid

flygte *v.: -ede* flee

flygtning *n.: -en, pl. -e* refugee

flytte *v.: -ede* move

flyve *v.: fløj, fløjet* fly; **flyvebåd** hovercraft

fløjte *v.: -ede* whistle; *n.: -n, pl. -r* whistle

fodbold *n.: -en, pl. -e* soccer ball; **fodboldbane** soccer field; **fodboldkamp** soccer game

fodgænger *n.: -en, pl. -e* pedestrian; **fodgængerovergang** pedestrian crossing

fodspor *n.: -et, pl. same* footprint

folk *n.: -et, pl. same* people

folkeafstemning *n.: -en, pl. -er* popular vote, referendum

folkedans *n.: -en* folk dance

folkedragt *n.: -en, pl. -er* regional or ethnic costume

folkehøjskole *n.: -n, pl. -r* folk high school (special curriculum with emphasis on personal development)

folkekirke *n.: -n* Danish National Evangelical Lutheran Church

folkepensionist *n.: -en, pl. -er* senior citizen

folkeregister *n.: -et* national register

folkesanger *n.: -en, pl. -e* folksinger

folkeskole *n.: -n, pl. -r* public grade/elementary school

folkestyre *n.: -t* representative government

folketing *n.: -et* Danish parliament (legislative branch)

folketingsmedlem *n.: -met, pl. -mer* member of parliament

foran *prep.* in front of

forbeholde *v.: forbeholdt, forbeholdt* reserve; **forbeholdt** reserved for

forberede *v.: -te* prepare

forbinde *v.: forbandt, forbundet* connect; bandage

forbyde *v.: forbød, forbudt* prohibit, forbid; **forbudt** forbidden

fordel *n.: -en, pl. -e* advantage

fordi *conj.* because

foredrag *n.: -et, pl. same* lecture

forelske sig *v.: -ede sig* fall in love

foreslå *v.: foreslog, foreslået* suggest

foretrække *v.: foretrak, foretrukket* prefer

forfatter *n.: -en, pl. -e* author

forgifte *v.: -ede* poison

forhindre *v.: -ede* prevent

forkert *adj.* wrong, inaccurate

forklare *v.: -ede* explain; **forklaring** *n.: -en, pl. -er* explanation

forkølelse *n.: -n, pl. -r* cold (illness); **at blive forkølet** to catch a cold

forlange *v.: -te* demand

forlovet *adj.* engaged, in a serious relationship

forlystelsespark *n.: -en, pl. -er* amusement park

formode *v.: -ede* assume, presume

formål *n.: -et, pl. same* purpose

fornavn *n.: -et, pl. -e* first name

fornærme *v.: -ede* insult, offend

fornøjelse *n.: -n, pl. -r* pleasure

forretningsmand *n.: -en, pl. forretningsmænd* businessman; **forretningskvinde** *n.: -n, pl. -r* businesswoman

forsamlingshus *n.: -et, pl. -e* community house (used for parties and community events)

forsigtig *adj.* careful, cautious

forsikre *v.: -ede* insure; assure

forsikring *n.: -en, pl. -er* insurance; **forsikringspolice** insurance policy

forsinke *v.: -ede* delay

forskel *n.: -len, pl. -le* difference; **forskellig** *adj.* different

forskrække *v.: -ede* scare, frighten

forskud *n.: -det, pl. same* advance payment; **på forskud** in advance

forslag *n.: -et, pl. same* suggestion

forstad *n.: -en, pl. forstæder* suburb

forstyrre *v.: -ede* disturb

forstørre *v.: -ede* enlarge

forstå *v.: forstod, forstået* understand

forsvinde *v.: forsvandt, forsvundet* disappear

forsæt *n.: -tet, pl. -ter* resolution, decision; **nytårsforsæt** New Year's resolution

forsøge *v.: -te* try, attempt

forsømt *adj.* neglected

forsørge *v.: -ede* provide for, support

fortage sig *v.: fortog, fortaget sig* abate, lessen

fortov *n.: -et, pl. same* sidewalk

fortryde *v.: fortrød, fortrudt* regret

fortsætte *v.: fortsatte, fortsat* continue

fortælle *v.: fortalte, fortalt* tell

forud *adv.* ahead

forurene *v.: -ede* pollute; **forurening** *n.: -en* pollution

forældre *n. (pl.)* parents

forære *v.: -ede* give (as a present, at no cost)

forår *n.: -et, pl. same* spring

forårsage *v.: -ede* cause

fotografere *v.: -ede* photograph, take pictures

frankere *v.: -ede* affix stamp, frank

fraregne *v.: -ede* deduct

fraråde *v.: -ede* caution against, advise against

fraskilt *adj.* divorced

fred *n.: -en* peace

fredag *n.* Friday; **om fredagen** on Fridays

fredelig *adj.* peaceful, quiet

fredet *adj.* protected, subject to conservation laws

fremad *adv.* forward

fremkalde *v.: -te* bring about, evoke; develop (film)

fremmed *adj.* foreign, strange; **fremmedarbejder** immigrant worker

fremtid *n.: -en* future

fri *adj.* free; **at have fri** to be off from work or school; **fribillet** complimentary ticket; **fridag** day off

fribadestrand *n.: -en, pl. -e* public nudist beach

frihed *n.: -en, pl. -er* freedom, liberty; **frihedsbevægelse** resistance movement

frikvarter *n.: -et, pl. -er* recess at school

friluftsmenneske *n.: -t, pl. -r* outdoor person

frimærke *n.: -t, pl. -r* stamp (letter)

frisk *adj.* fresh; **friskbagt brød** freshly baked bread; **friskmalet** freshly painted; freshly ground

frisør *n.: -en, pl. -er* hairdresser, barber

frokost *n.: -en, pl. -er* lunch

frost *n.: -en* frost; **frosset** *adj.* frozen

fryse *v.: frøs, frosset* freeze; to be cold

fugl *n.: -en, pl. -e* bird

fugtig *adj.* moist, humid; **luftfugtighed** *n.: -en* humidity

fuld *adj.* full; drunk

fuldautomatisk *adj.* fully automated

fuldmagt *n.: -en, pl. -er* power of attorney

fungere *v.: -ede* function; **fungere som** function as

fusion *n.: -en, pl. -er* merger; fusion (atomic physics)

fylde *v.: -te* fill; **fyldebøtte** heavy drinker and eater

Fyn *geog.* Fynen; **fynbo** native of Fynen

fyr *n.: -en, pl. -e* fellow, guy, boyfriend

fyraften *n.: -en, pl. -er* quitting time, end of a day's work

fyrre *num.* forty

fyrtårn *n.: -et, pl. -e* lighthouse

fyrværkeri *n.: -et* fireworks

fælles *adj.* shared, common

fængsel *n.: -et* or *fængslet, pl. fængsler* prison

fængsle *v.: -ede* imprison; captivate mentally

færdig *adj.* finished, ready

færdsel *n.: færdslen* traffic

færge *n.: -n, pl. -r* ferry

føde *n.: -n* food

føde *v.: -te* give birth to

fødeby *n.: -en, pl. -er* hometown; **fødejord** native soil; **fødested** birthplace

fødevare *n.: -n, pl. -r* food item

fødselsattest *n.: -en, pl. -er* birth certificate

fødselsdag *n.: -en, pl. -e* birthday; **fødselsdagskage** birthday cake

føle *v.: -te* feel

følelsesløs *adj.* numb

følge *v.: fulgte, fulgt* follow

før *adv.* before

føre *v.: -te* lead, be in the lead

føre *n.: -t* state of the roads; **dårligt føre** bad road conditions

først *adj., adv.* first

få *v.: fik, fået* get, receive

G

gade *n.: -n, pl. -r* street; **gadehjørne** street corner; **gadefest** block party

gal *adj.* angry; wrong; insane; bad; **at køre galt** to have an accident

galleri *n.: -et, pl. -er* gallery

gammel *adj.* old (**gammel, ældre, ældst** old, older, oldest)

gangsti *n.: -en, pl. -er* path, walkway

garanti *n.: -en, pl. -er* warranty; **garantibevis** *n.: -et, pl. -er* warranty certificate

gave *n.: -n, pl. -r* present

gebyr *n.: -et, pl. -er* fee

gemme *v.: -te* hide; **at lege gemme** to play hide-and-seek

genbo *n.: -en, pl. -er* neighbor on opposite side of street

genbruge *v.: -te* recycle, reuse; **genbrugsplads** recycling center

genere *v.: -ede* bother; **ugenert grund** secluded property

genert *adj.* shy

gennem *prep.* through

gennemgående *adv.* generally

gennemkørsel forbudt no through traffic

genstand *n.: -en, pl. -e* thing, object; one shot of alcohol

gentage *v.: gentog, gentaget* repeat

gift *n.: -en, pl. -e* poison; **giftig** *adj.* poisonous

gifte sig *v.: -ede sig* get married

gips *n.: -en* plaster, cast for broken bones

give *v.: gav, givet* give

glad *adj.* happy, satisfied

glas *n.: -set, pl. same* glass; **glaspuster** glassblower

glat *adj.* smooth; slippery

glemme *v.: -te* forget; **glemsom** forgetful

glide *v.: gled, gledet* slide

glæde *n.: -n, pl. -r* joy; **at glæde sig til** to look forward to

gløgg *n.: -en* Christmas punch (red wine, schnapps, sugar, lemon, spices, raisins, and almonds)

god *adj.* good

godartet *adj.* mild; benign (medical)

goddag *interj./greeting* hello (short versions: **dav, davs**)

godnat *interj./greeting* good night

gods *n.: -et, pl. -er* estate, manor; **godsejer** owner of estate or manor

gods *n.: -et* freight; belongings; **godstog** freight train

grad *n.: -en, pl. -er* degree (temperature or university degree)

gratis *adj.* free of cost

grav *n.: -en, pl. -e* grave

gravid *adj.* pregnant

greve *n.: -n, pl. -r* count; **grevinde** *n.: -n, pl. -r* countess

gribe *v.: greb, grebet* catch

grille *v.: -ede* grill; **grillstegt** cooked on grill

grine *v.: -ede* laugh

gris *n.: -en, pl. -e* pig; **grisekød** *n.: -et* pork

gro *v.: -ede* grow

grov *adj.* coarse; rude; **grofthakket** coarsely chopped; **en grov bemærkning** a rude comment

gruppe *n.: -n, pl. -r* group

gryde *n.: -n, pl. -r* saucepan; **grydeklar** ready to cook; **grydelap** pot holder

græde *v.: græd, grædt* cry; **grædefærdig** on the brink of tears

grænse *n.: -n, pl. -r* border, limit; **grænseløs** without limits

græs *n.: -set, pl. -ser* grasses; **græsplæne** lawn

grøft *n.: -en, pl. -er* ditch

grøn *adj.* green; **grøn koncert** music festivals held in a number of cities during the summer

Grønland *geog.* Greenland; **grønlænder** native to Greenland

grøntsag *n.: -en, pl. -er* vegetable; **grøntsagssuppe** vegetable soup

grå *adj.* gray; **gråvejr** *n.: -et* cloudy weather

gud *n.: -en, pl. -er* god

gudstjeneste *n.: -n, pl. -r* service; **gudmoder** godmother

gul *adj.* yellow

guld *n.: -et* gold; **guldmedalje** gold medal

guldbryllup *n.: -pet, pl. -per* 50th anniversary

gylden *adj.* golden

gyldig *adj.* valid

gylle *n.: -n* semiliquid manure spread on fields as organic fertilizer (has strong, foul odor)

gymnasium *n.: gymnasiet, pl. gymnasier* high school; **gymnasieelev** high-school student

gære *v.: -ede* ferment; **noget i gære** trouble brewing

gæst *n.: -en, pl. -er* guest; **gæstearbejder** immigrant worker; **gæsteværelse** guest room

gætte *v.: -ede* guess; **gætte krydsogtværs** do a cross-word puzzle

gø *v.: -ede* bark

gøg *n.: -en, pl. -e* cuckoo bird

gøre *v.: gjorde, gjort* do; **ikke noget at gøre** nothing we can do

gå *v.: gik, gået* walk; **gåtur** *n.: -en, pl. -e* walk

gård *n.: -en, pl. -e* farm; **gårdejer** *n.: -en, pl. -e* farmer

gårdhave *n.: -n, pl. -r* enclosed backyard

H

hade *v.: -ede* hate

hagl *n.: -et, pl. same* hail

halv *adj.* half

halvanden *num.* one and a half

halvfems *num.* ninety

halvfjerds *num.* seventy

halvtreds *num.* fifty

halvvejs *adv.* halfway

halvø *n.: -en, pl. -er* peninsula

hammer *n.: -en, pl. hamre* hammer

hamp *n.: -en* hemp

han *pron.* he; *n.: -nen, pl. -ner* male, man

handle *v.: -ede* trade, shop

haste *v.: -ede* be urgent; **haste af sted** hurry

hav *n.: -et, pl. -e* ocean, sea

have *v.: havde, haft (pre. har)* have

have *n.: -n, pl. -r* garden; **blomsterhave** flower garden; **køkkenhave** vegetable garden

havfrue *n.: -n, pl. -r* mermaid; **Den lille havfrue** the Little Mermaid

havn *n.: -en, pl. -e* harbor

hedde *v.: hed, heddet* be called

hede *n.: -n* heat; **hedeslag** heatstroke; **hedebølge** heat wave

hej *interj./greeting* hi

hejse *v.: -ede or -te* hoist

heks *n.: -en, pl. -e* witch

hel *adj.* whole

heldags *adj.* all-day; **heldagsjob** full-time job

heldig *adj.* lucky, fortunate

hellere *adv.* rather; **må hellere** had better

hellig *adj.* holy, religious; **helligdag** religious holiday; **Helligånden** The Holy Ghost

helst *adv.* preferably

helårshus *n.: -et, pl. -e* house suitable for occupancy year-round

her *adv.* here

herefter *adv.* hereafter, from now on

herfra *adv.* from here

heroverfor *adv.* opposite, on the other side

herovre *adv.* on this side, here

herpå *adv.* thereupon

herre *n.: -n, pl. -r* gentleman

herregård *n.: -en, pl. -e* manor; **herremand** owner of a manor

hest *n.: -en, pl. -e* horse; **hestekraft** horsepower

heteroseksuel *adj.* heterosexual

hikke *n.: -n* hiccups; **at have hikke** to have the hiccups

hilse *v.: -te* greet; **hilsen** *n.: -en, pl. -er* greeting

himmel *n.: himlen, pl. himle* sky; heaven; **himmerig** *n.: -et* Heaven, Paradise

hinanden *pron.* each other

historie *n.: -n, pl. -r* story; *n.: -n* history; **historisk** historical

hjelm *n.: -en, pl. -e* helmet; **cykelhjelm** bicycle helmet

hjem *n.: -met, pl. same* home; **plejehjem** nursing home

hjemme *adv.* at home; **hjemmelavet** *adj.* homemade; **hjemmemenneske** homebody; **hjemmehjælp** home aide

hjemmestyre *n.: -t* home rule (Greenland and the Faeroe Islands)

hjemve *n.: -en* homesickness

hjerne *n.: -n, pl. -r* brain; **hjernerystelse** concussion

hjerte *n.: -t, pl. -r* heart;
hjertetilfælde heart attack
hjælpe *v.: hjalp, hjulpet* help;
hjælpsom helpful
hjørne *n.: -t, pl. -r* corner;
hjørnespark corner kick
(soccer)
hof *n.: -fet, pl. -fer* royal
family; **hofleverandør**
purveyor to the royal
household
hold *n.: -et, pl. same* team,
group; **holdkammerat**
teammate
holde *v.: holdt, holdt* hold;
holde fest throw a party
homoseksuel *adj.*
homosexual
honorar *n.: -et, pl. -er* fee;
royalties
hoppe *v.: -ede* jump
hoved- *adj. pref.* main, chief,
the most important;
hovedkontor main office
hovednøgle *n.: -n, pl. -r*
master key
hovedperson *n.: -en, pl. -er*
main character,
protagonist; **hovedrolle**
leading role
hovedstad *n.: -en, pl.*
hovedstæder capital;
hovedstadsområdet metropolitan Copenhagen
hovedtrappe *n.: -n, pl. -r*
main staircase; **bagtrappe**
back stairs
hovedvej *n.: -en, pl. -e* main
road
hud *n.: -en, -er* hide; *n.: -en*
skin; **hudafskrabning**
abrasion
hul *n.: -let, pl. -ler* hole
hul *adj.* hollow
hule *n.: -n, pl. -r* cave;
hulebeboer caveman

humør *n.: -et* mood, spirits;
i godt humør in a good
mood
hun *pron.* she; *n.: -nen, pl.*
-ner female, woman
hund *n.: -en, pl. -e* dog; slang
for a 100 kr. bill;
hundehvalp puppy;
hundegalskab rabies
hundrede *num.* hundred;
hundredkroneseddel
100 kr. bill
hurtig *adj.* fast, quick
hus *n.: -et, pl. -e* house;
husdyr domestic animal
huske *v.: -ede* remember;
huskeseddel note,
shopping list
husmandsbrug *n.: -et, pl.*
same small farm
husmoder *n.: -en, pl.*
husmødre housewife
husstand *n.: -en, pl. -e* household
hustru *n.: -en, pl. -er* wife
hvad *pron.* what
hvem *pron.* who
hveps *n.: -en, pl. -e* wasp,
hornet; **hvepserede** wasp
nest
hver *pron.* each; **hver anden**
every other
hverdag *n.: -en, pl. -e*
weekday
hverken ... eller *adv.* neither
... nor
hvid *adj.* white
hvile *v.: -ede* rest
hvilken *pron.* which; **hvilken**
som helst any
hvis *pron.* whose
hvis *conj.* if
hviske *v.: -ede* whisper
hvor *adv.* where
hvordan *adv.* how

hvorfor adv. why

hvorfra adv. from where

hvorhen adv. where to

hvornår adv. when

hyggelig adj. cozy; **hjemlig hygge** coziness at home

hyrevogn n.: -en, pl. -e taxicab

hæk n.: -ken, pl. -ke hedge

hælde v.: -te pour; v.: -ede slant

hænge v.: hang, hængt (intr.) or hængte, hængt (tr.) hang; **hængekøje** hammock

hærværk n.: -et vandalism

hæve v.: -ede raise, lift up; withdraw (money); **hævekort** ATM card

hø n.: -et hay; **høfeber** hay fever

høflig adj. polite

høj n.: -en, pl. -e mound; **gravhøj** burial mound

høj adj. tall

Højesteret n.: -ten Supreme Court

højhælet adj. with high heels

højre adj. right; **højrehåndet** right-handed

højskole n.: -n, pl. -r folk high school (special curriculum with emphasis on personal development)

højsæson n.: -en peak season

højtid n.: -en, pl. -er religious holiday (esp. Christmas, Easter, and Whitsun)

højtidelig adj. solemn, ceremonious; **selvhøjtidelig** pompous, self-absorbed

højtryk n.: -ket, pl. same high pressure

højttaler n.: -en, pl. -e loudspeaker

høne n.: -n, pl. -r hen; **høns** (pl.) poultry; **hønsegård** chicken yard (outdoor)

høre v.: -te hear; **høreapparat** hearing aid

høste v.: -ede harvest; **høstfest** harvest festival; **høstgudstjeneste** harvest thanksgiving service in church

håbe v.: -ede hope; **håbløs** hopeless

hånd n.: -en, pl. hænder hand; **håndjern** handcuffs

håndklæde n.: -t, pl. -r towel

håndkøbsmedicin n.: -en over-the-counter medicine

håndskrift n.: -en, pl. -er handwriting; n.: -et, pl. -er handwritten manuscript

håndtag n.: -et, pl. same handle

håndtryk n.: -ket, pl. same handshake

håne v.: -ede taunt

hård adj. hard, difficult; **hårdkogt** hard-boiled

I

iberegne v.: -ede include; **alt iberegnet** everything included

idé n.: -en, pl. -er idea

identitetskort n.: -et, pl. same identification card; **id-kort** ID card

idræt n.: -ten sports, athletics; **Idrætsparken** main stadium in Copenhagen (also called **Parken**)

idrætscenter n.: -et or idrætscentret, pl. idrætscentre sports facility

idømme v.: -te sentence

igen adv. again

igennem prep., adv. through

ihjel *adv.* to death; **slå ihjel** to kill; **slå tiden ihjel** to kill time

ikke *adv.* not

ikke- *(before n. or adj.)* non-

ikon *n.: -et, pl. -er* icon

ild *n.: -en* fire; **ildebrand** *n.: -en, pl. -e* fire

ildelugtende *adj.* stinky, foul-smelling

ildslukker *n.: -en, pl. -e* fire extinguisher

ilt *n.: -en* oxygen

immun *adj.* immune; **immunforsvar** immune system

imponerende *adj.* impressive; **imponeret** *adj.* impressed

improvisere *v.: -ede* improvise

ind *adv.* in, into

indbrud *n.: -det, pl. same* burglary; **indbrudstyv** *n.: -en, pl. -e* burglar

indbydelse *n.: -en, pl. -er* invitation

indbygger *n.: -en, pl. -e* resident, inhabitant

indbygget *adj.* built-in

inden *adv.* before

indendørs *adj.* indoor

indenrigs *adj.* domestic

indflydelsesrig *adj.* influential

indfødsret *n.: -ten* right to citizenship

indhente *v.: -ede* catch up with

indholdsfortegnelse *n.: -n, pl. -r* table of contents

individuel *adj.* individual; **individ** *n.: -et, pl. -er* individual

indkomst *n.: -en, pl. -er* income; **indkomstskat** income taxes

indkvartere *v.: -ede* accommodate; **indkvartere i enkeltværelser** accommodate in single rooms

indkøbsvogn *n.: -en, pl. -e* shopping cart

indpakningspapir *n.: -et* wrapping paper

indregistrere *v.: -ede* register

indrejsetilladelse *n.: -n, pl. -r* entry permit (visa)

indrømme *v.: -ede* admit

indspille *v.: -ede* record (on tape or video)

indsprøjtning *n.: -en, pl. -er* injection

indtil *adv.* until

indtryk *n.: -ket, pl. same* impression

industri *n.: -en, pl. -er* industry; **industriarbejder** industrial worker

industriferie *n.: -n* three weeks in July when many businesses close for vacation

indvandrer *n.: -en, pl. -e* immigrant; **andengenerations-indvandrer** second-generation immigrant

indvendig *adj.* internal, inside, interior

ingen *pron.* nobody

ingenting *pron.* nothing

ingrediens *n.: -en, pl. -er* ingredient

inkludere *v.: -ede* include

inkompatibel *adj.* incompatible

insekt *n.: -et, pl. -er* insect; **insektpulver** insecticide

inspicere *v.: -ede* inspect

intet *n.* nothing

invalid *n.: -en, pl. -er*
disabled person; **invalid**
adj. disabled

is *n.: -en, pl. same* ice; ice
cream; **iskold** ice-cold;
isvaffel ice-cream cone

i stedet (for) *adv.* instead (of)

itu *adv., adj.* in pieces

ivrig *adj.* eager

iøjefaldende *adj.* conspicuous

J

ja *interj.* yes

jagt *n.: -en, pl. -er* hunt;
jagtgevær sporting gun;
jagthund hunting dog

januar *n.* January

jeg *pron.* I

jernbane *n.: -n, pl. -r*
railroad; **jernbanestation**
railroad station

jord *n.: -en* soil;
jordforbundet grounded
(electricity)

jordbær *n.: -ret, pl. same*
strawberry;
jordbærsyltetøj
strawberry jam

Jorden the Earth

journal *n.: -en, pl. -er* patient
record

jubilæum *n.: jubilæet, pl.
jubilæer* jubilee,
anniversary

jul *n.: -en* Christmas;
juleaften Christmas Eve;
juledag Christmas Day;
julegave Christmas
present

julemand *n.: -en, pl.
julemænd* Santa Claus;
julenisse *n.: -n, pl. -r* elf

julepynt *n.: -en* Christmas
decorations; **juletræ** *n.:
-et, pl. -er* Christmas tree

juli *n.* July

juni *n.* June

jura *n.: -en* jurisprudence,
law; **juridisk** *adj.* legal,
judicial

justere *v.: -ede* adjust;
justerbar *adj.* adjustable

justitsminister *n.: -en, pl.
justitsministre* attorney
general

Jylland *geog.* Jutland

jysk *adj.* pertaining to Jutland

jæger *n.: -en, pl. -e* hunter

jævn *adj.* even

jøde *n.: -n, pl. -r* Jew;
jødekage special Danish
Christmas cookie

K

kabel *n.: kablet, pl. kabler*
cable; **kabel-tv** cable
television

kaffe *n.: -n* coffee;
kaffekande coffeepot

kage *n.: -n, pl. -r* cake

kahyt *n.: -ten, pl. -ter* ship
cabin

kaj *n.: -en, pl. -er* quay

kalde *v.: -te* call

kalender *n.: -en, pl. -e*
calendar

kalkulere *v.: -ede* calculate

kalorie *n.: -n, pl. -r* calorie;
kaloriefattig low in
calories; **kaloriefri**
without calories

kam *n.: -men, pl. -me* comb

kammerat *n.: -en, pl. -er*
friend, companion

kamp *n.: -en, pl. -e* match,
fight, battle

kant *n.: -en, pl. -er* edge;
kantsten street curb

kaos *n.: -et* chaos; **trafikkaos**
traffic jam

kapel *n.: -let, pl. -ler* chapel;
mortuary

kapsel *n.: kapslen, pl. kapsler*
bottle cap; capsule

kaptajn *n.: -en, pl. -er*
captain

karet *n.: -en, pl. -er* coach
carriage; **kongelig karet**
royal coach

karriere *n.: -n, pl. -r* career

kartoffel *n.: kartoflen or -en,
pl. kartofler* potato

kaserne *n.: -n, pl. -r* military
barrack

kasse *n.: -n, pl. -r* box; cash
register

kasseapparat *n.: -et, pl. -er*
cash register

kassere *v.: -ede* throw away

kaste *v.: -ede* throw

kat *n.: -ten, pl. -te* cat

katalog *n.: -et, pl. -er* catalog

katastrofe *n.: -n, pl. -r*
catastrophe

kategori *n.: -en, pl. -er*
category

kedelig *adj.* boring

kende *v.: -te* know,
recognize; **kendetegn**
mark, characteristic

keramik *n.: -ken* ceramics

kernefamilie *n.: -n, pl. -r*
nuclear family

kigge *v.: -ede* look

kikkert *n.: -en, pl. -er*
binoculars

kilde *n.: -n, pl. -r* spring
(water); root, source;
kildevand spring water,
well water

kildre *v.: -ede* tickle

kilometer (km) *n.* kilometer

kinesisk *adj.* Chinese

kino *n.: -en, pl. -er* movie
theater

kiosk *n.: -en, pl. -er* kiosk

kirke *n.: -n, pl. -r* church;
kirkegænger churchgoer;
kirkeklokke church bell

klage *v.: -ede* complain; *n.:
-n, pl. -r* complaint

klam *adj.* moist, damp;
pathetic, unappealing
(slang)

klappe *v.: -ede* clap, applaud

klar *adj.* ready; clear,
transparent

klare *v.: -ede* manage,
handle, cope

klasse *n.: -n, pl. -r* class,
category; **klasseværelse**
classroom

klassesamfund *n.: -et, pl.
same* class society

klemme *v.: -te* squeeze, jam,
crush, pinch

klient *n.: -en, pl. -er* client,
customer

klikke *v.: -ede* click

klima *n.: -et, pl. -er* climate;
klimaanlæg *n.: -get, pl.
same* air conditioning

kloak *n.: -ken, pl. -ker* sewer

klog *adj.* smart, clever, intelligent, wise

klub *n.: -ben, pl. -ber* club;
tennisklub tennis club

klæbe *v.: -ede* stick; **klæbrig**
adj. sticky

klæde sig på *v.: -te sig på* get
dressed

klæg *adj.* doughy, sticky

klø *v.: -ede* itch

klø *n. (pl.)* beating; **få klø** be
beaten

knallert *n.: -en, pl. -er* moped

knap *n.: -pen, pl. -per* button

knap *adj.* scarce

knirke *v.: -ede* creak, squeak

kniv *n.: -en, pl. -e* knife;
knivskarp sharp as a razor

kno *n.: -en, pl. -er* knuckle;
knofedt elbow grease

knop *n.: -pen, pl. -per* bud
(botany); bump

knopsvane *n.: -n, pl. -r* mute swan *(Cygnus olor)* – Denmark's national bird

knude *n.: -n, pl. -r* knot

knus *n.: -et, pl. same* hug

knuse *v.: -te* crush

knæ *n.: -et, pl. same* knee

knække *v.: -ede* crack, break; **nøddeknækker** nutcracker

knæle *v.: -ede* kneel

ko *n.: -en, pl. køer* cow; **kogalskab** mad cow disease

koffein *n.: -et or -en* caffeine; **koffeinfri** caffeine free

koge *v.: -te* boil; **kogepunkt** boiling point

kok *n.: -ken, pl. -ke* chef; rooster

koket *adj.* flirtatious, coy

kold *adj.* cold

kollega *n.: -en, pl. -er or kolleger* colleague

kollegium *n.: kollegiet, pl. kollegier* college dorm

kollidere *v.: -ede* collide

komme *v.: kom, kommet* come

kommune *n.: -n, pl. -r* municipality

kompetent *adj.* competent

koncentrat *n.: -et, pl. -er* concentrate

koncert *n.: -en, pl. -er* concert

kondi *n.: -en* fitness, physical condition

konditori *n.: -et, pl. -er* café, pastry shop

kondolere *v.: -ede* condole

kondom *n.: -et, pl. -er* condom

kone *n.: -n, pl. -r* wife

konfekt *n.: -en, pl. -er* assorted chocolates, sweets, and marzipan

konference *n.: -n, pl. -r* conference

konfirmation *n.: -en, pl. -er* confirmation (religious)

konge *n.: -n, pl. -r* king; **kongedømme** kingdom, monarchy; **kongefamilie** royal family

kongelig *adj.* royal

konkurrence *n.: -n, pl. -r* competition

konsul *n.: -en, pl. -er* consul; **konsulat** *n.: -et, pl. -er* consulate

kontakt *n.: -en, pl. -er* contact; electrical outlet

konto *n.: -en, pl. -er or konti* account

kontor *n.: -et, pl. -er* office

konvolut *n.: -ten, pl. -ter* envelope

kopiere *v.: -ede* copy; **kopimaskine** copier

korn *n.: -et, pl. same* grain; **byg** barley; **havre** oats; **hvede** wheat; **rug** rye

kort *n.: -et, pl. same* map; playing cards

kort *adj.* short

kortslutning *n.: -en, pl. -er* short circuit

koste *v.: -ede* cost; **kostbar** *adj.* precious; expensive

kostskole *n.: -n, pl. -r* boarding school

kreditkort *n.: -et, pl. same* credit card

krig *n.: -en, pl. -e* war

kriminel *adj.* criminal

krise *n.: -n, pl. -r* crisis; **krisehjælp** emergency assistance

kristen *adj.* Christian

kro *n.: -en, pl. -er* inn

krone *n.: -n, pl. -er* Danish monetary unit

kronprins *n.: -n, pl. -r* crown prince; **kronprinsesse** *n.: -n, pl. -r* crown princess

krydstogt *n.: -et, pl. -er* cruise

kræsen *adj.* fastidious, particular about food

krøllet *adj.* curly (hair); wrinkled (clothes)

kuffert *n.: -en, pl. -er* suitcase

kuglepen *n.: -nen, pl. -ne* ballpoint pen

kulde *n.: -n* (the) cold

kultur *n.: -en, pl. -er* culture; **kulturel** *adj.* cultural

kulør *n.: -en, pl. -er* color; **kulørtvask** colorfast cottons

kun *adv.* only

kunde *n.: -n, pl. -r* customer, client; **kundeservice** customer service

kunne *v.: kunne, kunnet (pre. kan)* could

kunst *n.: -en* art; **kunstudstilling** art exhibit; **kunstner** artist

kunstig *adj.* artificial; **kunstigt åndedræt** CPR

kupon *n.: -en, pl. -er* coupon

kurere *v.: -ede* cure

kursus *n.: -et or kurset, pl. kurser* educational course

kuvert *n.: -en, pl. -er* envelope; **pris pr. kuvert** price per person (at a restaurant with a fixed price menu)

kvalificeret *adj.* qualified

kvalitet *n.: -en, pl. -er* quality

kvalme *n.: -n* nausea

kvartal *n.: -et, pl. -er* annual quarter

kvarter *n.: -et, pl. same* fifteen minutes; **boligkvarter** residential area

kvartfinale *n.: -n, pl. -r* quarterfinal

kvidre *v.: -ede* chirp, twitter

kvinde *n.: -n, pl. -r* woman; **kvindebevægelsen** the feminist movement

kvittering *n.: -en, pl. -er* receipt

kvæg *n.: -et* cattle

kvæste *v.: -ede* injure

kysse *v.: -ede* kiss; **kys** *n.: -set, pl. same* kiss; **kyssesyge** mononucleosis

kyst *n.: -en, pl. -er* coast; **kystpoliti** coast guard

kæde *n.: -n, pl. -r* chain; **kæderyger** chain-smoker

kælder *n.: -en, pl. kældre* basement

kælenavn *n.: -et, pl. -e* nickname

kær *adj.* dear; **kære** dear (salutation)

kæreste *n.: -n, pl. -r* boyfriend, girlfriend

kærlighed *n.: -en* love; **kærlig** *adj.* loving

kø *n.: -en, pl. -er* line; billiard cue; **stå i kø** wait in line; **kø-nummer** number in line

købe *v.: -te* buy

københavner *n.: -en, pl. -e* Copenhagener

købmand *n.: -en, pl. købmænd* grocer

kød *n.: -et* meat; **svinekød** pork; **lammekød** lamb; **oksekød** beef; **kalvekød** veal

køje *n.: -n, pl. -r* bunk bed

køkken *n.: -et, pl. -er* kitchen; **køkkenrulle** kitchen towel

køleskab *n.: -et, pl. -e* refrigerator

kølig *adj.* cool

køn *n.: -net, pl. same* sex, gender; **det modsatte køn** the opposite sex

køn *adj.* pretty

køre *v.: -te* drive; **kørekort** driver's license; **køresyg** carsick; **få kørelejlighed** catch a ride

køreplan *n.: -en, pl. -er* bus or train schedule

L

lade *v.: lod, ladet* or *ladt* let; **lade som om** give the impression, pretend

land *n.: -et, pl. -e* country, countryside; **på landet** in the countryside

landbrug *n.: -et, pl. same* agriculture; farm

lande *v.: -ede* land; **landingsbane** *n.: -n, pl. -r* runway

landevej *n.: -en, pl. -e* large country road; **lige ud ad landevejen** straightforward, easy to do

landgangsbro *n.: -en, pl. -er* gangplank; **gå i land** go ashore

landkort *n.: -et, pl. same* map

landmand *n.: -en, pl. landmænd* farmer

landsby *n.: -en, pl. -er* village

landshold *n.: -et, pl. same* national team

lang *adj.* long

langs *adv., prep.* along; **langs af sted** little by little

langsom *adj.* slow

lappe *v.: -ede* patch

larm *n.: -en* noise

lastbil *n.: -en, pl. -er* truck; **lastbilchauffør** *n.: -en, pl. -er* truck driver

latter *n.: -en* laughter; **lattermild** quick to laughter

lav *adj.* low

lavalder *n.: -en* minimum age; **seksuel lavalder** age of consent; **kriminel lavalder** age of criminal responsibility

lave *v.: -ede* do; make

lavprisvarehus *n.: -et, pl. -e* discount department store

lede (efter) *v.: -te (efter)* search for, look for something

leder *n.: -en, pl. -e* leader, manager; newspaper editorial; **lede** *v.: -te* lead, manage

ledig *adj.* vacant, empty; unemployed

ledning *n.: -en, pl. -er* cord; **forlængerledning** extension cord

lege *v.: -ede* play (games, with toys); **legeplads** playground; **legetøj** toys

legoklods *n.: -en, pl. -er* lego; **Legoland** amusement park in Billund with impressive lego displays and rides

leje *v.: -ede* rent; rent out; **lejemål** *n.: -et, pl. same* lease

lejlighed *n.: -en, pl. -er* apartment

lejr *n.: -en, pl. lejre* camp; **sommerlejr** summer camp; **slå lejr** set up camp; **lejrbål** campfire

let *adj.* easy

letsindig *adj.* rash, irresponsible, foolhardy

leve *v.: -ede* live, be alive

levere *v.: -ede* deliver

leverpostej *n.: -en, pl. -e* liver pâté

lide *v.: led, lidt* suffer; **kunne lide** *v.: kunne, kunnet lide* like *(pre. kan lide)*

lidt *adj.* little
lige *adj.* straight
ligeglad *adj.* indifferent
ligesom *adj., adv.* like
ligge *v.: lå, ligget* lie
ligne *v.: -ede* look like
lilla *adj.* purple
lillejuleaften *n.: -en, pl. -er* evening of December 23
lim *n.: -en* glue; **lime** *v.: -ede* glue
linie *n.: -n, pl. -r* line; **lineal** *n.: -en, pl. -er* ruler
linned *n.: -et* linen; underwear
liter *n.: -en, pl. same* liter (approximately one quart)
litteratur *n.: -en* literature; **faglitteratur** non-fiction; **skønlitteratur** fiction
lodret *adj.* vertical
lodseddel *n.: -en* or *lodsedlen, pl. lodsedler* lottery or raffle ticket
lokal *adj.* local; **lokalhistorie** local history
lokale *n.: -t, pl. -r* room, meeting room
lomme *n.: -n, pl. -r* pocket; **lommetyv** *n.: -en, pl. -e* pickpocket; **lommeregner** *n.: -en, pl. -e* calculator
lommelygte *n.: -n, pl. -r* flashlight
lommetørklæde *n.: -t, pl. -r* handkerchief; **papirlommetørklæde** facial tissue
loppe *n.: -n, pl. -r* flea
losseplads *n.: -en, pl. -er* dump, landfill
lotteri *n.: -et, pl. -er* lottery; **lotteriseddel** lottery ticket
lov *n.: -en, pl. -e* law; **få lov (til at)** *v.: fik, fået lov (til at)* get permission (to do something)

love *v.: -ede* promise
lovlig *adj.* legal; *adv.* a little, too, rather
luft *n.: -en* air; **luftmadras** air mattress
lugte *v.: -ede* smell, stink; **lugte af** smell like
lukke *v.: -ede* close; **lukke op** open; **lukke i** close; **lukketid** closing time (shops)
luksuriøs *adj.* luxurious
lun *adj.* lukewarm, tepid
lup *n.: -pen, pl. -per* magnifying glass
lurmærke trademark for certain Danish agricultural products
lus *n.: -en, pl. same* lice
lygte *n.: -n, pl. -r* light; **lygtetændingstid** time of day before dark when bicycle lights must be turned on
lykønske *v.: -ede* congratulate; **tillykke med fødselsdagen** happy birthday
lyn *n.: -et, pl. same* bolt of lightning; **lynafleder** lightning rod
lyng *n.: -en* heather
lynlås *n.: -en, pl. -e* zipper
lys *n.: -et, pl. same* light; **stearinlys** candle
lyse- *adj. pref.* light; **lyseblå** light blue
lysestage *n.: -n, pl. -r* candlestick
lyst *adj.* light
lyst *n.: -en, pl. -er* desire
læ *n.: -et* shelter; **læ for vinden** shelter from the wind
læge *n.: -n, pl. -r* doctor
lægge *v.: lagde, lagt* lay, put down; **lægge sig** lie down

lækker *adj.* delicious, tasty; exquisite; lovely, sweet, pretty

længe *adv.* for a long time

lære *v.: -te* learn; teach

lærer *n.: -en, pl. -e* teacher; **folkeskolelærer** public school teacher

lærke *n.: -n, pl. -r* lark

læse *v.: -te* read; **læsebriller** reading glasses

løbe *v.: løb, løbet* run; **løbehjul** scooter; **løbebånd** treadmill

løfte *v.: -ede* lift

lørdag *n.: -en, pl. -e* Saturday

løs *adj.* loose

låne *v.: -te* borrow; lend

lås *n.: -en, pl. -e* lock; **låsesmed** locksmith

M

mad *n.: -en* food; **madforgiftning** food poisoning

mad *n.: -den, pl. -der* open-faced sandwich; **ostemad** with cheese; **spegepølsemad** with salami

madame-pose *n.: -n, pl. -r* plastic bag in restrooms for tampons and sanitary napkins

madpakke *n.: -n, pl. -r* brown-bag lunch

madras *n.: -sen, pl. -ser* mattress

madro *n.: -en* peace and quiet during a meal

mager *adj.* skinny, lean

magnet *n.: -en, pl. -er* magnet; **magnetisk** *adj.* magnetic

maj *n.* May

majestæt *n.: -en, pl. -er* majesty; **Hendes Majestæt Dronning Margrethe II** Her Majesty Queen Margrethe II

majs *n.: -en, pl. same* corn; **majskolbe** corn on the cob

male *v.: -ede* paint; grind

maler *n.: -en, pl. -e* painter (houses); **kunstmaler** painter (art)

malke *v.: -ede* milk; **malkeko** *n.: -en, pl. malkekøer* dairy cow

man *pron.* you, one

mand *n.: -en, pl. mænd* man

mandag *n.: -en, pl. -e* Monday

mange *adj., pron.* many, numerous

mangle *v.: -ede* lack; be in need of; be missing

maratonløb *n.: -et, pl. same* marathon

Marguerit-ruten scenic route that runs throughout Denmark

marinere *v.: -ede* marinate; **marinerede sild** pickled herring

mark *n.: -en, pl. -er* field; **græsmark** pasture; **kornmark** grainfield

markspiller *n.: -en, pl. -e* field player (as opposed to goalkeeper)

marts *n.* March

meddelelse *n.: -n, pl. -r* message

medicin *n.: -en* medicine

medlem *n.: -met, pl. -mer* member; **MF (medlem af folketinget)** member of parliament

medlidenhed *n.: -en* pity, compassion, sympathy; **medlidenhedsdrab** euthanasia

medmindre *adv.* unless

medregne *v.: -ede* include, take into account

medvind *n.: -en* tailwind

meget *adj., adv.* very, a great deal, a lot

mejeri *n.: -et, pl. -er* dairy; **mejeriprodukt** *n.: -et, pl. -er* dairy product

mekaniker *n.: -en, pl. -e* mechanic

mellem *prep.* between; among

mellem- in compound words to express medium quality or something in between; **mellemnavn** middle name

men *conj.* but

mene *v.: -te* think, believe; **meningsmåling** opinion poll

menneske *n.: -t, pl. -r* person, human being

mens *conj.* while

menu *n.: -en, pl. -er* menu

mere *adj.* more

mesterskab *n.: -et, pl. -er* championship; **VM** world championship; **EM** European championship

meter *n.: -en, pl. same* meter (39.37 inches); **metervarer** yard goods

middag *n.: -en, pl. -e* dinner; **middagsselskab** dinner party

middel- in compound words to express medium position; **middelklasse** middle class

midlertidig *adj.* temporary

midte *n.: -n* middle

mild *adj.* mild

militær *n.: -et* military

miljø *n.: -et, pl. -er* environment; **miljøbeskyttelse** environmental protection

milliard *n.: -en, pl. -er* billion

mindre *adj.* smaller, less

minut *n.: -tet, pl. -ter* minute; **i minuttet** per minute

misforstå *v.: misforstod, misforstået* misunderstand

miste *v.: -ede* lose

mjød *n.: -n* mead (fermented honey dissolved in water)

mobiltelefon *n.: -en, pl. -er* cellular phone

modbydelig *adj.* disgusting, nasty, foul, repulsive

mode *n.: -n* fashion; **moderne** *adj.* fashionable

moden *adj.* ripe; mature

modgift *n.: -en* antidote

modsat *adj.* opposite

modtage *v.: modtog, modtaget* receive

modvind *n.: -en* headwind

moms *n.: -en* value-added tax

morgen *n.: -en, pl. -er* morning; **morgenmad** breakfast; **morgenavis** morning paper

muggen *adj.* moldy

mulig *adj.* possible

mund *n.: -en, pl. -e* mouth

mur *n.: -en, pl. -e* wall

mus *n.: -en, pl. same* mouse; **musestille** as quiet as a mouse

museum *n.: museet, pl. museer* museum; **museumsudstilling** museum exhibit

musik *n.: -ken* music; **musiker** *n.: -en, pl. -e* musician

myg *n.:* -gen, pl. same
mosquito; **myggestik**
mosquito bite;
myggebalsam bug
repellent

myldretid *n.:* -en rush hour;
i myldretiden during
rush hour

myndig *adj.* of age; authorita-
tive; **blive myndig** come
of age

myre *n.:* -n, pl. -r ant;
myregift ant poison

mælk *n.:* -en milk; **sødmælk**
whole milk; **letmælk** 2%
milk; **skummetmælk**
skim milk; **kærnemælk**
buttermilk

mærke *v.:* -ede feel; **bide
mærke i** take notice of

mæt *adj.* full

møbel *n.:* møblet, pl. møbler
furniture

møde *v.:* -te meet; **møde** *n.:*
-t, pl. -r meeting

mølle *n.:* -n, pl. -r mill;
vandmølle water mill;
vindmølle windmill

mønster *n.* mønstret, pl.
mønstre pattern

mønt *n.:* -en, pl. -er coin

mønttelefon *n.:* -en, pl. -er
pay phone

møntvaskeri *n.:* -et, pl. -er
Laundromat

mørk *adj.* dark

mørke *n.:* -t dark; **ved
mørkets frembrud** at
dusk

måle *v.:* -te measure;
målebånd tape measure

måltid *n.:* -et, pl. -er meal

måne *n.:* -n, pl. -r moon;
måneskin moonlight;
måneformørkelse eclipse
of the moon

måske *adv.* perhaps

måtte *v.:* måtte, måttet (pre.
må) may, be allowed to;
have to

N

nabo *n.:* -en, pl. -er neighbor;
nabolag *n.:* -et, pl. same
neighborhood

narkoman *n.:* -en, pl. -er
drug addict

narkotika *n.:* -en drugs,
narcotics;
narkotikamisbrug drug
abuse

nat *n.:* -ten, pl. nætter night

nationalitet *n.:* -en, pl. -er
nationality

natur *n.:* -en nature; **natursti**
n.: -en, pl. -er nature path

naturlig *adj.* natural

naturmedicin *n.:* -en natural
medicine, herbal medicine

navle *n.:* -n, pl. -r belly
button

navn *n.:* -et, pl. -e name;
fornavn first name;
efternavn last name;
mellemnavn middle
name

nazist *n.:* -en, pl. -er Nazi;
nynazist neo-Nazi

ned *adv.* down

nedbør *n.:* -en precipitation

nedslidt *adj.* worn, run-down,
worn-out

negl *n.:* -en, pl. -e nail;
neglelak nail polish

nej *interj.* no; **nejsiger**
naysayer

nem *adj.* easy, simple

ni *num.* nine; **niende** ninth

nitten *num.* nineteen;
nittende nineteenth

node *n.:* -n, pl. -r musical
note

nok *adv.* enough
nord *n.* north
november *n.* November
nu *adv.* now; **nulevende**
living, existing,
contemporary
nul *num.* zero; **nulstille** *v.:*
-ede reset
nummer (nr.) *n.: -et, pl.*
numre number
nummerplade *n.: -n, pl. -r*
license plate
ny *adj.* new; **nybegynder** *n.:*
-en, pl. -e beginner,
novice, rookie
nyhed *n.: -en, pl. -er* news
nyse *v.: -te* sneeze
nysgerrig *adj.* curious
nyttig *adj.* useful
nytår *n.: -et, pl. same* New
Year; **nytårsaften** New
Year's Eve; **nytårsforsæt**
New Year's resolution
nær *adj.* close; **i nærheden**
close by
nærig *adj.* stingy
nærkøb
(nærkøbsforretning) *n.*
convenience store
næse *n.: -n, pl. -r* nose;
næseblod nosebleed
næste *adj.* next; **i næste uge**
next week
næsten *adv.* almost, close to
nævne *v.: -te* or *-ede*
mention; **nævneværdig**
worth mentioning
nød *n.: -den, pl. -der* nut;
nøddeknækker
nutcracker
nød *n.: -en* need; **lide nød** *v.*
suffer, be in dire need
nødudgang *n.: -en, pl. -e*
emergency exit;
nødlanding emergency
landing

nødvendig *adj.* necessary
nøgen *adj.* naked;
nøgenbadning nude
bathing, skinny-dipping
nøgle *n.: -n, pl. -r* key
nøjsom *adj.* frugal; humble
nål *n.: -en, pl. -e* needle;
nåletræ pine tree; **nål og
tråd** needle and thread
når *adv., conj.* when; **når
som helst** any time

O

obligatorisk *adj.* mandatory
offentlig *adj.* public; **offentlig
transport** public
transportation
offentlig *adj.* having to do
with government; **det
offentlige** public
authorities, government
ofte *adv.* often
og *conj.* and
også *adv.* too, as well
oktantal *n.: -let, pl. same*
octane rating
oktober *n.* October
oldtid *n.: -en* antiquity
olie *n.: -n* oil; **skifte olie**
change the oil
olympisk *adj.* Olympic; **De
Olympiske Lege** the
Olympic Games
omadressere *v.: -ede*
forward, redirect (letter,
shipment)
ombestemme sig *v.: -te sig*
change one's mind
omfangsrig *adj.* extensive,
bulky, voluminous
omfatte *v.: -ede* include,
consist of
omgængelig *adj.*
approachable, sociable
omgående *adv.* immediately
omklædningsrum *n.: -met,
pl. same* locker room

omkostning *n.: -en, pl. -er* expense, cost

omkørsel *n.: -en* or *omkørslen, pl. omkørsler* detour

område *n.: -t, pl. -r* area; **områdenummer** area code

omtrent *adv.* circa, about

ond *adj.* evil; **ondartet** malignant

onsdag *n.: -en, pl. -e* Wednesday

op *adv., adj., prep.* up

opdage *v.: -ede* discover

opdatere *v.: -ede* update

operere *v.: -ede* perform surgery

opfinde *v.: opfandt, opfundet* invent

ophold *n.: -et, pl. same* stay; **opholdstilladelse** residence permit

opholdsvejr *n.: -et* period of time without rain

opkald *n.: -et, pl. same* phone call

oplukker *n.: -en, pl. -e* bottle opener

opløse *v.: -te* dissolve

optage *v.: optog, optaget* accept into a program; record; **båndoptager** tape recorder

optaget *adj.* busy (telephone); in use (for ex. bathroom)

optog *n.: -et, pl. same* parade, procession

opvartning *n.: -en* service

opvask *n.: -en* dirty dishes

orange *adj.* orange

ord *n.: -et, pl. same* word

ordbog *n.: -en, pl. ordbøger* dictionary

ordinere *v.: -ede* prescribe medicine; **lægeordineret medicin** prescription medicine

os *pron.* us

ost *n.: -en, pl. -e* cheese; **ostehøvl** cheese slicer

osv. (og så videre) *abbr.* and so on, etc.

otte *num.* eight; **ottende** eighth

ovenfor *adv.* above

ovenfra *adv.* from above

oveni *adv.* on top of

ovenover *adv.* above

ovenpå *adv.* on top of

over *adv., prep.* above; across; more than

overalt *adv.* everywhere

overbevise *v.: -te* convince; **overbevisende** convincing

overfølsom *adj.* allergic, sensitive

overførsel *n.: overførslen, pl. overførsler* transfer; **bankoverførsel** wire transfer

overhale *v.: -ede* pass; **overhalingsbane** *n.: -n, pl. -r* fast lane

overholde *v.: overholdt, overholdt* observe, keep, abide by

overhovedet *adv.* at all; altogether

overmorgen: i overmorgen the day after tomorrow

overnatte *v.: -ede* stay overnight

overskyet *adj.* cloudy

overstige *v.: oversteg, oversteget* exceed

oversvømmelse *n.: -n, pl. -r* flood

oversætte *v.: oversatte, oversat* translate

overtale *v.: -te* persuade

overtræde *v.: overtrådte, overtrådt* break, violate, breach; **overtræde loven** break the law

overvægtig *adj.* overweight

P

pakke *n.:* *-n, pl. -r* package, parcel; **en pakke cigaretter** a pack of cigarettes

pakke *v.:* *-ede* pack; **pakke ud** unwrap, unpack

panik *n.:* *-ken* panic; **panikslagen** *adj.* panic-stricken

pap *n.:* *-pen* or *-pet* cardboard; **papbæger** paper cup; **paptallerken** paper plate; **papkasse** cardboard box

papir *n.:* *-et, pl. -er* paper; **papirkurv** wastepaper basket; **papirslommetørklæde** facial tissue

paragraf *n.:* *-fen, pl. -fer* section, clause, article; **klare paragrafferne** cope with a situation

parallel *adj.* parallel; **løber parallelt med** runs parallel to

paraply *n.:* *-en, pl. -er* umbrella

parat *adj.* ready

parcelhus *n.:* *-et, pl. -e* single-family house with a garden

park *n.:* *-en, pl. -er* park

parkere *v.:* *-ede* park; **parkeringsplads** parking lot; **parkering forbudt** no parking

pas *n.:* *-set, pl. same* passport

passager *n.:* *-en, pl. -er* passenger

passe *v.:* *-ede* look after; **passe børn** look after children

passe *v.:* *-ede* fit; be true

pas på *interj.* watch out!

passere *v.:* *-ede* pass

patient *n.:* *-en, pl. -er* patient

pege *v.:* *-ede* point to

pels *n.:* *-en, pl. -e* fur, fur coat

pendler *n.:* *-en, pl. -e* commuter

penge *n. (pl.)* money; **pengeinstitut** bank; **pengeoverførsel** money transfer

pensionist *n.:* *-en, pl. -er* senior citizen

per (pr.) *prep.* **pr. luftpost** by airmail; **pr. stk.** apiece; **to gange pr. dag** twice a day; **betales pr.** pay by

periode *n.:* *-n, pl. -r* period of time

perron *n.:* *-en, pl. -er* platform; **afgang fra perron 1** departure from platform number one

person *n.:* *-en, pl. -er* person; **personnummer (CPR-nr.)** social security number

pibe *n.:* *-n, pl. -r* pipe (for smoking)

pilsner *n.:* *-en, pl. -e* lager beer

PIN-kode *n.:* *-n, pl. -r* personal identification number

plakat *n.:* *-en, pl. -er* poster

planlægge *v.:* *planlagde, planlagt* plan, arrange

plante *n.:* *-n, pl. -r* plant; **plante** *v.:* *-ede* plant

pleje *v.:* *-ede* nurse, take care of, tend to; **plejeforældre** foster parent; **plejehjem** nursing home

pleje at gøre *v.:* *-ede at gøre* usually do something, accustomed to doing something a certain way

plet *n.: -ten, pl. -ter* spot;
pletfri spotless;
pletrensning spot
removal

pligtopfyldende *adj.*
conscientious;
pligtmenneske dutiful
person

plombere *v.: -ede* fill a
cavity; seal a CD (for
return or exchange
purposes)

pludselig *adj., adv* sudden,
suddenly

plukke *v.: -ede* pick, pluck;
håndplukke handpick

plæne *n.: -n, pl. -r* lawn;
plæneklipper lawn mower

pløje *v.: -ede* plow; **pløjeland**
arable land

pokal *n.: -en, pl. -er* cup,
trophy

politi *n.: -et* police;
politibetjent policeman;
polititilhold restraint
order; **politibeskyttelse**
police protection

politiker *n.: -en, pl. -e* politi-
cian

pollental *n.: -let, pl. same*
pollen count

polyp *n.: -pen, pl. -per* polyp,
adenoids

pornoblad *n.: -et, pl. -e*
pornographic magazine;
pornofilm pornographic
film

pose *n.: -n, pl. -r* bag; **plastic-
pose** plastic bag

postbud *n.: -et, pl. -e*
mailman

posthus *n.: -et, pl. -e* post
office

postkasse *n.: -n, pl. -r*
mailbox

postkort *n.: -et, pl. same*
postcard

postnummer *n.: -et, pl. postnumre* zip code

postvæsen *n.: -et* postal
service

pragtfuld *adj.* magnificent,
splendid

pressen *n.* the press;
pressefotograf press pho-
tographer; **pressemøde**
press conference

prins *n.: -en, pl. -er* prince;
kronprins crown prince

prinsesse *n.: -n, pl. -r*
princess; **kronprinsesse**
crown princess

pris *n.: -en, pl. -er* price;
prisskilt price tag

privat *adj.* private

problematisk *adj.*
problematic

procent *n.: -en, pl. -er* percent

promillekørsel *n.:*
promillekørslen drunk driving (0.05–0.12%)

prostitueret kvinde *n.*
prostitute

præsident *n.: -en, pl. -er*
president

præst *n.: -en, pl. -er* priest,
minister

prævention *n.: -en, pl. -er*
birth control

prøve *v.: -ede* try

P-skive (parkeringsskive) *n.:*
-n, pl. -r clock-like dial
placed in cars to indicate
time of parking

psykologisk *adj.*
psychological; **psykolog**
psychologist; **psykiater**
psychiatrist

puls *n.: -en* pulse

pung *n.: -en, pl. -e* wallet;
scrotum

puslerum *n.: -met, pl. same*
room for changing diapers

pynte *v.:* *-ede* decorate; **julepynt** Christmas decorations

pæn *adj.* nice-looking, nice, good, decent, respectable

pære *n.:* *-n, pl. -r* pear; lightbulb

pæredansk *adj.* very Danish

pølse *n.:* *-n, pl. -r* sausage, hotdog; **pølsevogn** hotdog stand

på *prep.* on; **på stedet** right then and there

pålæg *n.:* *-get* cold cuts, cheese, etc. for sandwiches

påpege *v.:* *-ede* point out, mention

pårørende *n. (pl.)* relatives

påske *n.:* *-n* Easter; **påskedag** Easter Sunday; **påskehare** Easter bunny; **påskeæg** Easter egg

Q

quilte *v.:* *-ede* quilt; **quiltet tæppe** quilted blanket

quizze *v.:* *-ede* quiz

R

rabat *n.:* *-ten, pl. -ter* discount; **grupperabat** group discount

rabat *n.:* *-ten, pl. -ter* road shoulder

race *n.:* *-n, pl. -r* race, breed; **racisme** racism

race *n.:* *-t, pl. same* race; **racerbane** racetrack

radio *n.:* *-en, pl. -er* radio; **radioavis** radio news broadcast

ramme *v.:* *-te* hit a target

ramme *n.:* *-n, pl. -r* frame; **referenceramme** frame of reference

rampe *n.:* *-n, pl. -r* ramp; **rampelys** spotlight; **i offentlighedens rampelys** in the limelight

rask *adj.* quick; healthy; **blive rask igen** recover from illness

rav *n.:* *-et* amber

rav- *prefix used for emphasis*; **tale ravjysk** speak with a heavy Jutland accent

reb *n.:* *-et, pl. same* rope; **rebstige** rope ladder

recept *n.:* *-en, pl. -er* prescription

redde *v.:* *-ede* save; **livredder** lifeguard; **redningsbåd** lifeboat

rede *v.:* *-te* comb

rede *n.:* *-n, pl. -r* nest

rede *adj.* ready

refundere *v.:* *-ede* refund

regel *n.:* *-en* or *reglen, pl. regler* rule; **færdselsregler** traffic regulations

regelmæssig *adj.* regular

regent *n.:* *-en, pl. -er* ruler, sovereign; **regentparret** the royal couple

regn *n.:* *-en* rain; **regnbue** rainbow; **regnbyge** shower; **regnjakke** raincoat

regning *n.:* *-en, pl. -er* bill, invoice

rejse *v.:* *-te* travel; **rejsebureau** travel agency; **rejsecheck** traveler's check

reklame *n.:* *-n, pl. -r* advertisement

ren *adj.* clean, pure

rengøring *n.:* *-en* cleaning

renovation *n.* garbage collection; **renovationsvogn** garbage truck

renovere *v.:* *-ede* fix up, remodel

rense *v.:* *-ede* clean, purify; **renseri** dry cleaner

rente *n.:* *-n, pl. -r* interest, interest rate

reparere *v.:* *-ede* fix, repair

replik *n.:* *-ken, pl. -ker* reply, remark, repartee; line (theater)

reservere *v.:* *-ede* reserve, book

restaurant *n.:* *-en, pl. -er* restaurant; also **restauration** *n.:* *-en, pl. -er*

resultat *n.:* *-et, pl. -er* result

ret *n.:* *-ten, pl. -ter* dish, course; **tre retter mad** three courses

ret *adj.* straight, right, proper; **det rette øjeblik** the right moment

ret *n.:* *-ten* court of law; **retsstridig** unlawful

retfærdig *adj.* fair, just

rettighed *n.:* *-en, pl. -er* right; **retssikkerhed** legal rights

retur *adv.* back; **sende retur** send back; **returbillet** return ticket; **returflaske** returnable bottle

returnere *v.:* *-ede* return, give back

revisor *n.:* *-en, pl. -er* accountant

revne *v.:* *-ede* crack, split open; **revnefærdig** ready to burst

ride *v.:* *red, redet* ride; **rideskole** riding school

ridse *v.:* *-ede* scratch

rig *adj.* rich

rigelig *adj.* plentiful, more than enough

Rigshospitalet main research and teaching hospital in Denmark

rigtig *adj.* correct, appropriate

rim *n.:* *-en* rime, frost

rime *v.:* *-ede* rhyme; **rim** *n.:* *-et, pl. same* rhyme

rimelig *adj.* reasonable, fair

rimelig *adv.* fairly, relatively, reasonably

ring *n.:* *-en, pl. -e* ring

ringe *v.:* *-ede* ring; **opringning** telephone call

ringe *adj.* of poor quality, bad

ris *n.:* *-en* rice; **risalamande** Danish Christmas rice pudding

risikabel *adj.* risky

riste *v.:* *-ede* grill, roast; **ristede pølser** grilled sausages, hotdogs

ro *n.:* *-en* peace and quiet; **rolig** *adj.* peaceful and quiet

ro *v.:* *-ede* row; **robåd** rowboat

roe *n.:* *-n, pl. -r* beet; **roemark** field with beets; **sukkerroe** sugar beet

rolle *n.:* *-n, pl. -r* role; **rollemodel** role model

roman *n.:* *-en, pl. -er* novel

romantisk *adj.* romantic

romertal *n.:* *-let, pl. same* roman numeral

rose *n.:* *-n, pl. -r* rose

rotte *n.:* *-n, pl. -r* rat

rude *n.:* *-n, pl. -r* pane, window; **rudekonvolut** window envelope

rullestol *n.:* *-en, pl. -e* wheelchair

rund *adj.* round

rundkirke *n.:* *-n, pl. -r* round church found on the island of Bornholm

rundkørsel *n.: -en or rundkørslen, pl. rundkørsler* traffic circle, roundabout

rundvisning *n.: -en. pl. -er* guided tour

rune *n.: -n, pl. -r* runic letter; **runesten** runic stone

rust *n.: -en* rust; **rusten** *adj.* rusty; **rustbehandle** rustproof

rustik *adj.* rustic

rute *n.: -n, pl. -r* route; **rutebil** rural bus

ryge *v.: røg, røget* smoke; **rygning forbudt** no smoking

række *n.: -n, pl. -r* row

rækkefølge *n.: -n* order; **i den rigtige rækkefølge** in the right order

rækkehus *n.: -et, pl. -e* townhouse

rød *adj.* red; **rødvin** red wine

rødme *v.: -ede* blush

røg *n.: -en* smoke; **røgalarm** smoke detector

røge *v.: -ede* smoke; **røget sild** smoked herring

røntgenbillede *n.: -t, pl. -r* X-ray; **røntgenfotografere** *v.: -ede* x-ray

røre *v.: -te* touch; move; stir

rå *adj.* raw

råbe *v.: -te* shout, call; **råbe om hjælp** call for help

rådden *adj.* rotten

rådhus *n.: -et, pl. -e* city hall; **Rådhuspladsen** city square in Copenhagen

S

saft *n.: -en, pl. -er* juice; sap; **saftevand** fruit juice; **saftig** juicy

sagfører *n.: -en, pl. -e* lawyer

saks *n.: -en, pl. -e* scissors; **neglesaks** nail scissors

salg *n.: -et, pl. same* sale; **ikke til salg** not for sale

salme *n.: -n, pl. -r* hymn; **salmebog** *n.: -en, pl. salmebøger* hymnal

salt *n.: -et* salt; **saltbøsse** saltshaker; **saltvand** salt water

samfund *n.: -et, pl. same* society; **samfundsmæssig** societal

samle *v.: -ede* assemble; collect; **samle frimærker** collect stamps

samleje *n.: -t, pl. -r* sexual intercourse

samles *v.: samledes, samlet* gather

samme *adj.* same

sammen *adv.* together; **tale sammen** talk to each other

sammenligne *v.: -ede* compare

sammenskudsgilde *n.: -t, pl. -r* potluck party

sammenstød *n.: -et, pl. same* collision; argument

samtale *n.: -n, pl. -r* conversation; **samtaleanlæg** intercom

samtidig *adj., adv.* at the same time, contemporary, simultaneous(ly)

sand *n.: -et* sand; **sandbund** sandy bottom; **sandstrand** sandy beach

sand *adj.* true; **sandhed** *n.: -en, pl. -er* truth

sang *n.: -en, pl. -e* song; **sangbog** songbook

sankthansaften Midsummer Eve (June 23) — celebrated with bonfires, singing, and speeches

S-bane *n.: -n, pl. -r* subway;
S-tog *n.: -et, pl. same*
subway train
se *v.: så, set* see
seddel *n.: -en* or *sedlen, pl.
sedler* note; bill (money)
sej *adj.* tough, chewy;
stubborn, tough; cool,
neat (slang)
sejle *v.: -ede* sail
seks *num.* six; **sjette** sixth
seksten *num.* sixteen;
sekstende sixteenth
seksualliv *n.: -et* sex life
sekund *n.: -et, pl. -er* second
selskab *n.: -et, pl. -er* party;
company, firm;
companionship
selvbetjening *n.: -en*
self-service
selverhvervende *adj.* self-
employed
selvforsvar *n.: -et* self-
defense
selvfølgelig *adj.* natural,
inevitable
selvfølgelig *adv.* of course
selvklæbende *adj.* self-
adhesive, self-sealing
selvrisiko *n.: -en, pl. -er* or
risici insurance deductible
sen *adj.* late; **komme for sent**
be late
sende *v.: -te* send, broadcast
seng *n.: -en, pl. -e* bed;
sengeliggende bedridden;
sengetid bedtime
SE-nummer *n.: -et, pl. SE-
numre* tax identification
number for business
servere *v.: -ede* serve (food)
servicestation *n.: -en, pl. -er*
gas station

sidde *v.: sad, siddet* sit
side *n.: -n, pl. -r* side;
sidegade side street;
ved siden af next to, on
the side
side *n.: -n, pl. -r* page; **sidetal**
page number
siden *adv., conj.* since
sidst *adj., adv., conj.* last;
hans sidste ord his last
words; **sidst** last time
sig *pron.* oneself; **gøre det af
sig selv** do it on own
initiative; **være lidt for
sig selv** be a little strange
sige *v.: sagde, sagt* say
signere *v.: -ede* sign
sikker *adj.* safe, certain, sure;
sikkerhedssele seat belt
sikkerhedsnål *n.: -en, pl. -e*
safety pin
sikring *n.: -en, pl. -er* fuse
sild *n.: -en, pl. same* herring;
flot sild pretty girl
(slang); **død sild** dud,
boring person
sin, sit, sine *pron.* his, hers,
one's
sjælden *adj.* rare; **sjældent**
adv. rarely, seldom
skade *v.: -ede* injure, damage;
komme til skade get
injured
skadestue *n.: -n, pl. -r*
emergency room
skakt *n.: -en, pl. -er* chute;
affaldsskakt garbage
chute
skarp *adj.* sharp
skat *n.: -ten, pl. -ter* tax;
skatteprocent tax rate
skat *n.: -ten, pl. -te* treasure;
sweetie, honey, darling
ske *v.: -te* happen, take place

skib *n.: -et, pl. -e* ship;
  skibsrederi shipping
  company; **skibsværft**
  shipyard
skifte *v.: -ede* change
skiftevis *adv.* by turns
skille (ad) *v.: -te* separate,
  take apart; **skilsmisse** *n.:*
  -n, pl. -r divorce
skilt *n.: -et, pl. -e* sign;
  færdselsskilt traffic sign
skind *n.: -et, pl. same* skin,
  hide
skinne *v.: -ede* shine; **solskin**
  sunshine
skive *n.: -n, pl. -r* slice;
  pålæg i skiver sliced cold
  cuts
skjule *v.: -te* hide
skole *n.: -n, pl. -r* school;
  skolebus school bus;
  skolelærer teacher
skov *n.: -en, pl. -e* forest,
  woods; **skovjordbær** wild
  strawberry; **skovsnegl**
  black slug *(Arion ater)*
skrald *n.: -et* garbage;
  skraldespand garbage can
skrive *v.: skrev, skrevet* write;
  skrivebord desk
skrotte *v.: -ede* scrap, throw
  out
skrue *n.: -n, pl. -r* screw;
  skruenøgle wrench;
  skruetrækker
  screwdriver; **have en**
  skrue løs be crazy
skrup- *prefix used for*
  emphasis; **skrupskør**
  totally crazy;
  skrupkedelig extremely
  boring
skrædder *n.: -en, pl. -e* tailor;
  skræddersyet tailor-
  made, custom-made
skrælle *v.: -ede* peel

skrå *adj.* slanted, tilted,
  sloping
skrå *v.: -ede* chew tobacco
skråsikker *adj.* cocksure,
  certain
skuffe *n.: -n, pl. -r* drawer;
  luk skuffen be quiet,
  shut up
skuffe *v.: -ede* disappoint;
  skuffelse *n.: -n, pl. -r*
  disappointment
skulle *v.: skulle, skullet (pre.*
  skal) should
sky *n.: -en, pl. -er* cloud;
  skydække cloud cover
skyde *v.: skød, skudt* shoot
skygge *n.: -n* shade; *n.: -n, pl.*
  -r shadow
skyld *n.: -en* guilt; **skyldig**
  adj. guilty
skylde *v.: -te* owe
skynde sig *v.: -te sig* hurry
skæg *adj.* funny, entertaining
skæg *n.: -get, pl. same* beard
skænke *v.: -ede* pour; give,
  grant
skære *v.: skar, skåret* cut;
  skærebræt cutting board
skål *interj.* cheers
skål *n.: -en, pl. -e* bowl
slags *n.: -en, pl. same* kind,
  type
slagsmål *n.: -et, pl. same*
  fight, brawl
slappe af *v.: -ede af* relax
slet ikke *adv.* not at all
slik *n.: -ket* candy
slikke *v.: -ede* lick;
  slikkepind lollipop
slot *n.: -tet, pl. -te* castle,
  palace
sluge *v.: -te* swallow
slukke *v.: -ede* turn off; put
  out; quench, satisfy
slut *adj.* finished, over

slægt *n.: -en, pl. -er* family; **være af god slægt** be of good stock; **slægtsgård** family farm

slægtsforskning *n.: -en* genealogy; **slægtshistorie** family history

slå *v.: slog, slået* hit, beat; **slå telt op** pitch a tent

smage *v.: -te* taste; **smagsprøve** *n.: -n, pl. -r* taste, sample

smal *adj.* narrow

smelte *v.: -ede* melt

smerte *n.: -n, pl. -r* pain; **smertefuld** *adj.* painful

smile *v.: -ede or -te* smile; **smil** *n.: -et, pl. same* smile; **smilehul** *n.: -let, pl. -ler* dimple

smittefarlig *adj.* contagious

smuk *adj.* beautiful

smør *n.: -ret* butter

smørrebrød *n. (pl.)* open-faced sandwiches

snakke *v.: -ede* talk, chat

snaps *n.: -en, pl. -e* schnapps

snart *adv.* soon

snavset *adj.* dirty

sne *n.: -en* snow; **sneskovl** snow shovel

snes *n.: -en, pl. -e* score (group of 20)

snor *n.: -en, pl. -e* string; **snorlige** completely straight

snorke *v.: -ede* snore

snyde *v.: snød, snydt* cheat

sodavand *n.: -en, pl. same* soda pop

sogn *n.: -et, pl. -e* parish

sol *n.: -en, pl. -e* sun

solbriller *n. (pl.)* sunglasses

soldat *n.: -en, pl. -er* soldier

solenergi *n.: -en* solar energy

solid *adj.* solid

solnedgang *n.: -en, pl. -e* sunset

solopgang *n.: -en, pl. -e* sunrise

solskin *n.: -net* sunshine

solskoldet *adj.* sunburned; **solstik** sunstroke; **solcreme** sunscreen

solægte *adj.* fadeless

sommer *n.: -en, pl. somre* summer; **sommerferie** summer vacation; **sommerhus** vacation home

sommerfugl *n.: -en, pl. -e* butterfly

sommetider *adv.* sometimes

soppe *v.: -ede* paddle, wade; **soppebassin** wading pool

sorg *n.: -en, pl. -r* sorrow, grief

sort *adj.* black; **sortbørshandel** black market transactions; **sortliste** *v.: -ede* blacklist

sove *v.: sov, sovet* sleep; **sovepose** *n.: -n, pl. -r* sleeping bag

spare *v.: -ede* save; **sparebøsse** piggy bank

sparke *v.: -ede* kick

spegepølse *n.: -n, pl. -r* salami

spejl *n.: -et, pl. -e* mirror; **spejlglat** very slippery

spids *adj.* pointed

spilde *v.: -te* spill; **spildtid** wasted time; **spild af tid** waste of time

spille *v.: -ede* play (ball games or instruments)

spiritus *n.: -en or -sen* alcohol

spirituskørsel drunk driving (over 0.12%)

spise *v.: -te* eat

springe *v.: sprang, sprunget* jump; burst

sprød *adj.* crisp

spørge *v.: spurgte, spurgt* ask; **stille et spørgsmål** ask a question

stadigvæk *adv.* still

stadion *n.: -et, pl. -er* stadium

stald *n.: -en, pl. -e* stable

standse *v.: -ede* stop

starte *v.: -ede* start, begin

statsborger *n.: -en, pl. -e* citizen; **statsborgerskab** citizenship

statsminister *n.: -en, pl. statsministre* prime minister

statsstøttet *adj.* state-supported, government-assisted

stave *v.: -ede* spell (words)

stearinlys *n.: -et, pl. same* candle

stejl *adj.* steep

stemme *v.: -te* vote; **stemmeret** the right to vote; **stemmeseddel** ballot

stemme *n.: -n, pl. -r* voice

sten *n.: -en, pl. same or -e* stone; **stenalderen** Stone Age; **stensikker** *adj.* dead certain

stentøj *n.: -et* stoneware

stereoanlæg *n.: -get, pl. same* stereo system

sti *n.: -en, pl. -er* path

stikke *v.: stak, stukket* sting

stikkontakt *n.: -en, pl. -er* power outlet

stille *adj.* quiet

stiv *adj.* stiff; **stivkrampe** tetanus

stjerne *n.: -n, pl. -r* star; **stjernekaster** sparkler

stjæle *v.: stjal, stjålet* steal

stoppe *v.: -ede* stop

stor *adj.* big; **Storkøbenhavn** Copenhagen metropolitan area; **stormagasin** department store

straks *adv., conj.* at once, right away

stram *adj.* tight

strand *n.: -en, pl. -e* beach

streg *n.: -en, pl. -er* line; **stregkode** bar code

strøm *n.: -men, pl. -me* current; **strømafbrydelse** power outage; **understrøm** undertow

studentereksamen *n.: -en, pl. -er or eksaminer* high school education

studere *v.: -ede* study

stuepige *n.: -n, pl. -r* chambermaid

stykke *n.: -t, pl. -r* piece; **pr. stk.** apiece

stærk *adj.* strong

støj *n.: -en* noise; **støjende** *adj.* noisy

størrelse *n.: -n, pl. -r* size

stå *v.: stod, stået* stand

suite *n.: -en, pl. -er* suite; **brudesuite** honeymoon suite

sukker *n.: -et* sugar; **sukkerfri** sugarless; **sukkersyge** diabetes

sulten *adj.* hungry

sund *adj.* healthy; **usund** unhealthy

sur *adj.* cranky, in a bad mood; sour

svare *v.: -ede* answer; **telefonsvarer** answering machine

svede *v.: -te* sweat

svimmel *adj.* dizzy

svin *n.: -et, pl. same* pig; **svinekød** pork; **skovsvin** litterbug

svømme *v.:* *-ede* swim; **svømmebassin** swimming pool

syd *n.:* *-en* south

syg *adj.* ill; **sygehus** hospital; **sygeforsikring** health insurance

synes *v.:* *syntes, syntes* think; **synes om** like

synge *v.:* *sang, sunget* sing

syv *num.* seven; **syvende** seventh

sælge *v.:* *solgte, solgt* sell

sær *adj.* strange, weird

sær- *prefix meaning special*; **særskilt** separate; **særbehandling** special treatment

særlig *adj.* particular, special

sæson *n.:* *-en, pl. -er* season; **sæsonkort** season ticket; **sæsonbestemt** seasonal

sø *n.:* *-en, pl. -er* lake, pond

sød *adj.* sweet; **kunstigt sødemiddel** artificial sweetener

sølv *n.:* *-et* silver; **sølvbryllup** 25th anniversary

søm *n.:* *-met, pl. same* nail; **ramme hovedet på sømmet** hit the nail on the head

søm *n.:* *-men, pl. -me* hem, seam

søndag *n.:* *-en, pl. -e* Sunday

søskende *n. (pl.)* siblings

så *conj.* so (also adj. and adv. with context-determined meaning)

således *adv.* like that, in that way

T

tabe *v.:* *-te* lose, drop

tag *n.:* *-et, pl. -e* roof; **stråtag** thatched roof

tage *v.:* *tog, taget* take

tak *interj.* thank you; **takkekort** thank-you note

taknemmelig *adj.* grateful

takst *n.:* *-en, pl. -er* rate, fare

tal *n.:* *-let, pl. same* number

tale *v.:* *-te* speak, talk; **tale** *n.:* *-n, pl. -r* speech

tand *n.:* *-en, pl. tænder* tooth; **tandlæge** dentist

tanke *n.:* *-n, pl. -r* thought

tankstation *n.:* *-en, pl. -er* service station, gas station; **tanke** *v.:* *-ede* pump gas

tegne *v.:* *-ede* draw; **tegnefilm** *n.:* *-en, pl. same* cartoon; **det tegner godt** it looks promising

tegnsprog *n.:* *-et* sign language

tekst *n.:* *-en, pl. -er* text; **tekstbehandling** word processing

telefon *n.:* *-en, pl. -er* telephone; **telefonbog** phonebook; **telefonnummer** phone number

telefonbruser *n.:* *-en, pl. -e* hand-held shower

telt *n.:* *-et, pl. -e* tent

temperatur *n.:* *-en, pl. -er* temperature

termoflaske (bottle), **termokande** (for coffee or tea) *n.:* *-n, pl. -r* thermos

termostat *n.:* *-en, pl. -er* thermostat

ti *num.* ten; **tiende** tenth

tid *n.:* *-en, pl. -er* time; **tidsfrist** deadline; **tidszone** time zone; **tidspunkt** point in time; **til tider** sometimes

tidlig *adj.* early

til *prep.* to, for (multiple meanings depending on context)

tilbage *adv.* back, backwards; **tre gæster tilbage** three guests left; **tilbagevirkende** retroactive

tilberede *v.: -te* prepare

tilbringe *v.: tilbragte, tilbragt* spend time

tilbud *n.: -et, pl. same* special offer

tilbyde *v.: tilbød, tilbudt* offer

tilfreds *adj.* satisfied

tilfældig *adj.* accidental, coincidental, random

tilgodeseddel *n.: -en, pl. tilgodesedler* credit note

tilkalde *v.: -te* call; **tilkalde en ambulance** call an ambulance

tillade *v.: tillod, tilladt* allow; **tilladelse** *n.: -n, pl. -r* permission

tillykke *interj.* congratulations; **tillykke med fødselsdagen** happy birthday

tilovers *adv.* left, left over

tilsammen *adv.* altogether

tilskuer *n.: -en, pl. -e* spectator, member of the audience

time *n.: -n, pl. -r* hour; **timebetaling** hourly pay; **timeglas** hourglass

ting *n.: -en, pl. same* thing

tirsdag *n.: -en, pl. -e* Tuesday

titel *n.: titlen, pl. titler* title

tiøre *n.: -n, pl. -r* coin (10 øre)

tja *interj.* well, maybe, yes and no

tjener *n.: -en, pl. -e* waiter

tjeneste *n.: -n, pl. -r* favor

to *num.* two; **tosproget** *adj.* bilingual

tobak *n.: -ken* tobacco; **tobaksrygning forbudt** no smoking

tog *n.: -et, pl. -e* train; **tage med toget** take the train

toilet *n.: -tet, pl. -ter* toilet; **toiletpapir** toilet paper

told *n.: -en* duty, customs; **toldfri** duty-free

tolk *n.: -en, pl. -e* interpreter

tolv *num.* twelve; **tolvte** twelfth

tom *adj.* empty

torden *n.: -en* thunder; **tordenskrald** clap of thunder

torsdag *n.: -en, pl. -e* Thursday

trafik *n.: -ken* traffic; **trafikprop** traffic jam

traktor *n.: -en, pl. -er* tractor

trappe *n.: -n, pl. -r* staircase; **trappestige** stepladder

tre *num.* three; **tredje** third

tredive *num.* thirty; **tredvte** thirtieth

tretten *num.* thirteen; **trettende** thirteenth

tro *n.: -en* faith, belief, persuasion; **trosretning** religious denomination

trone *n.: -n, pl. -r* throne; **tronfølger** heir to the throne; **den danske trone** the Danish throne

trykke *v.: -ede* or *-te* print; *v.: -ede* press; push

træffe *v.: traf, truffet* meet, run into, hit the target

trække *v.: trak, trukket* pull

træt *adj.* tired

tung *adj.* heavy

turist *n.: -en, pl. -er* tourist

tusind *num.* thousand

tv-udsendelse *n.: -n, pl. -r*
TV program

tygge *v.: -ede* chew;
tyggegummi chewing gum

tyk *adj.* thick; fat, overweight

tynd *adj.* thin

tyv *n.: -en, pl. -e* thief;
tyvekoster stolen goods

tyve *num.* twenty; **tyvende**
twentieth

tælle *v.: talte, talt* count

tændstik *n.: -ken, pl. -ker*
match (to light something)

tænke *v.: -te* think

tø *v.: -ede* thaw; **tø op** defrost

tøj *n.: -et* clothing; **tøjsnor**
clothesline; **tøjklemme**
clothespin

tør *adj.* dry; **tørretumbler**
clothes dryer

tørklæde *n.: -t, pl. -r* scarf

tørstig *adj.* thirsty

tørvejr *n.: -et* dry weather

tåge *n.: -en* fog; **tågehorn**
foghorn

tåle *v.: -te* tolerate

tårn *n.: -et, pl. -e* tower, steeple

U

uafbrudt *adj.* continuous,
uninterrupted, constant

uafgjort *adj.* undecided,
inconclusive, tied

uafhængig *adj.* independent,
sovereign, self-governing

ualmindelig *adj.* uncommon,
unusual

uanmeldt *adj.* unannounced

uanset *prep.* irrespective of,
no matter what

uansvarlig *adj.* irresponsible

ubegrænset *adj.* unlimited

ubehagelig *adj.* unpleasant,
distasteful, awkward,
annoying

ubekvem *adj.* uncomfortable,
awkward, inconvenient

ubeskadiget *adj.* unharmed

ubetinget *adj.* unqualified,
unconditional

ubetydelig *adj.* insignificant,
slight, negligible

ubetænksom *adj.* thoughtless

ubrugelig *adj.* useless

ud *prep.* out; **udgang** *n.: -en,
pl. -e* exit

uddannelse *n.: -n, pl. -r*
education

udeblive *v.: udeblev,
udeblevet* to be absent, to
be a no-show

uden *prep.* without

udendørs *adj.* outdoors

udenpå *adv.* on the outside

udenrigsfly *n.: -et, pl. same*
international flight

udfylde *v.: -te* fill out

udgift *n.: -en, pl. -er* expense

udkomme *n.: -et* outcome

udleje *v.: -ede* rent out;
udlejningsbil rental car

udlænding *n.: -en, pl. -e*
foreigner

udløbe *v.: udløb, udløbet*
expire; **udløbsdato**
expiration date

udsalg *n.: -et, pl. same* sale

udskifte *v.: -ede* change,
replace

udskyde *v.: udskød, udskudt*
postpone

udslæt *n.: -tet* rash, skin
eruption

udsmider *n.: -en, pl. -e*
bouncer

udspring *n.: -et, pl. same*
dive; jump; source,
headwaters

udstede *v.: -te* issue, make

udstilling *n.: -en, pl. -er*
exhibit

udstyr *n.: -et* equipment
udvendig *adj.* exterior, on the outside
ufarlig *adj.* safe, not dangerous
uformel *adj.* informal
uge *n.: -n, pl. -r* week; **ugeavis** weekly paper; **ugeblad** weekly magazine; **ugedag** weekday; **ugentlig** weekly
ugenert *adj.* secluded; free and easy, uninhibited
ugift *adj.* unmarried
ugyldig *adj.* invalid
uheld *n.: -et, pl. same* accident, mishap
ujævn *adj.* rough, uneven, irregular
ulovlig *adj.* illegal
ulykke *n.: -n, pl. -r* accident
ulæselig *adj.* illegible
umulig *adj.* impossible
under *prep.* under
underholdning *n.: -en* entertainment
underrette *v.: -ede* inform, notify
underskrift *n.: -en, pl. -er* signature
undersøge *v.: -te* investigate, examine
undervejs *adv.* on the way
undskyldning *n.; -en, pl. -er* apology; **undskyld** I am sorry; excuse me
undtagelse *n.: -n, pl. -r* exception; **gøre en undtagelse** make an exception
undtagen *prep., conj.* except
undvære *v.: -ede* do without
ung *adj.* young; **ungkarl** bachelor
uregelmæssig *adj.* irregular
usikker *adj.* uncertain, unsafe, insecure, doubtful

usund *adj.* unhealthy
usynlig *adj.* invisible
usødet *adj.* unsweetened
utilpas *adj.* uneasy, unwell
utro *adj.* unfaithful
utydelig *adj.* vague, indistinct
uægte *adj.* artificial, false, phony, insincere
uærlig *adj.* dishonest
uåbnet *adj.* unopened

V

vaccinere *v.: -ede* vaccinate
vagtlæge *n.: -n, pl. -r* doctor on call
vagtskifte *n.: -t* changing of the guard
valg *n.: -et, pl. same* choice; election; **folketingsvalg** parliamentary election
valgfri *adj.* optional
valgret *n.: -ten* the right to vote; **valgretsalder** voting age
valutakurs *n.: -en, pl. -er* exchange rate
vand *n.: -et* water; **vandtæt** waterproof
vandhane *n.: -n, pl. -r* faucet
vandmand *n.: -en, pl. vandmænd* jellyfish
vandmærke *n.: -t, pl. -r* watermark
vandmølle *n.: -n, pl. -r* water mill
vandskræk *adj.* afraid of water
vanskelig *adj.* difficult
vare *v.: -ede* last
vare *n.: -n, pl. -r* product, article, item, commodity; **varemærke** trademark
varm *adj.* warm
varme *n.: -n* heat; **varme** *v.: -ede* heat

vaske *v.: -ede* wash; **vaskbar** washable; **vaskeægte** colorfast, washable; **vasketøj** laundry

vaskemaskine *n.: -n, pl. -r* washing machine; **møntvaskeri** Laundromat

vegetar *n.: -en, pl. -er* vegetarian; **vegetarisk** *adj.* vegetarian; **vegetarmad** vegetarian food

vej *n.: -en, pl. -e* road; **vejar-bejde** road construction

veje *v.: -ede* weigh

vejkryds *n.: -et, pl. same* intersection

vejr *n.: -et* weather; **vejrudsigt** weather forecast

veksle *v.: -ede* change, exchange

velbekomme *interj.* you are welcome

velfærd *n.: -en* welfare; **velfærdsstat** welfare society

velhavende *adj.* wealthy

velkommen *interj.* welcome

velopdragen *adj.* well-behaved, well-mannered

velplejet *adj.* well-groomed, well taken care of

velsignelse *n.: -n, pl. -r* blessing; **velsigne** *v.: -ede* bless

ven *n.: -nen, pl. -ner* friend (male); **veninde** *n.: -n, pl. -r* friend (female); **vennekreds** circle of friends

venlig *adj.* kind, friendly; **venlig hilsen** kind regards

venskab *n.: -et, pl. -er* friendship

venstre *adj.* left

vente *v.: -ede* wait; **venteliste** waiting list; **venteværelse** waiting room

verden *n.: -en, pl. -er* world

vest *n.* west

vi *pron.* we

vide *v.: vidste, vidst* know; **viden** *n.: -en* knowledge

vidne *n.: -t, pl. -r* witness; **vidne** *v.: -ede* testify

vigtig *adj.* important

vikar *n.: -en, pl. -er* substitute, temp

viking *n.: -en, pl. -er* Viking

vild *adj.* wild; **fare vild** get lost

ville *v.: ville, villet (pre. vil)* will

villig *adj.* willing

vin *n.: -en, pl. -e* wine

vind *n.: -en, pl. -e* wind; **vindmølle** windmill; **vindtæt** windproof

vinde *v.: vandt, vundet* win

vindue *n.: -t, pl. -r* window; **vinduesplads** window seat

vinke *v.: -ede* wave

vinter *n.: -en, pl. vintre* winter; **vintergæk** snowdrop; **vinterhave** conservatory

virke *v.: -ede* work, function

virksomhed *n.: -en, pl. -er* business

vise *v.: -te* show

voksen *adj.* adult, mature

vold *n.: -en* violence

voldtægtsmand *n.: -en, pl. voldtægtsmænd* rapist; **voldtægt** rape

vred *adj.* angry

vægt *n.: -en, pl. -e* weight; scale

væk *adv.* away, absent, gone

vække v.: -ede wake somebody

vækkeur n.: -et, pl. -e alarm clock

vænne sig til v.: -ede sig til get used to

værdi n.: -en, pl. -er value; **værdigenstande** valuables

være v.: var, været (pre. er) be

værelse n.: -t, pl. -r room

værksted n.: -et, pl. -er repair shop

værktøj n.: -et, pl. -er or same tool; **værktøjskasse** toolbox

vært n.: -en, pl. -er host; **værtinde** n.: -n, pl. -r hostess

værtshus n.: -et, pl. -e bar, pub

våben n.: -et or våbnet, pl. same weapon

våd adj. wet; **våddragt** n.: -en, pl. -er wet suit

vågen adj. awake

vågne (op) v.: -ede wake up

W

wienerbrød n.: -et sweet pastry

wienerpølse n.: -n, pl. -r small hotdog

windsurfing n. windsurfing

Y

yde v.: -ede yield; give, contribute; perform

yderlighed n.: -en, pl. -er extreme

ydermere adv. furthermore

ydmyg adj. humble

yndefuld adj. graceful

yndig adj. lovely, pretty, sweet, charming

yt adj. no longer fashionable, passé

Z

zenit n.: -et zenith

zinksalve n.: -n zinc ointment

zone n.: -n, pl. -r zone

zoneterapi n.: -en reflexology

zoologisk have n. zoo

zoomlinse n.: -n, pl. -r zoom lens

Æ

æble n.: -t, pl. -r apple

æbleskive n.: -n, pl. -r small, round cake made from waffle-like batter and fried in a special pan

æde v.: åd, ædt eat, guzzle

ædel adj. noble, generous, pure; **ædelsten** precious stone

ædru adj. sober

æg n.: -get, pl. same egg; **æggeblomme** yolk; **æggehvide** egg white

ægte adj. real, sincere, genuine

ægteskab n.: -et, pl. -er marriage

ækel adj. nasty, disgusting

ækvator n.: -en equator

ældreforsorg n.: -en care of the elderly

ændre v.: -ede change, alter

ære n.: -n honor; **ærefuld** honorable

æresord n.: -et, pl. same word of honor

æresport n.: -en, pl. -e arch of branches and flowers to honor newlyweds

ærinde n.: -t, pl. -r errand

ærlig adj. honest

æske n.: -n, pl. -r box

Ø

ø *n.: -en, pl. -er* island;
øgruppe group of islands

øde *adj.* deserted, empty,
barren

ødelægge *v.: ødelagde,
ødelagt* destroy, wreck,
spoil, smash, ruin

øge *v.: -ede* increase, extend

øjeblik *n.: -ket, pl. -ke*
moment; **øjeblikkelig**
adv.: at once, instantly,
momentarily

øjenkontakt *n.: -en* eye
contact

øjensynlig *adj.* apparent,
evident, obvious

øjenvidne *n.: -t, pl. -r*
eyewitness

økologisk *adj.* organic,
ecological

økonomi *n.: -en, pl. -er*
economy

øl *n.: -len, pl. -ler* beer; *n.:*
-let beer (mass noun)

øm *adj.* sore; loving,
affectionate

ønske *v.: -ede* wish;
ønskeseddel wish list;
ønskehus dream house

øre *n.: -n, pl. -r* 1/100 of one
krone

øre *n.: -t, pl. -r* ear; **ørepine**
earache

øse ned *v.: -ede* or *-te ned*
pour, rain cats and dogs

øst *n.* east

øve *v.: -ede* practice

øverst *adj.* on top

øvrighed *n.: -en, pl. -er*
authority

Å

å *n.: -en, pl. -er* stream, large
creek

åben *adj.* open

åbne *v.: -ede* open;
åbningstider store hours

ånde *n.: -n* breath; **dårlig
ånde** bad breath

ånde *v.: -ede* breathe

åndelig *adj.* spiritual, intellec-
tual, mental

åndsfrisk *adj.* lively, alert,
having unimpaired mental
faculties

åndssvag *adj.* mentally hand-
icapped; idiotic, silly

år *n.: -et, pl. same* year;
årlig(t) yearly; **i årevis**
for years

århundrede *n.: -t, pl. -r* century; **århundredeskifte**
n.: -t turn of the century

årsag *n.: -en, pl. -er* reason,
cause

ENGLISH-DANISH DICTIONARY

A

abbreviation *n.* forkortelse
-*n, pl. -r*
able (to be able to) *v.* kunne
kunne, kunnet (pre. kan)
aboard *adv.* om bord
about *adv.* cirka; **about to**
prep. tæt på at
above *prep.* over
abrupt *adj.* pludselig
absent *adj.* fraværende
abstract *adj.* abstrakt;
abstract art abstrakt
kunst
abuse *v.* mishandle -*ede*
accept *v.* acceptere -*ede*
acceptable *adj.* acceptabel
access *n.* adgang
accessory *n.* tilbehør -*et, pl.
same*
accident *n.* ulykke -*n, pl. -r*
accommodations *n.* logi -*et,
pl. -er*
account (bank account) *n.*
konto -*en, pl. konti*
accuse *v.* beskylde -*te*
accustomed to *adj.* vant til
acquaintance *n.* bekendt *den
bekendte, pl. -e*
across *adv.* tværs over, over
across from *prep.* på den
modsatte side af, overfor
activity *n.* aktivitet -*en, pl. -er*
adapter *n.* adapter -*en, pl. -e*
add *v.* lægge sammen *lagde
sammen, lagt sammen*;
tilføje -*ede*
addicted (to) *adj.* afhængig
(af)
additional *adj.* ekstra

additive *n.* tilsætningsstof
-*fet, pl. -fer*
address *n.* adresse -*n, pl. -r*
adequate *adj.* tilstrækkelig,
nok
adhesive *n.* klæbemiddel
*klæbemidlet, pl.
klæbemidler*
adjacent *adj.*
sammenstødende,
sammenhængende
admire *v.* beundre -*ede*
admission *n.* adgang (access);
indlæggelse (hospital);
optagelse (school);
indrømmelse (confession)
admission ticket *n.* entrébillet
-*ten, pl. -ter*,
indgangsbillet -*ten, pl. -ter*
admit *v.* indrømme (tell the
truth) -*ede*; give adgang
(let in) *gav, givet adgang*
adult *adj.* voksen; **adult
ticket** *n.* voksenbillet -*ten,
pl. -ter*
adult *n.* voksen *den voksne,
pl. voksne*
advance *v.* gå videre *gik, gået
videre*; **in advance** på
forhånd
advantage *n.* fordel -*en, pl. -e*
advertisement *n.* reklame -*n,
pl. -r*; annonce -*n, pl. -r*
advise *v.* vejlede -*te*, råde
-*ede*
afford (be able to) *v.* have
råd til *havde, haft råd til*;
affordable price
overkommelig pris
afraid *adj.* bange
after *prep., adv., conj.* efter

afternoon *n.* eftermiddag *-en, pl. -e*

again *adv.* igen

against *prep., adv.* imod, mod

age *n.* alder *-en, pl. aldre*; **to come of age** at blive myndig

ago *adj., adv.* for ... siden; **three years ago** for tre år siden

agree *v.* være enig *var, været* enig

agreement *n.* aftale *-n, pl. -r*

agriculture *n.* landbrug *-et, pl. same*

ahead *prep.* foran, længere fremme

air *n.* luft *-en*

air conditioning *n.* klimaanlæg *-get, pl. same*

airmail *n.* luftpost *-en*; **by airmail** med luftpost

airplane *n.* flyver *-en, pl. -e*, flyvemaskine *-n, pl. -r*

airport *n.* lufthavn *-en, pl. -e*

alarm clock *n.* vækkeur *-et, pl. -e*

alcohol *n.* alkohol *-en, pl. -er*

alcoholic *n.* alkoholiker *-en, pl. -e*

alcoholic *adj.* alkoholholdig (containing alcohol)

alike *adj.* ens

alive *adj.* i live, levende

all *adj.* alle

allergic to *adj.* allergisk overfor

allowed *adj.* tilladt

almost *adv.* næsten

alone *adj.* alene

along *prep.* langs med (sail along the coast); på (stopped along the way)

already *adv.* allerede

also *adv.* også

alternate *v.* skifte mellem *-ede mellem*

alternative *n.* alternativ *-et, pl. -er*

although *conj.* skønt

altogether *adv.* tilsammen, i det hele taget

always *adv.* altid

ambassador *n.* ambassadør *-en, pl. -er*

ambulance *n.* ambulance *-n, pl. -r*

American *n.* amerikaner *-en, pl. -e*; *adj.* amerikansk

among *prep.* mellem, blandt

amount *n.* mængde *-n, pl. -r*

and *conj.* og

angel *n.* engel *-en or englen, pl. engle*

angle *n.* vinkel *-en or vinklen, pl. vinkler*

angry *adj.* vred

animal *n.* dyr *-et, pl. same*

annually *adv.* årligt

another *adj.* en anden (some other); en mere (one more)

answer *n.* svar *-et, pl. same*

answer *v.* svare *-ede*

answering machine *n.* telefonsvarer *-en, pl. -e*

antique *n.* antikvitet *-en, pl. -er*

antique *adj.* antik

anyone *pron.* enhver

anything *pron.* hvad som helst

apartment *n.* lejlighed *-en, pl. -er*

apologize *v.* sige undskyld *sagde, sagt undskyld*

applaud *v.* klappe *-ede*

appointment *n.* aftale *-n, pl. -r*; tid (with a doctor) *-en, pl. -er*

appreciate v. sætte pris på
(be appreciative of) *satte,*
sat pris på; stige
(appreciate in value)
steg, steget

appreciative adj.
taknemmelig

appropriate adj. passende,
behørig

archaeology n. arkæologi *-en*

architecture n. arkitektur *-en,*
pl. -er

area n. område *-t, pl. -r*

argue v. argumentere (debate)
-ede; skændes (quarrel)
skændtes, skændtes

around prep. rundt om

arrival n. ankomst *-en, pl. -er*

artifact n. artefakt *-et, pl. -er*

artificial adj. kunstig

artist n. kunstner (male) *-en,*
pl. -e, kunstnerinde
(female) *-n, pl. -r*

ashtray n. askebæger *-et* or
askebægret, pl. -e or
askebægre

ask v. spørge *spurgte, spurgt*

asleep (to be) v. sove *sov,*
sovet

as long as conj. så længe, når
bare

assemble v. samle (put something together or collect)
-ede; samles (gather,
meet) *samledes*

assess v. bedømme *-te*

assist v. hjælpe *hjalp, hjulpet*

assume v. formode *-ede*

as well as adv. tilligemed

at all adv. overhovedet; **not
at all** overhovedet ikke

at least i det mindste

at once adv. med det samme,
øjeblikkeligt

attach v. fastgøre *fastgjorde,*
fastgjort

attack n. angreb *-et, pl. same*

attack v. angribe *angreb,*
angrebet

attend v. deltage i *deltog,*
deltaget i

attorney n. advokat *-en, pl. -er*

audience n. publikum *-et,*
pl. -er

August n. august

automatic adj. automatisk

automobile n. bil *-en, pl. -er*

available adj. til rådighed

average n. gennemsnit *-tet,*
pl. same

avoid v. undgå *undgik, undgået*

awake adj. vågen

awake v. vække (wake
someone up) *-ede*; **wake
up** v. vågne *-ede*

away adj. bortrejst (away
from home); *adj., adv.*
væk (absent); **throw
away** v. smide væk *smed,*
smidt væk

awful adj. frygtelig,
forfærdelig

B

baby n. baby *-en, pl. -er*

babysitter n. barnepige *-n,*
pl. -r

backpack n. rygsæk *-ken,*
pl. -ke

backstairs n. bagtrappe *-n,*
pl. -r

backward(s) adv. baglæns

bad adj. dårlig, slem

bag n. pose *-n, pl. -r*

baggage n. bagage *-n*

bail n. kaution *-en, pl. -er*

bake v. bage *-te*

ball n. bold (for sports) *-en,*
pl. -e; bal (dance) *-let,*
pl. -ler

ban v. forbyde *forbød,*
forbudt

Band-Aid *n.* hæfteplaster *-et,*
  pl. hæfteplastre
bank *n.* bank *-en, pl. -er,*
  pengeinstitut *-tet, pl. -ter*
bar *n.* bar (place to drink)
  -en, pl. -er
barber *n.* herrefrisør *-en,*
  pl. -er
bar code *n.* stregkode *-n, pl. -r*
barefoot *adj.* barfodet
barely *adv.* kun lige
bark *v.* gø *-ede*
barn *n.* lade *-n, pl. -r*
bartender *n.* bartender *-en,*
  pl. -e
basement *n.* kælder *-en, pl.*
  kældre
basket *n.* kurv *-en, pl. -e*
bath *n.* bad *-et, pl. -e*
bathroom *n.* badeværelse *-t,*
  pl. -r
battery *n.* batteri *-et, pl. -er*
be *v.* være *var, været*
beach *n.* strand *-en, pl. -e*
beard *n.* skæg *-get, pl. same*
beat *v.* slå *slog, slået*
beautiful *adj.* smuk
beauty salon *n.* damefrisør
  -en, pl. -er
because *conj.* fordi
because of *prep.* på grund af
become *v.* blive *blev, blevet*
bed *n.* seng *-en, pl. -e*
bedroom *n.* soveværelse *-t,*
  pl. -r
bedtime *n.* sengetid *-en,*
  pl. -er
bee *n.* bi *-en, pl. -er;* **bee
  sting** bistik *-ket, pl. same*
beef *n.* oksekød *-et, pl. same*
beeper *n.* personsøger *-en,*
  pl. -e
beer *n.* øl *-len, pl. -ler; -let
  (collective noun)*
before *prep.* før

beforehand *adv.* på forhånd
begin *v.* begynde *-te*
beginner *n.* nybegynder *-en,*
  pl. -e
behind *prep.* bag, bagved,
  bagefter
believe *v.* tro *-ede*
bell *n.* klokke *-n, pl. -r*
belonging(s) *n.* ejendel *-en,*
  pl. -e
belong to *v.* tilhøre *-te*
below *prep.* under
bench *n.* bænk *-en, pl. -e*
bend *n.* sving (in a road) *-et,*
  pl. same
bend *v.* bøje *-ede*
beneath *adj.* under; *adv.*
  nedenunder, nedenfor
beneficial *adj.* fordelagtig,
  gavnlig
benign *adj.* venlig (friendly);
  godartet (medicine)
besides *adv.* desuden
best *adj.* bedst
bet *n.* væddemål *-et, pl. same*
bet *v.* vædde *-ede*
better *adj.* bedre
between *prep.* mellem
beware *v.* være opmærksom på
  var, været opmærksom på
beyond *prep.* ud over
bicycle *n.* cykel *-en* or *cyklen,
  pl. cykler;* **bike path**
  cykelsti *-en, pl. -er*
big *adj.* stor
bilingual *adj.* tosproget
bill *n.* regning (at restaurant)
  -en, pl. -er; seddel (money)
  -en or *sedlen, pl. sedler*
bind *v.* binde (to tie) *bandt,
  bundet*
binoculars *n.* kikkert *-en,*
  pl. -er
biodegradable *adj.* biologisk
  nedbrydelig

bird *n.* fugl *-en, pl. -e*
birth certificate *n.*
  fødselsattest *-en, pl. -er*
birth control *n.* prævention
birthday *n.* fødselsdag *-en,*
  pl. -e
birthplace *n.* fødested *-et,*
  pl. -er
bite *n.* bid *-det, pl. same*
bite *v.* bide *bed, bidt*
bitter *adj.* bitter
black *adj.* sort
blame *v.* beskylde *-te*
blanket *n.* tæppe *-t, pl. -r*
bleed *v.* bløde *-te*
blend *v.* blande *-ede;* mikse
  v. -ede
bless *v.* velsigne *-ede*
blind *adj.* blind
blink *v.* blinke *-ede*
blister *n.* vable *-n, pl. -r*
blond *adj.* blond, lyshåret
blood *n.* blod *-et*
blood bank *n.* blodbank *-en,*
  pl. -er
blood donor *n.* bloddonor
  -en, pl. -er
blood pressure *n.* blodtryk
  -ket
blood type *n.* blodtype *-n,*
  pl. -r
bloom *v.* blomstre *-ede*
blow *v.* blæse *-te*
blue *adj.* blå
blunt *adj.* sløv (knife)
boast *v.* prale *-ede*
boat *n.* båd *-en, pl. -e*
body *n.* krop *-pen, pl. -pe*
boil *v.* koge *-te*
bold *adj.* modig (brave); fed
  (in typed material)
bomb *n.* bombe *-n, pl. -r*
bomb threat *n.* bombetrussel
  -en or *bombetruslen, pl.*
  bombetrusler

bone *n.* knogle *-n, pl. -r*
book *n.* bog *-en, pl. bøger*
bookstore *n.* boghandel *-en,*
  pl. boghandler
boot *n.* støvle *-n, pl. -r*
border *n.* grænse *-n, pl. -r*
borderline *adj.* på grænsen til
born *adj.* født
borrow *v.* låne *-te*
both *pron.* begge (both are
  here); *adv.* både ... og
  (both he and she came)
bottle *n.* flaske *-n, pl. -r*
bottom *n.* bund *-en, pl. -e*
bouquet *n.* buket *-ten, pl. -ter*
bow *v.* bukke *-ede*
box *n.* kasse *-n, pl. -r*
boxing *n.* boksning *-en*
box office *n.* billetkontor *-et,*
  pl. -er
boy *n.* dreng *-en, pl. -e*
boyfriend *n.* kæreste *-n, pl. -r*
brag *v.* prale *-ede*
brake *v.* bremse *-ede*
branch *n.* gren *-en, pl. -e*
brand-new *adj.* splinterny
brave *adj.* modig
brawl *n.* slåskamp *-en, pl. -e*
bread *n.* brød *-et, pl. same*
break *v.* gå itu (something
  breaks) *gik itu, gået itu;*
  slå i stykker (break something) *slog, slået i stykker*
breakfast *n.* morgenmad *-en*
breast-feed *v.* amme *-ede*
breathe *v.* trække vejret *trak,*
  trukket vejret
breeze *n.* brise *-n, pl. -r*
brew *v.* brygge *-ede*
bric-a-brac *n.* nips *-et*
bridge *n.* bro *-en, pl. -er*
brief *adj.* kort
bright *adj.* lys, strålende
broad *adj.* bred

broad-minded *adj.* tolerant, frisindet, rummelig

broken *adj.* i stykker

broker *n.* mægler *-en, pl. -e*

broom *n.* kost *-en, pl. -e*

brothel *n.* bordel *-let, pl. -ler*

brother *n.* broder *-en, pl. brødre*

brown *adj.* brun

brush *v.* børste *-ede*

bucket *n.* spand *-en, pl. -e*

build *v.* bygge *-ede*

building *n.* bygning *-en, pl. -er*

bulb *n.* pære (electrical) *-n, pl. -r*; blomsterløg (plant) *-et, pl. same*

bunch *n.* bundt *-et, pl. -er*

bureau *n.* bureau *-et, pl. -er*

burn *v.* brænde *-te*

burst *v.* springe *sprang, sprunget*

bury *v.* begrave *-ede*

bus *n.* bus *-sen, pl. -ser*

bush *n.* busk *-en, pl. -e*

business *n.* forretning *-en, pl. -er*

bus station *n.* busstation *-en, pl. -er*

bus stop *n.* busstoppested *-et, pl. -er*

busy *adj.* travl, optaget

but *conj.* men

butcher *n.* slagter *-en, pl. -e*

button *n.* knap *-pen, pl. -per*

buy *v.* købe *-te*

C

cab *n.* taxi *-en, pl. -er*, taxa *-en, pl. -er*

cable TV *n.* kabel-tv

café *n.* café *-en, pl. -er*

caffeine *n.* koffein *-en* or *-et*

cage *n.* bur *-et, pl. -e*

cake *n.* kage *-n, pl. -r*

calculate *v.* beregne *-ede*

calculator *n.* lommeregner *-en, pl. -e*

calendar *n.* kalender *-en, pl. -e*

call (telephone) *v.* ringe *-ede*

calm *adj.* rolig

calorie *n.* kalorie *-n, pl. -r*

camera *n.* kamera *-et, pl. -er*, fotografiapparat *-et, pl. -er*

camp *n.* lejr *-en, pl. -e*; **campfire** *n.* lejrbål *-et, pl. same* ·

camp *v.* campere *-ede*

camper *n.* campingvogn (portable dwelling) *-en, pl. -e*; campist (one who camps) *-en, pl. -er*

can *n.* dåse *-n, pl. -r*

can *v.* kunne *kunne, kunnet (pre. kan)*

cancel *v.* aflyse *-te*

cancer *n.* kræft *-en*

candle *n.* stearinlys *-et, pl. same*

candy *n.* slik *-ket, pl. same (collective noun)*

capable *adj.* dygtig, kompetent

capacity *n.* kapacitet *-en, pl. -er*

capital *n.* kapital *-en, pl. -er*

captain *n.* kaptajn *-en, pl. -er*

caption *n.* undertekst (film) *-en, pl. -er*; billedtekst (picture) *-en, pl. -er*

captivating *adj.* vindende, fængslende

car *n.* bil *-en, pl. -er*

card *n.* kort *-et, pl. same*; **birthday card** fødselsdagskort *-et, pl. same*

cardboard *n.* pap *-pet, pl. -per*; **cardboard box** papkasse *-n, pl. -r*

careful *adj.* omhyggelig (with care); forsigtig (cautious)

carry *v.* bære *bar, båret*

carry-on luggage *n.*
håndbagage *-n*

carsick *adj.* køresyg

case *n.* tilfælde *-t, pl. same*; **in case** i tilfælde af

cash *n.* kontanter, rede penge *pl.*

cash register *n.* kasseapparat *-et, pl. -er*

cassette *n.* kassettebånd *-et, pl. same*

cast *n.* gips (on broken bone) *-en*; rollebesætning (theater) *-en, pl. -er*

castle *n.* borg *-en, pl. -e*

casual *adj.* uformel

cat *n.* kat *-ten, pl. -te*

catalog *n.* katalog *-et, pl. -er*

catch *v.* fange *-ede*

category *n.* kategori *-en, pl. -er*

caution *v.* advare *-ede*

cautious *adj.* forsigtig

cavity *n.* hul (in tooth) *-let, pl. -ler*

celebrate *v.* fejre *-ede*

celebrity *n.* berømthed *-en, pl. -er*, celebritet *-en, pl. -er*

cell *n.* celle *-n, pl. -r*

cemetery *n.* kirkegård *-en, pl. -e*

century *n.* århundrede *-t, pl. -r*

ceramics *n.* keramik *-ken*

certain *adj.* bestemt

change *v.* skifte *-ede*, ændre *-ede*

change *n.* forandring *-en, pl. -er*, ændring *-en, pl. -er*

channel *n.* kanal *-en, pl. -er*

charcoal *n.* trækul *-let, pl. same*

cheap *adj.* billig

cheat *v.* snyde *snød, snydt*

check *n.* check *-en, pl. checks*

check *v.* checke, tjekke *-ede*

cheer for *v.* heppe på *-ede på*

cheerful *adj.* glad, i godt humør

cheering crowd *n.* heppekor *-et, pl. same*

cheers *interj.* skål; **to say cheers** *v.* skåle *-ede*

cheese *n.* ost *-en, pl. -e*

chef *n.* kok *-ken, pl. -ke*

chew *v.* tygge *-ede*

chewing gum *n.* tyggegummi *-et*

child *n.* barn *-et, pl. børn*

childproof *adj.* børnesikret

chilly *adj.* kølig

choice *n.* valg *-et, pl. same*

choose *v.* vælge *valgte, valgt*

Christmas *n.* jul *-en*; **during Christmas** i julen

church *n.* kirke *-n, pl. -r*

cigar *n.* cigar *-en, pl. -er*

cigarette *n.* cigaret *-ten, pl. -ter*

citizen *n.* borger *-en, pl. -ere*, indbygger *-en, pl. -e*

city *n.* by *-en, pl. -er*

clean *adj.* ren

client *n.* kunde *-n, pl. -r*

climate *n.* klima *-et, pl. -er*

clock *n.* ur *-et, pl. -e*

clockwise *adv.* med uret

clog *v.* tilstoppe *-ede*; **clogged** tilstoppet

close *adv., adj.* tæt på, nær ved

close *v.* lukke *-ede*; **closed** lukket

closet *n.* skab *-et, pl. -e*

clothes *n.* tøj *-et, pl. same*

coat hanger *n.* bøjle *-n, pl. -r*

coffee *n.* kaffe *-n*

coin *n.* mønt *-en, pl. -er*

coincidental *adj.* tilfældig (random); samtidig (simultaneous)

cold *adj.* kold
cold *n.* kulde (temperature) *-n*;
forkølelse (illness) *-n, pl. -r*
cold sore *n.* forkølelsessår *-et,*
pl. same
collaborate *v.* samarbejde *-ede*
colleague *n.* kollega *-en, pl.*
kolleger
collect *v.* indsamle, samle *-ede*
collision *n.* sammenstød *-et,*
pl. same
color *n.* farve *-n, pl. -r*
come *v.* komme *kom, kommet*
comfortable *adj.*
komfortabel, behagelig
commercial *adj.* kommerciel
common *adj.* almindelig
(plain); fælles (shared)
commuter *n.* pendler *-en, pl. -e*
company *n.* firma (firm) *-et,*
pl. -er; selskab (firm or
social gathering) *-et, pl. -er*
compare *v.* sammenligne *-ede*
compatible *adj.* kompatibel
complain *v.* klage *-ede,*
beklage sig *-ede sig*
complimentary *adj.* rosende
(praising); smigrende
(flattering); gratis (free)
concentrate *v.* koncentrere
sig *-ede sig*
concert *n.* koncert *-en, pl. -er*
condole *v.* kondolere *-ede*
confess *v.* indrømme
(admit) *-ede*
confirm *v.* bekræfte *-ede*
confuse *v.* forvirre *-ede*
congratulate *v.* lykønske *-ede*
congratulations *interj.*
tillykke; **happy birthday**
tillykke med fødselsdagen
conspicuous *adj.* iøjefaldende
constant *adj.* konstant;
constantly *adv.* konstant
constitution *n.* forfatning *-en,*
pl. -er, grundlov *-en, pl. -e*

consumption *n.* forbrug *-et*;
consumer forbruger *-en,*
pl. -e
contact lens *n.* kontaktlinse
-n, pl. -r
contagious *adj.* smitsom
contemporary *adj.* moderne
(modern)
continue *v.* fortsætte *fortsatte,*
fortsat
contraceptive *n.*
præventionsmiddel
præventionsmidlet, pl.
præventionsmidler
cookbook *n.* kogebog *-en, pl.*
kogebøger
cookie *n.* småkage *-n, pl. -r*
cooperative *adj.*
samarbejdsvillig
copy *n.* kopi *-en, pl. -er*
copy *v.* kopiere *-ede*
cork *n.* prop *-pen, pl. -per*
corkscrew *n.* proptrækker
-en, pl. -e
corner *n.* hjørne *-t, pl. -r*
corrugated cardboard *n.*
bølgepap *-pet* or *-pen*
cost *n.* pris *-en, pl. -er*
cost *v.* koste *-ede*
cough *v.* hoste *-ede*
count *v.* tælle *talte, talt*
country *n.* land *-et, pl. -e*
cover *v.* dække *-ede*
cow *n.* ko *-en, pl. køer*
cozy *adj.* hyggelig
cranky *adj.* umulig, sur,
urolig
crash *n.* ulykke *-n, pl. -r*
crash *v.* forulykke *-ede*
crazy *adj.* skør, tosset, tåbelig
credit card *n.* kreditkort *-et,*
pl. same
crime *n.* forbrydelse *-n, pl. -r*
criminal *adj.* kriminel
crisis *n.* krise *-n, pl. -r*

criticize v. kritisere -ede
crooked adj. bøjet, skæv
crucial adj. vigtig, afgørende
cruel adj. ond, ondskabsfuld
cruise n. krydstogt -et, pl. -er
cry v. græde græd, grædt
culinary adj. kulinarisk
curious adj. nysgerrig
currency n. valuta -en, pl. -er
custom n. skik (tradition)
    -ken, pl. -ke
customer n. kunde -n, pl. -r
customer service n.
    kundeservice -n
custom-made adj.
    skræddersyet
cut n. flænge (wound) -n, pl.
    -r; snit (opening made with
    sharp tool) -tet, pl. same
cut v. skære skar, skåret
cycle n. cyklus -en, pl. -er

D

dad n. far -en, pl. fædre
daily adj. daglig
damage n. skade -n, pl. -r
damage v. beskadige -ede
damp adj. fugtig
dance n. dans -en, pl. -e
dance v. danse -ede
dandelion n. mælkebøtte -n,
    pl. -r
dandruff n. skæl -let, pl. same
Dane n. dansker -en, pl. -e
danger n. fare -n, pl. -r
dangerous adj. farlig
dare v. turde turde, turdet
    (pre. tør)
dark adj. mørk
darkness n. mørke -t
data processing n.
    databehandling -n
date n. dato (point in time)
    -en, pl. -er

date n. aftale -n, pl. -r;
    stævnemøde (romantic
    date) -t, pl. -r
date v. komme sammen med
    (go out with) kom,
    kommet sammen med
date v. datere (put a date on)
    -ede
dawn n. daggry -et
day n. dag -en, pl. -e
daycare n. dagpleje -n
daylight n. dagslys -et
daylight-saving time n.
    sommertid
dead adj. død
deadline n. afleveringsfrist
    -en, pl. -er, deadline -n
deaf adj. døv
dear adj. kær; kære (in letter)
death n. død (death occurred)
    -en; dødsfald (a death in
    the family) -et, pl. same
debate n. debat -ten, pl. -ter
debit card n. betalingskort
    -et, pl. same
debt n. gæld -en
decade n. årti -et, pl. -er
decaffeinated adj. koffeinfri
December n. december
decent adj. anstændig
decide v. beslutte -ede
decision n. beslutning -en,
    pl. -er
declare v. erklære (make
    statement) -ede; fortolde
    (at customs) -ede
decrease v. aftage aftog,
    aftaget, svinde svandt,
    svundet
deep adj. dyb
deep-fried adj. friturestegt
deep-frozen adj. dybfrossen
defective adj. defekt,
    mangelfuld
defend v. forsvare -ede

defrost *v.* tø op -*ede op*
degree *n.* grad -*en, pl.* -*er*
delay *v.* forsinke -*ede;*
  delayed forsinket
delete *v.* slette -*ede*
deliberate *v.* overveje
  (consider) -*ede;* drøfte
  (discuss) -*ede*
deliberately *adv.* med fuldt
  overlæg, med vilje
delicious *adj.* velsmagende,
  lækker
deliver *v.* levere (bring) -*ede;*
  føde (give birth) -*te*
demand *v.* kræve -*ede*
democracy *n.* demokrati -*et,*
  pl. -*er*
dentist *n.* tandlæge -*n, pl.* -*r*
deny *v.* benægte -*ede*
department *n.* afdeling -*en,*
  pl. -*er*
department store *n.*
  stormagasin -*et, pl.* -*er*
departure *n.* afgang -*en, pl.* -*e*
dependable *adj.* pålidelig
dependent *adj.* afhængig
deposit *n.* depositum -*et,*
  pl. -*er*
deposit *v.* sætte ind (in a
  bank) *satte, sat ind*
depressed *adj.* deprimeret
describe *v.* beskrive *beskrev,*
  beskrevet
deserve *v.* fortjene -*te*
dessert *n.* dessert -*en, pl.* -*er*
develop *v.* udvikle -*ede*
diaper *n.* ble -*en, pl.* -*er*
dictionary *n.* ordbog -*en, pl.*
  ordbøger
die *v.* dø -*de*
diet *n.* diætmad (special diet)
  -*en;* slankekur (to lose
  weight) -*en, pl.* -*e*
different *adj.* anderledes,
  forskellig

difficult *adj.* svær,
  kompliceret
dilute *v.* fortynde -*ede*
dining room *n.* spisestue -*n,*
  pl. -*r*
dinner *n.* aftensmad -*en*
direct *adj.* direkte
dirty *adj.* beskidt, snavset
disabled *adj.* handicappet
disagree *v.* være uenig *var,*
  været uenig
disappear *v.* forsvinde
  forsvandt, forsvundet
disco *n.* diskotek -*et, pl.* -*er*
discount *n.* rabat -*ten, pl.* -*ter*
discover *v.* opdage -*ede*
discuss *v.* diskutere -*ede*
disease *n.* sygdom -*men,*
  pl. -*me*
disembark *v.* gå fra borde
  gik, gået fra borde
dishonest *adj.* uærlig
disinfect *v.* desinficere -*ede*
dislike *v.* ikke kunne lide
dislocate *v.* få af led *fik, fået*
  af led
disobedient *adj.* ulydig
display *v.* udstille -*ede*
disposable *adj.* disponibel
  (available for use);
  engangs- (discarded
  after use)
dissatisfied *adj.* utilfreds
distance *n.* afstand -*en, pl.* -*e*
distribute *v.* distribuere -*ede,*
  dele ud -*te ud*
disturb *v.* forstyrre -*ede*
dive *v.* springe ud (from
  diving board) *sprang,*
  sprunget ud; dykke (go to
  bottom) -*ede*
divide *v.* dele -*te;* dividere
  (mathematics) -*ede*
divorce *n.* skilsmisse -*n, pl.* -*r*
divorced *adj.* skilt

dizzy *adj.* svimmel
do *v.* gøre *gjorde, gjort*
doctor *n.* doktor *-en, pl. -er*
dog *n.* hund *-en, pl. -e*
dominant *adj.* dominerende
door *n.* dør *-en, pl. -e*
dormitory *n.* kollegium (student housing) *kollegiet, pl. kollegier;* sovesal (hostel) *-en, pl. -e*
double *adj.* dobbelt
doubt *v.* tvivle på *-ede på*
doubtful *adj.* tvivlsom
doubtless *adv.* utvivlsomt, uden tvivl
down *prep.* ned
downhill *adv.* ned ad bakke
downstairs *adv.* nedenunder
downtown area *n.* centrum *-met, pl. -mer,* bymidte *-n*
dozen *n.* dusin *-et, pl. same*
drain *n.* afløb (in sink, etc.) *-et, pl. same*
draw *v.* tegne (picture) *-ede;* trække (lottery) *trak, trukket*
dream *n.* drøm *-men, pl. -me*
dream *v.* drømme *-te*
dress *n.* kjole *-n, pl. -r*
dress *v.* tage tøj på *tog, taget tøj på*
drink *v.* drikke *drak, drukket*
drive *v.* køre *-te*
driver's license *n.* kørekort *-et, pl. same*
drizzle *v.* støvregne *-ede*
drop *v.* tabe *-te*
drought *n.* tørke *-n, pl. -r*
drown *v.* drukne *-ede*
drugs *n.* medicin (medicine) *-en;* narkotika (narcotics) *-en*
drunk *adj.* fuld, beruset
drunk driving *n.* promillekørsel, spirituskørsel

dry *adj.* tør
dry *v.* tørre *-ede*
dry cleaner *n.* renseri *-et, pl. -er*
dry ice *n.* tøris *-en*
dumb *adj.* dum, uklog
durable *adj.* varig, holdbar, solid
duration *n.* varighed *-en, pl. -er*
during *prep.* under, i løbet af
dusk skumring *n. -en, pl. -er,* mørkning *-en*
dust *n.* støv *-et*
duty *n.* pligt *-en, pl. -er*
dye *v.* farve *-ede*

E

each *adv.* hver (apiece)
each other *pron.* hinanden
early *adj.* tidlig; *adv.* tidligt
earn *v.* tjene *-te*
east *n.* øst *-en*
easy *adj.* let, nem
eat *v.* spise *-te*
ecstatic *adj.* ekstatisk, begejstret, henrykt
edge *n.* kant *-en, pl. -er*
editor *n.* redaktør *-en, pl. -er*
educate *v.* uddanne *-ede*
education *n.* uddannelse *-n, pl. -r*
effective *adj.* effektiv
effort *n.* indsats *-en, pl. -er*
eight *num.* otte
eighteen *num.* atten
eighty *num.* firs
either ... or *conj.* enten ... eller
elastic *adj.* elastisk
electricity *n.* elektricitet *-en*
electronic *adj.* elektronisk
elevator *n.* elevator *-en, pl. -er*

eleven *num.* elleve

elsewhere *adv.* andetsteds

E-mail *n.* e-mail, e-post *-en*

embarrassed *adj.* flov

embassy *n.* ambassade *-n, pl. -r*

embrace *v.* omfavne *-ede*

emergency *n.* nødstilfælde *-t, pl. same*

emergency exit *n.* nødudgang *-en, pl. -e*

emergency room *n.* skadestue *-n, pl. -r*

empty *adj.* tom

end *n.* ende *-n, pl. -r*

end *v.* slutte *-ede*, ende *-te*

energetic *adj.* energisk

energy *n.* energi *-en*

engaged *adj.* forlovet (betrothed); engageret, involveret (committed)

engine *n.* motor *-en, pl. -er*

enjoy *v.* nyde *nød, nydt*

enlarge *v.* forstørre *-ede*

enormous *adj.* enorm, kæmpestor

enough *adj.* nok

ensure *v.* garantere *-ede*, sikre *-ede*

entail *v.* medføre (involve) *-te*

enter *v.* gå ind *gik, gået ind*; indtaste (data) *-ede*

entertain *v.* underholde *underholdt, underholdt*

entertainment *n.* underholdning *-en*

entrance *n.* indgang *-en, pl. -e*

envelope *n.* kuvert *-en, pl. -er*, konvolut *-ten, pl. -ter*

envious *adj.* misunderlig

environment *n.* miljø *-et, pl. -er*

equipment *n.* udstyr *-et*

erase *v.* slette *-ede*; viske ud (with eraser) *-ede ud*

erotic *adj.* erotisk

error *n.* fejl *-en, pl. same*

escalator *n.* rullende trappe *pl. rullende trapper*

escape *v.* undslippe *undslap, undsluppet*

Eskimo *n.* eskimo *-en, pl. -er*

Europe *n.* Europa

European *adj.* europæisk; *n.* europæer *-en, pl. -e*

evacuate *v.* evakuere *-ede*

evening *n.* aften *-en* or *aftnen, pl. -er* or *aftner*

every *adj.* hver

everyone *pron.* enhver

everything *pron.* alt, det hele

everywhere *adv.* overalt, over det hele

evil *adj.* ond

exact *adj.* nøjagtig, lige; **exact change** lige penge

exaggerate *v.* overdrive *overdrev, overdrevet*

except *prep., conj.* undtagen

exception *n.* undtagelse *-n, pl. -r*

exchange *v.* bytte *-ede*, udveksle *-ede*

exchange rate *n.* valutakurs *-en, pl. -er*

excuse *n.* undskyldning *-en, pl. -er*

excuse *v.* undskylde *-te*

exercise *v.* motionere *-ede*

exhausted *adj.* udmattet, udkørt

exhibition *n.* udstilling *-en, pl. -er*

exit *n.* udgang *-en, pl. -e*

expect *v.* forvente *-ede*

expensive *adj.* dyr

experience *n.* erfaring *-en, pl. -er*

expert *n.* ekspert *-en, pl. -er*

expire *v.* udløbe *udløb, udløbet*

explain v. forklare -ede
express adv. ekspres (at high speed)
express v. udtrykke -te
extinguish v. slukke -ede; **fire extinguisher** n. ildslukker -en, pl. -e
extra adj. ekstra
eyeglasses n. briller (pl.)
eyewitness n. øjenvidne -t, pl. -r

F

face n. ansigt -et, pl. -er
factory n. fabrik -ken, pl. -ker
faculty n. fakultet (at learning institution) -et, pl. -er
fail v. fejle -ede
faint v. besvime -ede
fairy tale n. eventyr -et, pl. same
faith n. tro -en
fall n. efterår -et, pl. same; fald (act of falling) -et, pl. same
fall v. falde faldt, faldet
false adj. falsk
family n. familie -n, pl. -r; **family history** n. slægtshistorie -n
family farm n. slægtsgård -en, pl. -e
family planning n. familieplanlægning -en
famous adj. berømt
far adv. langt; **far away** adj. langt væk, fjern
farm n. gård -en, pl. -e
farmer n. gårdejer -en, pl. -e
farming n. landbrug -et, pl. same
farsighted adj. langsynet (eyesight); vidtskuende, fremsynet
fashion n. mode -n, pl. -r

fashionable adj. moderne
fast adj. hurtig (quick)
fast v. faste -ede
fat n. fedt -et
fat adj. tyk, kraftig, fed
fatal adj. dræbende, dødbringende (resulting in death); skæbnesvanger (disastrous); **fate** n. skæbne -n, pl. -r
father n. far -en, pl. fædre
fatigue n. træthed -en
favor n. tjeneste -n, pl. -r
favorable adj. gunstig
favorite n. yndling -en, pl. -er; **favorite poem** yndlingsdigt
favorite n. favorit (most likely to win) -ten, pl. -ter
fear n. frygt -en
fear v. frygte -ede
February n. februar
fee n. afgift -en, pl. -er
feel v. føle -te
feeling n. følelse -n, pl. -r
female adj. kvindelig, af hunkøn
fence n. hegn -et, pl. same
ferry n. færge -n, pl. -r
fertile adj. frugtbar
fever n. feber -en, pl. febre
few n., adj. få
fiction n. skønlitteratur (books) -en
fictional adj. opdigtet
field n. mark (on farm) -en, pl. -er; felt (computer or form) -et, pl. -er
fifteen num. femten
fifth num. femte
fifty num. halvtreds
fight v. slås sloges, sloges
fight n. slåskamp -en, pl. -e
file n. fil -n, pl. -r
fill v. fylde -te

film *n.* film *-en, pl. same*

final *adj.* endelig definitiv; sidst (last in order)

find *v.* finde *fandt, fundet*

fine *n.* bøde *-n, pl. -r*

fine *adj.* fin, i orden

finger *n.* finger *-en, pl. fingre*

fingerprint *n.* fingeraftryk *-ket, pl. same*

finish *v.* afslutte *-ede*

fire *n.* ildebrand (destructive burning) *-en, pl. -e*; bål (campfire) *-et, pl. same*

fire department *n.* brandvæsen *-et*

fire engine *n.* brandbil *-en, pl. -er*

fire escape *n.* brandtrappe *-n, pl. -r*

firefighter *n.* brandmand *-en, pl. brandmænd*

fireproof *adj.* brandsikker

fireworks *n.* fyrværkeri *-et*

firm *adj.* fast

first *adj., adv., num.* først

first aid *n.* førstehjælp *-en*

fish *n.* fisk *-en, pl. same*

fisherman *n.* fisker *-en, pl. -e*

fist *n.* knytnæve *-n, pl. -r*

fit *adj.* i god kondition (in good physical shape)

fit *v.* passe (right size) *-ede*

five *num.* fem

fix *v.* reparere *-ede*

flag *n.* flag *-et, pl. same*; Dannebrog (the Danish flag)

flame *n.* flamme *-n, pl. -r*

flashlight *n.* lommelygte *-n, pl. -r*

flat *adj.* flad

flavor *n.* smag *-en*

flea *n.* loppe *-n, pl. -r*

flee *v.* flygte *-ede*

fleet *n.* flåde *-n, pl. -r*

flicker *v.* flimre *-ede*

float *v.* flyde *flød, flydt*

floor *n.* gulv *-et, pl. -e*

flourish *v.* trives *trivedes*

flow *v.* strømme (water) *-ede*

flower *n.* blomst *-en, pl. -er*

flu *n.* influenza *-en, pl. -er*

flue *n.* trækkanal *-en, pl. -er*

fluid *n.* væske *-n, pl. -r*

flush *v.* skylle *-ede*

fly *n.* flue (insect) *-n, pl. -r*

fly *v.* flyve *fløj, fløjet*

flyswatter *n.* fluesmækker *-en, pl. -e*

fog *n.* tåge *-n*

foghorn *n.* tågehorn *-et, pl. same*

folksinger *n.* folkesanger *-en, pl. -e*

follow *v.* følge *fulgte, fulgt*

food *n.* mad *-en*

foot *n.* fod *-en, pl. fødder*

forbid *v.* forbyde *forbød, forbudt*; **forbidden** forbudt

foreign *adj.* fremmed, udenlandsk

foreigner *n.* udlænding *-en, pl. -e*

forest *n.* skov *-en, pl. -e*

forever *adv.* altid, i al evighed

forget *v.* glemme *-te*

forgive *v.* tilgive *tilgav, tilgivet*

formal *adj.* formel

fortunate *adj.* heldig

forty *num.* fyrre

forward *adv.* fremad

fountain *n.* springvand *-et, pl. same*

four *num.* fire

fourteen *num.* fjorten

fourth *num.* fjerde

fracture *v.* brække *-ede*

fragile adj. skrøbelig, skør (breakable)

free adj. fri, løs (free to move); gratis (at no cost)

freedom n. frihed -en, pl. -er

freeway n. motorvej -en, pl. -e

freeze v. fryse frøs, frosset

French fry n. pomfrit -ten, pl. -ter

fresh adj. frisk

Friday n. fredag; **on Fridays** om fredagen

fridge n. køleskab -et, pl. -e

friend n. ven (male) -nen, pl. -ner; veninde (female) -n, pl. -r

friendly adj. rar, venlig

frighten v. forskrække -ede

frightened adj. bange, forskrækket

frisk v. kropsvisitere -ede

from prep. fra

frost n. frost -en

frostbite n. forfrysning -en, pl. -er

frozen adj. frossen

fruit n. frugt -en

fry v. stege -te

fuel n. brændstof -fet, pl. -fer

full adj. fuld

full moon n. fuldmåne -n

full-time adj. fuldtids-

function v. fungere -ede

funeral n. begravelse -n, pl. -r

funny adj. sjov

fur n. pels -en, pl. -e

furnace n. fyr -et

furniture n. møbler (pl.)

fuse n. sikring -en, pl. -er

future n. fremtid -en

G

gallery n. galleri -et, pl. -er

game n. kamp (match) -en, pl. -e; spil (such as board game) -let, pl. same

gangplank n. landgangsbro -en, pl. -er

garage n. garage -n, pl. -r

garbage n. affald -et

garden n. have -n, pl. -r

gas n. benzin (fuel) -en

gas station n. tankstation -en, pl. -er

gate n. låge -n, pl. -r; gate (airport) -n

gather v. samle (collect) -ede; samles (social gathering) samledes

gay adj. homoseksuel

gender n. køn -net, pl. same

genealogy n. slægtsforskning -en

general adj. generel

generous adj. gavmild

genius n. geni -et, pl. -er

gentle adj. blid, mild

genuine adj. ægte

geographically adv. geografisk set

get v. få fik, fået

gift n. gave -n, pl. -r

giggle v. fnise -ede

girl n. pige -n, pl. -r

girlfriend n. kæreste -n, pl. -r

give v. give gav, givet

glad adj. glad, lykkelig

glass n. glas -set, pl. same

glasses n. briller (eye) (pl.)

glossy adj. blank

glue n. lime -n

gold n. guld -et; **goldsmith** n. guldsmed -en, pl. -e

good adj. god

good-bye n. farvel -let

government n. regering (administration) -en, pl. -er; myndighed (authority) -en, pl. -er

graduate v. tage afsluttende eksamen tog, taget afsluttende eksamen

grain n. korn -et
grass n. græs -set, pl. -ser
grateful adj. taknemmelig
gratuity n. drikkepenge (pl.)
grave n. grav -en, pl. -e
gravity n. tyngdekraft -en
great adj. stor, storartet, storslået
greenhouse n. drivhus -et, pl. -e
grief n. sorg -en
grieve v. sørge -ede
grill v. grille -ede; n. grill -en, pl. -er
groundwater n. grundvand -et
group n. gruppe -n, pl. -r
grow v. vokse -ede
grumpy adj. gnaven, sur
guarantee v. garantere -ede
guess v. gætte -ede
guest n. gæst -en, pl. -er
guide n. guide -n, pl. -r
guilty adj. skyldig
gun n. skydevåben -et or skydevåbnet, pl. same
gutter n. tagrende (on roof) -n, pl. -r; rendesten (along street) -en, pl. -e

H

habit n. vane -n, pl. -r
hair n. hår -et
hairdresser n. frisør -en, pl. -er
half n. halvdel -en, pl. -e
ham n. skinke -n, pl. -r
hammer n. hammer -en, pl. -e or hamre
hammock n. hængekøje -n, pl. -r
hand n. hånd -en, pl. hænder
handbag n. håndtaske -n, pl. -r
handcuffs n. håndjern -et, pl. same

handle v. håndtere -ede
handmade adj. håndlavet
handshake n. håndtryk -ket, pl. same
handwriting n. håndskrift -en, pl. -er
handy adj. praktisk (practical); lethåndterlig (easy to handle)
hang v. intr. hænge hang, hængt; v. tr. hænge hængte, hængt
hangover n. tømmermænd (pl.)
happen v. ske -te
happiness n. lykke -n, glæde -n
happy adj. glad, lykkelig
harbor n. havn -en, pl. -e
hard adj. hård
hardly adv. næppe, næsten ikke
harm v. skade -ede
harvest n. høst -en; v. høste -ede
hate n. had -et
hate v. hade -ede
have v. have havde, haft (pre. har)
hay n. hø -et; **haystack** n. høstak -ken, pl. -ke
hay fever n. høfeber -en
hazy adj. diset
he pron. han
health n. helbred -et
healthy adj. sund, rask
hear v. høre -te; **hearing aid** n. høreapparat -et, pl. -er
heart n. hjerte -t, pl. -r
heat n. varme -n
heavy adj. tung
hedge n. hæk -ken, pl. -ke
height n. højde -n, pl. -r
heir n. arving -en, pl. -er
hello interj. hallo (telephone); goddag (greeting); hej (informal greeting)

helmet *n.* hjelm *-en, pl. -e*
help *n.* hjælp *-en*
help *v.* hjælpe *hjalp, hjulpet*
her *pron.* hende (object), hendes (possessive)
herb *n.* krydderurt *-en, pl. -er*
here *adv.* her
hereditary *adj.* arvelig
hero *n.* helt *-en, pl. -e*
heroine *n.* heltinde *-n, pl. -r*
herring *n.* sild *-en, pl. same*
hers *pron.* hendes
hesitant *adj.* tøvende
hesitate *v.* tøve *-ede*
hiccups *n.* hikke *-n;* **to have the hiccups** at have hikke
hide *v.* gemme *-te,* skjule *-te*
high *adj.* høj
high school *n.* gymnasium *gymnasiet, pl. gymnasier*
highway *n.* motorvej *-en, pl. -e*
hill *n.* bakke *-n, pl. -r*
hippie *n.* hippie *-n, pl. -r,* provo *-en, pl. -er*
hire *v.* ansætte *ansatte, ansat,* hyre *-ede*
historical *adj.* historisk; **historically** *adv.* historisk set
hit *v.* slå *slog, slået;* ramme (hit the target) *-te*
hit-and-run driver *n.* flugtbilist *-en, pl. -er*
hitchhike *v.* tage den på stop *tog, taget den på stop*
hobby *n.* hobby *-en, pl. -er,* fritidsinteresse *-n, pl. -r*
hold *v.* holde *holdt, holdt*
hole *n.* hul *-let, pl. -ler*
holiday *n.* ferie *-n, pl. -r*
hollow *adj.* hul
holy *adj.* hellig
home *n.* hjem *-met, pl. same*
homegrown *adj.* hjemmeavlet

homeless *adj.* hjemløs
homemade *adj.* hjemmelavet
homesickness *n.* hjemve *-en*
homework *n.* lektier *(pl.),* hjemmearbejde *-t*
homosexual *adj.* homoseksuel
honest *adj.* ærlig
honeymoon *n.* bryllupsrejse *-n, pl. -r*
hope *n.* håb *-et, pl. same;* **in hopes that** i håbet om
hope *v.* håbe *-ede*
hopefully *adv.* forhåbentlig
horticulture *n.* havebrug *-et, pl. same*
hospital *n.* hospital *-et, pl. -er,* sygehus *-et, pl. -e*
host *n.* vært (male) *-en, pl. -er,* værtinde (female) *-n, pl. -r*
hostage *n.* gidsel *-et* or *gidslet, pl. gidsler*
hostel *n.* vandrerhjem *-met, pl. same*
hostile *adj.* uvenlig, fjendtlig
hot *adj.* varm, hed
hot dog *n.* pølse *-n, pl. -r,* hotdog *-gen, pl. -s*
hotel *n.* hotel *-let, pl. -ler*
hour *n.* time *-n, pl. -r;* **hourglass** timeglas *-set, pl. same*
house *n.* hus *-et, pl. -e*
housekeeper *n.* husholderske *-n, pl. -r*
housewife *n.* husmor *-en, pl. husmødre*
how *adv.* hvordan
however *adv.* imidlertid
hug *n.* knus *-et, pl. same*
humidity *n.* luftfugtighed *-en*
humiliate *v.* ydmyge *-ede*
humorous *adj.* humoristisk; **humor** humoristisk sans

hundred *num.* hundrede
hunger *n.* sult -en
hungry *adj.* sulten
hunter *n.* jæger -en, pl. -e
hurrah *interj.* hurra
hurry *v.* skynde sig -te sig
hurt *v.* skade -ede
husband *n.* ægtemand -en, pl. ægtemænd
hygiene *n.* hygiejne -n

I

ice *n.* is -en
ice cream *n.* is -en, pl. same
ice-cream cone *n.* isvaffel -en or isvaflen, pl. isvafler
ice skating *n.* isskøjteløb -et
ice storm *n.* isslag -et
icicle *n.* istap -pen, pl. -pe or -per
idea *n.* idé -en, pl. -er
identical *adj.* identisk
idiom *n.* talemåde -n, pl. -r
if *conj.* hvis
ignorant *adj.* uvidende
ill *adj.* syg
illegal *adj.* ulovlig
illiteracy *n.* analfabetisme -n
illness *n.* sygdom -men, pl. -me
imagination *n.* fantasi -en, pl. -er
imagine *v.* forestille sig -ede sig
imitate *v.* imitere -ede, efterligne -ede
immature *adj.* umoden
immediately *adv.* øjeblikkeligt, med det samme
immigrant *n.* immigrant -en, pl. -er, indvandrer -en, pl. -e
immoral *adj.* umoralsk
immune *adj.* immun

Immune system *n.* immunforsvar -et
immunize *v.* immunisere -ede, vaccinere -ede
impact *n.* virkning -en, pl. -er
impatient *adj.* utålmodig
impersonal *adj.* upersonlig
important *adj.* vigtig
impossible *adj.* umulig
impractical *adj.* upraktisk
impressive *adj.* imponerende
improper *adj.* upassende
improve *v.* forbedre -ede
impulsive *adj.* impulsiv
inaccessible *adj.* utilgængelig
inaccurate *adj.* upræsis, unøjagtig
inadequate *adj.* utilstrækkelig
inappropriate *adj.* upassende, malplaceret, uhensigtsmæssig
incentive *n.* incitament -et, pl. -er
incident *n.* tilfælde -t, pl. same
incidental *adj.* tilfældig
include *v.* inkludere -ede
income *n.* indtægt -en, pl. -er, indkomst -en, pl. -er
income tax *n.* indkomstskat -ten, pl. -ter
incompatible with *adj.* uforenelig med; inkompatibel (computer)
incompetent *adj.* ukvalificeret, uduelig
incomprehensible *adj.* uforståelig, ubegribelig
inconceivable *adj.* utænkelig
inconsiderate *adj.* ubetænksom
inconsistent *adj.* inkonsistent, svingende
inconvenient *adj.* upraktisk, ubelejliget
incorrect *adj.* ukorrekt

increase v. tiltage *tiltog, tiltaget,* vokse *-ede,* stige *steg, steget*

incredible adj. utrolig

independent adj. uafhængig

indifferent adj. ligeglad

indispensable adj. uundværlig

indoor adj. indendørs

industrious adj. arbejdsom

industry n. industri *-en, pl. -er*

inedible adj. uspiselig, uegnet til menneske føde

inefficient adj. ineffektiv

inevitable adj. uundgåelig

inexpensive adj. billig

inexperienced adj. uerfaren

infant n. spædbarn *-et, pl. spædbørn*

infection n. infektion *-en, pl. -er,* betændelse *-n*

infidelity n. utroskab *-en, pl. -er*

infinite adj. uendelig

influence v. påvirke *-ede*

influence n. påvirkning, indflydelse *-en, pl. -er;* **under the influence** i påvirket tilstand

information n. oplysning *-en, pl. -er*

infrastructure n. infrastruktur *-en, pl. -er*

ingredient n. ingrediens *-en, pl. -er*

inherit v. arve *-ede*

inhospitable adj. ugæstfri (about hostess); uvenlig, barsk (about climate)

inhuman adj. umenneskelig

initially adv. i begyndelsen, til at begynde med

injection n. indsprøjtning *-en, pl. -er*

injure v. skade *-ede;* komme til skade (get injured)

ink n. blæk *-ket*

innocent adj. uskyldig

insecticide n. insektmiddel *insektmidlet, pl. insektmidler*

inseparable adj. uadskillelige

insignificant adj. ubetydelig

insist v. insistere *-ede*

insofar as conj. såfremt

install v. installere *-ede*

instantly adv. øjeblikkeligt, med det samme

instead (of) adv. i stedet (for)

insufficient adj. utilstrækkelig

insult v. fornærme *-ede*

insurance n. forsikring *-en, pl. -er*

insure v. forsikre *-ede*

intentional adj. med vilje, forsætlig

intercourse n. samleje *-t, pl. -r*

interest n. interesse *-n, pl. -r*

interest v. interessere *-ede*

interested adj. interesseret

interesting adj. interessant

intermission n. pause *-n, pl. -r*

interpreter n. tolk *-en, pl. -e*

interrupt v. afbryde *afbrød, afbrudt*

intersection n. vejkryds *-et, pl. same*

intimate adj. intim

into prep. ind i

introduce v. præsentere *-ede*

invalid adj. ugyldig

invaluable adj. uvurderlig, kostbar

invent v. opfinde *opfandt, opfundet*

invest v. investere *-ede*

investigate v. undersøge *-te*

invisible adj. usynlig

invitation n. indbydelse *-n, pl. -r,* invitation *-en, pl. -er*

invite v. invitere -ede
invoice n. faktura -en, pl. -er
involuntary adj. ufrivillig
iron n. jern (metal) -et;
    strygejern (for ironing
    clothes) -et, pl. same
irresistible adj. uimodståelig
irresponsible adj. uansvarlig
irritate v. irritere -ede
island n. ø -en, pl. -er
issue v. udstede -te
it pron. den/det (common/nt.
    gender)
itch n. kløe -n
itch v. klø -ede
itinerary n. rejseplan -en,
    pl. -er

J

jail n. fængsel -et or fængslet,
    pl. fængsler
January n. januar
jealous adj. jaloux
jewelry n. smykker (pl.)
job n. job -bet, pl. same
jog v. jogge -ede
joke n. vittighed -en, pl. -er
joke v. spøge -te; **tell a joke**
    fortælle en vittighed
journey n. rejse -n, pl. -r
joy n. glæde -n, pl. -r
joyful adj. glad, lykkelig
jubilee n. jubilæum jubilæet,
    pl. jubilæer
judge n. dommer -en, pl. -e
judge v. bedømme (assess) -te
juice n. juice -n, pl. -r
juicy adj. saftig
July n. juli
jump v. hoppe -ede
June n. juni
just adv. lige, netop, for
    nylig

K

kayak n. kajak -ken, pl. -ker
keep v. beholde -te
key n. nøgle -n, pl. -r
keyboard n. tastatur -et, pl. -er
kick v. sparke -ede
kill v. dræbe -te, slå ihjel slog,
    slået ihjel
kind adj. rar, venlig
kindergarten n.
    børnehaveklasse -n, pl. -r
king n. konge -n, pl. -r
kingdom n. kongerige -t, pl. -r
kiosk n. kiosk -en, pl. -er
kiss n. kys -set, pl. same
kiss v. kysse -ede
kitchen n. køkken -et, pl. -er
kneel v. knæle -ede
knife n. kniv -en, pl. -e
knock v. banke på (on door)
    -ede på
knot n. knude -n, pl. -r
know v. vide (knowledge)
    vidste, vidst; kende
    (familiarity) -te

L

label n. mærkat -et, pl. -er,
    etiket -ten, pl. -ter
lace n. blonde -n, pl. -r
lack v. mangle -ede
lacking adj. mangelfuld
ladder n. stige -n, pl. -r
lady n. dame -n, pl. -r
lake n. sø -en, pl. -er
lamb n. lammekød -et; lam
    (animal) -met, pl. same
landfill n. losseplads -en,
    pl. -er
landlord n. vært -en, pl. -er
landscape n. landskab -et,
    pl. -er
language n. sprog -et, pl. same
large adj. stor
last v. vare -ede

last *adv.* sidst
late *adj.* sen; **at the latest** senest
laugh *v.* le *lo, leet,* grine *-ede*
Laundromat *n.* møntvask *-en*
laundry *n.* vasketøj *-et*
law *n.* lov *-en, pl. -e*
lawn *n.* græsplæne *-n, pl. -r*
lawn mower *n.* plæneklipper *-en, pl. -e*
lawyer *n.* advokat *-en, pl. -er*
laxative *n.* afføringsmiddel *afføringsmidlet, pl. afføringsmidler*
lay *v.* lægge *lagde, lagt*
lazy *adj.* doven
lead *n.* bly *-et*
lead *v.* lede *-te;* **be in the lead** ligge i spidsen
leaf *n.* blad *-et, pl. -e*
leak *n.* utæthed *-en, pl. -er*
lean *adj.* mager
learn *v.* lære *-te*
lease *n.* lejemål *-et, pl. same*
leash *n.* snor *-en, pl. -e*
least *adj.* mindst
left *adj.* venstre
left-handed *adj.* venstrehåndet
leftovers *n.* levning *-en, pl. -er*
legal *adj.* lovlig
legible *adj.* læselig
leisure time *n.* fritid *-en*
lend *v.* låne *-te*
length *n.* længde *-n, pl. -r*
lens *n.* linse *-n, pl. -r*
lesbian *adj.* lesbisk
less *adj.* mindre
let *v.* lade *lod, ladet*
letter *n.* brev *-et, pl. -e*
library *n.* bibliotek *-et, pl. -er*
lick *v.* slikke *-ede*
lie *n.* løgn *-en, pl. -e*
lie *v.* ligge *lå, ligget;* lyve (tell a lie) *løj, løjet*

life *n.* liv *-et, pl. same*
lifeguard *n.* livredder *-en, pl. -e*
lift *v.* løfte *-ede*
light *n.* lys *-et, pl. same*
light *adj.* let
lighter *n.* lighter *-en, pl. -e*
like *v.* kunne lide *kunne, kunnet lide (pre. kan lide)*
likely *adj.* sandsynlig
liquid *n.* væske *-n, pl. -r*
liquid *adj.* flydende
liquor *n.* spiritus *-en*
listen *v.* lytte *-ede*
literature *n.* litteratur *-en*
little *adj.* lille; lidt
live *v.* leve (be alive) *-ede;* bo (reside) *-ede*
lively *adj.* livlig
living room *n.* dagligstue *-n, pl. -r*
load *v.* læsse *-ede*
local *adj.* lokal
lock *n.* lås *-en, pl. -e*
lock *v.* låse *-ede* or *-te*
locksmith *n.* låsesmed *-en, pl. -e*
lollipop *n.* slikkepind *-en, pl. -e*
lonely *adj.* ensom
long *adj.* lang
long for *v.* længes efter *længtes efter*
longing *n.* længsel *længslen, pl. længsler*
look *v.* se *så, set,* kigge *-ede*
loose *adj.* løs
loosen *v.* løsne *-ede*
lose *v.* tabe *-te,* miste *-ede*
lost and found *n.* glemte sager *(pl.)*
loud *adj.* højlydt
loudspeaker *n.* højtaler *-en, pl. -e*
love *n.* kærlighed *-en*
love *v.* elske *-ede*
lover *n.* elsker *-en, pl. -e*

loving *adj.* kærlig

low *adj.* lav

luck *n.* held *-et*

luckily *adv.* heldigvis

lucky *adj.* heldig

luggage *n.* bagage *-n*

lunch *n.* frokost *-en, pl. -er*

luxurious *adj.* luksuriøs

luxury *n.* luksus *-en*

M

machine *n.* maskine *-n, pl. -r*

mad *adj.* vred (angry); tosset (crazy)

magazine *n.* blad *-et, pl. -e*

magnetic *adj.* magnetisk

magnify *v.* forstørre *-ede*

mail *n.* post *-en*

mailbox *n.* postkasse *-n, pl. -r*

main *adj.* hoved-

maintain *v.* vedligeholde *vedligeholdt, vedligeholdt*

maintenance *n.* vedligeholdelse *-n*

majesty *n.* majestæt *-en, pl. -er*; **Her Majesty Queen Margrethe II** Hendes Majestæt Dronning Margrethe II

majority *n.* flertal *-let*

make *v.* lave *-ede*

malignant *adj.* ondartet

malpractice *n.* uagtsomhed *-en*

man *n.* mand *-en, pl. mænd*

manager *n.* leder *-en, pl. -e,* manager *-en, pl. -e*

mandatory *adj.* obligatorisk

manual *adj.* manuel

manual *n.* instruktionsbog *-en, pl. instruktionsbøger*

many *adj.* mange

map *n.* kort *-et, pl. same*

marathon *n.* maratonløb *-et, pl. same*

March *n.* marts

marijuana *n.* marihuana *-en*

marriage *n.* ægteskab *-et, pl. -er*

marriage license *n.* vielsesattest *-en, pl. -er*

married *adj.* gift

masseur *n.* massør *-en, pl. -er*; **masseuse** *n.* massøse *-n, pl. -r*

mass media *n.* massemedie *-t, pl. -r*

master key *n.* universalnøgle, hovednøgle *-n, pl. -r*

match *n.* kamp (game) *-en, pl. -e*; ligemand (equal) *-en, pl. ligemænd*

match *n.* tændstik (for lighting) *-ken, pl. -ker*

maternity leave *n.* barselsorlov *-en*

May *n.* maj

maybe *adv.* måske

meal *n.* måltid *-et, pl. -er*

mean *v.* mene *-te*

mean *adj.* ond (nasty)

meaning *n.* betydning *-en, pl. -er*

meanwhile *adv.* i mellemtiden

measure *v.* måle *-te*

meat *n.* kød *-et*

mechanic *n.* mekaniker *-en, pl. -e*

medal *n.* medalje *-n, pl. -r*

medicine *n.* medicin *-en*

meet *v.tr.* møde *-te; v.intr.* mødes *mødtes, mødtes*

meeting *n.* møde *-t, pl. -r*

melt *v.* smelte *-ede*

member *n.* medlem *-met, pl. -mer*

memory *n.* hukommelse *-n, pl. -r*

menopause *n.* overgangsalder *-en*

mention v. nævne -te or -ede
menu n. menukort -et, pl. same
mermaid n. havfrue -n, pl. -r;
  The Little Mermaid Den
  lille Havfrue
message n. besked -en, pl.
  -er, meddelelse -n, pl. -r
microphone n. mikrofon -en,
  pl. -er
midnight n. midnat
midsummer n. midsommer;
  Midsummer Night's Eve
  sankthansaften (June 23)
mild adj. mild
military n. militær -et
millennium n. årtusind -et,
  pl. -er
millionaire n. millionær -en,
  pl. -er
mine n. mine -n, pl. -r
mine pron. min/mit/mine
  (common gender, sing./nt.
  sing./pl.)
minister n. minister (gov.
  official) -en, pl. ministre;
  præst (church) -en, pl. -er
minority n. minoritet -en,
  pl. -er
minute n. minut -tet, pl. -ter;
  per minute i minuttet
mirror n. spejl -et, pl. -e
misbehave v. optræde
  upassende optrådte,
  optrådt upassende; være
  uartig (children) var,
  været uartig
miscellaneous adj. diverse
misdemeanor n. forseelse -n,
  pl. -r; lovovertrædelse
  (small crime) -n, pl. -r
misjudge v. fejlbedømme -te
misplace v. fejlplacere
  (wrong place) -ede;
  forlægge (mislay)
  forlagde, forlagt

miss v. savne (long for) -ede;
  ramme ved siden af (fail
  to hit) -te ved siden af
mistake n. fejl -en, pl. same,
  fejltagelse -n, pl. -r
mistress n. elskerinde -n, pl. -r
misunderstand v. misforstå
  misforstod, misforstået
misunderstanding n.
  misforståelse -n, pl. -r
mix v. blande -ede, mikse -ede
moat n. voldgrav -en, pl. -e
modern adj. moderne
modesty n. blufærdighed -en
moist adj. fugtig
moldy adj. muggen
moment n. øjeblik -ket, pl.
  -ke; **in a moment** om et
  øjeblik
monarchy n. monarki -et,
  pl. -er
Monday n. mandag
money n. penge (pl.)
month n. måned -en, pl. -er
moon n. måne -n, pl. -r
moonlight n. måneskin -net
more adj. mere
moreover adv. desuden
morning n. morgen -en,
  pl. -er
mosquito n. myg -gen, pl.
  same
most adj. mest; adv. meget,
  særdeles; **most surprising**
  særdeles overraskende
mostly adv. hovedsagelig
motel n. motel -let, pl. -ler
mother n. mor -en, pl. mødre
motherland n. fædreland -et,
  pl. -e
motorcycle n. motorcykel
  -en or motorcyklen,
  pl. motorcykler
mourn v. sørge -ede
mouse n. mus -en, pl. same

move *n.* flytning *-en, pl. -er*
move *v.* flytte *-ede*
movie *n.* film *-en, pl. same*
Mr. hr.
Mrs. fru
Ms. frøken (frk.)
much *adv.* meget
mud *n.* mudder *-et*
mug *v.* overfalde *overfaldt, overfaldet*
multiply *v.* multiplicere *-ede*
murder *n.* mord *-et, pl. same*
museum *n.* museum *museet, pl. museer*
music *n.* musik *-ken*
musician *n.* musiker *-en, pl. -e*
must *v.* skulle *skulle, skullet (pre. skal)*
mute *adj.* stum
mutual *adj.* gensidig
my *pron.* min/mit/mine *(common gender, sing./nt. sing./pl.)*
myself *pron.* mig selv

N

nail *n.* negl (finger) *-en, pl. -e*; søm (hardware) *-met, pl. same*
naked *adj.* nøgen
name *n.* navn *-et, pl. -e*
nap *n.* lur *-en*
napkin *n.* serviet *-ten, pl. -ter*
narcotics *n.* narkotika *-en*
narrow *adj.* smal
narrow-minded *adj.* snæversynet, smalsporet
nation *n.* nation *-en, pl. -er*
nationality *n.* nationalitet *-en, pl. -er*
native *adj.* indfødt
natural *adj.* naturlig
natural gas *n.* naturgas *-sen*
nature *n.* natur *-en*
nausea *n.* kvalme *-n*

Nazi *n.* nazist *-en, pl. -er*;
  neo-Nazi nynazist
near *adj.* tæt på, nær
nearby *adv.* i nærheden
nearly *adv.* næsten
nearsighted *adj.* nærsynet
neat *adj.* ordentlig
necessary *adj.* nødvendig
necessity *n.* nødvendighed *-en, pl. -er*
need *v.* behøve *-ede*
needle *n.* nål *-en, pl. -e*
needless *adj.* unødig, unødvendig
neglect *v.* forsømme *-te*
negligent *adj.* skødesløs; uagtsom (law)
negligible *adj.* ubetydelig
neighbor *n.* nabo (same side of street) *-en, pl. -er*; genbo (across the street) *-en, pl. -er*
neighborhood *n.* nabolag *-et, pl. same*
neither ... nor *conj.* hverken ... eller
nervous *adj.* nervøs
nest *n.* rede *-n, pl. -r*
neurotic *adj.* neurotisk
neutral *adj.* neutral
neutralize *v.* neutralisere *-ede*
never *adv.* aldrig
nevertheless *adv.* ikke desto mindre
new *adj.* ny
newborn *adj.* nyfødt
news *n.* nyhed *-en, pl. -er*
newspaper *n.* avis *-en, pl. -er*
New Year's Eve *n.* nytårsaften
next *adj.* næste
nice *adj.* rar (kind); pæn (nice-looking)
nickname *n.* kælenavn *-et, pl. -e*
nicotine *n.* nikotin *-en*

night *n.* nat *-ten, pl. nætter*
nightlife *n.* natteliv *-et*
nightmare *n.* mareridt *-et, pl. same*
nine *num.* ni
nineteen *num.* nitten
ninety *num.* halvfems
no *interj.* nej
nobility *n.* adel *-en*
noble *adj.* adelig
nobleman *n.* adelsmand *-en, pl. adelsmænd*
nobody *pron.* ingen
nod *v.* nikke *-ede*
noise *n.* støj *-en;* **noise pollution** støjforurening
noisy *adj.* støjende
nonalcoholic *adj.* alkoholfri
none *pron.* ingen
nonfat *adj.* fedtfri
nonsense *n.* vrøvl *-et*
Nordic *adj.* nordisk
normal *adj.* normal
north *n.* nord *-en*
northern lights *n.* nordlys *-et*
not *adv.* ikke
notary public *n.* notar *-en, pl. -er*
noteworthy *adj.* bemærkelsesværdig, værd at lægge mærke til
nothing *pron.* intet, ingenting
notice *v.* lægge mærke til *lagde, lagt mærke til,* bemærke *-ede*
noticeable *adj.* mærkbar, synlig
notify *v.* underrette *-ede,* informere om *-ede om*
nourishment *n.* næring *-en*
novel *adj.* ny (new); usædvanlig (unusual)
November *n.* november
now *adv.* nu
nowadays *adv.* nu om dage

nowhere *adv.* ingensteds, intetsteds
nuclear power *n.* atomkraft *-en*
nude *adj.* nøgen, upåklædt
nudist beach *n.* nudiststrand *-en, pl. -e*
nuisance *n.* ulempe (inconvenience) *-n, pl. -r;* plage (pest) *-n, pl. -r*
numb *adj.* følelsesløs
number *n.* nummer *-et, pl. numre*
numerous *adj.* talrige
nurse *n.* sygeplejerske *-n, pl. -r*
nursery school *n.* børnehave *-n, pl. -r*
nursing home *n.* plejehjem *-met, pl. same*
nut *n.* nød *-den, pl. -der*
nutcracker *n.* nøddeknækker *-en, pl. -e*

O

oath *n.* ed *-en, pl. -er;* **under oath** under ed; **the Hippocratic oath** lægeløftet
obedient *adj.* lydig
obese *adj.* fed, overvægtig
obituary *n.* dødsannonce *-n, pl. -r*
obligation *n.* forpligtelse *-n, pl. -r*
oblong *adj.* aflang
obsession *n.* besættelse *-n, pl. -r,* tvangstanke *-n, pl. -r*
obstetrics *n.* obstetrik *-ken*
obstinate *adj.* stædig
obtain *v.* opnå *-ede*
obvious *adj.* åbenbar, indlysende
occasionally *adv.* lejlighedsvis
occupation *n.* stilling *-en, pl. -er*

occupied *adj.* besat, optaget

occur *v.* ske *-te*

ocean *n.* hav *-et, pl. -e,* ocean *-et, pl. -er*

octane rating *n.* oktantal *-let, pl. same*

October *n.* oktober

odd *adj.* mærkelig

odor *n.* lugt *-en, pl. -e*

of *prep.* af

of course *adv.* selvfølgelig, naturligvis

offend *v.* fornærme *-ede*

offer *v.* tilbyde *tilbød, tilbudt*

office *n.* kontor *-et, pl. -er*

official *adj.* officiel

often *adv.* ofte, tit

oil *n.* olie *-n*

old *adj.* gammel

old-fashioned *adj.* gammeldags

Olympic Games *n.* Olympiade *-n*

omit *v.* udelade *udelod, udeladt*

once *adv.* én gang (once); engang (formerly)

one *num.* en

oneself *pron.* sig selv

one-way *adj.* ensrettet

only *adv.* kun

open *v.* åbne *-ede*

open *adj.* åben

operation *n.* operation *-en, pl. -er*

opinion *n.* mening *-en, pl. -er*; opinion poll meningsundersøgelse, meningsmåling

opportunity *n.* mulighed *-en, pl. -er*

opposite *adj.* modsat

orchard *n.* frugtplantage *-n, pl. -r*

orchestra *n.* orkester *-et, pl. orkestre*

order *v.* bestille (arrange to receive) *-te*; befale (command) *-ede*

ordinary *adj.* almindelig

organic *adj.* økologisk

organization *n.* organisation *-en, pl. -er*

original *adj.* original, oprindelig

other *adj.* anden/andet/andre *(common gender, sing./nt. sing./pl.)*

otherwise *conj.* ellers

ought to *v.* burde *burde, burdet (pre. bør)*

our *pron.* vores (informal); vor/vort/vore (formal) *(common gender, sing./nt. sing./pl.)*

out *prep.* ud

outdoors *adj.* udendørs

outrageous *adj.* fantastisk (fantastic); skandaløs, skammelig (beyond decency)

oven *n.* ovn *-en, pl. -e*

over *prep.* over

overeat *v.* spise for meget *-te for meget*

overnight *adv.* natten over

overseas *adj.* oversøisk, udenlandsk

oversleep *v.* sove for længe *sov, sovet for længe*

over-the-counter medicine *n.* håndkøbsmedicin *-en*

overtime *n.* overtid *-en* (work); forlanget spilletid (sports)

overweight *adj.* overvægtig

overwhelming *adj.* overvældende

owe *v.* skylde *-te*

own *v.* eje *-ede*

own *pron.* egen/eget/egne *(common gender, sing./nt. sing./pl.)*

owner *n.* ejer *-en, pl. -e*

oxygen *n.* ilt *-en*

P

pack *v.* pakke -*ede*

package *n.* pakke -*n, pl. -r*

padlock *n.* hængelås -*en, pl. -e*

page *n.* side -*n, pl. -r*

pager *n.* personsøger -*en, pl. -e*

pain *n.* smerte -*n, pl. -r*

paint *n.* maling -*en*

paint *v.* male -*ede*

painter *n.* maler -*en, pl. -e*

painting *n.* maleri -*et, pl. -er*

pair *n.* par -*ret, pl. same*

pale *adj.* bleg

panhandle *v.* tigge på gaden -*ede på gaden*

panic *n.* panik -*ken*

panic *v.* gå i panik *gik, gået i panik*

paper *n.* papir -*et, pl. -er*

paperback (book) *n.* billigbog -*en, pl. billigbøger*

parallel *adj.* parallel

parents *n.* forældre *(pl.)*

park *n.* park -*en, pl. -er*

park *v.* parkere -*ede*

parking lot *n.* parkeringsplads -*en, pl. -er*

part *n.* del -*en, pl. -e*

participant *n.* deltager -*en, pl. -e*

participate *v.* deltage *deltog, deltaget*

partly *adv.* delvis

party *n.* fest (celebration) -*en, pl. -er*; selskab (celebration or group) -*et, pl. -er*

pass *v.* overhale (on road) -*ede*; række (give) *rakte, rakt*

passenger *n.* passager -*en, pl. -er*

passport *n.* pas -*set, pl. same*

pastime *n.* fritidsbeskæftigelse, adspredelse -*n, pl. -r*

pastry *n.* wienerbrød -*et*

path *n.* sti -*en, pl. -er*

patient *adj.* tålmodig

patient *n.* patient -*en, pl. -er*

pause *n.* pause -*n, pl. -r*

pay *v.* betale -*te*

payment *n.* betaling -*en, pl. -er*

peace *n.* fred -*en*

peaceful *adj.* fredelig

peculiar *adj.* underlig, mærkelig

pedestrian *n.* fodgænger -*en, pl. -e*

peel *v.* skrælle -*ede*

penalty *n.* straf -*fen, pl. -fe*

pencil *n.* blyant -*en, pl. -er*

people *n.* folk *(pl.)*; the people folket

percent *n.* procent -*en, pl. -er*

perhaps *adv.* måske

period *n.* periode -*n, pl. -r*

periodically *adv.* periodevis, i perioder

perishable *adj.* letfordærvelig

permanent *adj.* vedvarende (long time); stedsevarende (forever)

permission *n.* tilladelse -*n, pl. -r*

personal *adj.* personlig

perspire *v.* svede -*te*, perspirere -*ede*

persuade *v.* overtale -*te*

perverse *adj.* pervers

pesticide *n.* pesticid -*et, pl. -er*

pet *n.* kæledyr -*et, pl. same*

pharmacy *n.* apotek -*et, pl. -er*

philanthropy *n.* filantropi -*en*, velgørenhedsarbejde -*t*

philosophy *n.* filosofi -*en,*
pl. -*er*

phone *n.* telefon -*en, pl.* -*er*

phone book *n.* telefonbog
-*en, pl. telefonbøger*

photocopy *n.* fotokopi -*en,*
pl. -*er*

photocopy *v.* fotokopiere -*ede*

photograph *n.* fotografi -*et,*
pl. -*er*

photograph *v.* fotografere -*ede*

physical *adj.* fysisk

pick *v.* vælge (choose) *valgte,*
valgt; plukke (pick apples,
etc.) -*ede*

pickpocket *n.* lommetyv -*en,*
pl. -*e;* **beware of**
pickpockets pas på
lommetyve

picture *n.* billede -*t, pl.* -*r*

picturesque *adj.* malerisk,
pittoresk

piece *n.* stykke -*t, pl.* -*r;*
apiece stykket

pig *n.* gris -*en, pl.* -*e*

pill *n.* pille -*n, pl.* -*r*

pillow *n.* hovedpude -*n, pl.* -*r*

pilot *n.* pilot -*en, pl.* -*er*

pin *n.* nål -*en, pl.* -*e;* **safety**
pin sikkerhedsnål

pinch *v.* nappe -*ede*

pitch a tent *v.* slå telt op *slog,*
slået telt op

place *n.* sted -*et, pl.* -*er*

place *v.* placere -*ede*

place-name *n.* stednavn -*et,*
pl. -*e*

plain *adj.* almindelig

plan *n.* plan -*en, pl.* -*er*

plan *v.* planlægge *planlagde,*
planlagt

plane *n.* flyvemaskine -*n, pl.* -*r*

plant *n.* plante -*n, pl.* -*r*

play *n.* skuespil (theater) -*let,*
pl. same

play *v.* spille (instrument, ball
game) -*ede;* lege
(children) -*ede*

playground *n.* legeplads -*en,*
pl. -*er*

playmate *n.* legekammerat
-*en, pl.* -*er*

pleasant *adj.* dejlig (nice);
behagelig (comfortable)

pleasure *n.* fornøjelse -*n, pl.* -*r*

plentiful *adj.* rigelig

pliers *n.* tang -*en, pl. tænger*

plug *n.* stik -*ket, pl. same*

plunger *n.* svuppert -*en,*
pl. -*er*

pocket *n.* lomme -*n, pl.* -*r*

poem *n.* digt -*et, pl.* -*e*

poison *n.* gift -*en*

poisonous *adj.* giftig

police *n.* politi -*et*

policeman *n.* politibetjent
-*en, pl.* -*e*

police station *n.* politistation
-*en, pl.* -*er*

polite *adj.* høflig

political *adj.* politisk

polluted *adj.* forurenet

pond *n.* dam -*men, pl.* -*me;* sø
(lake) -*en, pl.* -*er*

poor *adj.* fattig (penniless);
ringe (low quality)

popsicle *n.* ispind -*en, pl.* -*e*

popular *adj.* populær

population *n.* befolkning -*en,*
pl. -*er*

porcelain *n.* porcelæn -*et*

pork *n.* svinekød -*et*

portable *adj.* transportabel,
bærbar

porter *n.* drager -*en, pl.* -*e*

portrait *n.* portræt -*tet, pl.* -*ter*

possibility *n.* mulighed -*en,*
pl. -*er*

possible *adj.* mulig

postage *n.* porto -*en*

postcard *n.* postkort *-et, pl. same*

post office *n.* posthus *-et, pl. -e*

postpone *v.* udsætte *udsatte, udsat*

potluck *n.* sammenskudsgilde *-t, pl. -r*

poultry *n.* fjerkræ *-et*

pour *v.* hælde (from jar) *-te;* skænke (wine) *-ede;* øse ned (rain) *-ede ned*

poverty *n.* fattigdom *-men*

power outage *n.* strømsvigt *-et, pl. same*

practical *adj.* praktisk

practice *v.* øve sig *-ede sig*

pragmatic *adj.* pragmatisk

praise *v.* rose *-te*

pray *v.* bede *bad, bedt*

prayer *n.* bøn *-nen, pl. -ner*

preach *v.* prædike *-ede*

precede *v.* gå forud for *gik, gået forud for*

precious *adj.* kostbar, værdifuld (valuable); dyrebar (beloved)

precious stone *n.* ædelsten *-en, pl. -e*

precipitation *n.* nedbør *-en*

precise *adj.* præcis, nøjagtig

predetermine *v.* forudbestemme *-te*

predict *v.* forudsige *forudsagde, forudsagt*

prefer *v.* foretrække *foretrak, foretrukket*

pregnant *adj.* gravid

prejudice *n.* fordom *-men, pl. -me*

prepare *v.* forberede *-te;* tilberede (food) *-te*

prepay *v.* forudbetale *-te*

prescribe *v.* ordinere *-ede;* **medicine prescribed by doctor** lægeordineret medicin

prescription *n.* recept *-en, pl. -er*

present *n.* gave *-n, pl. -r*

present *adj.* tilstedeværende

president *n.* præsident *-en, pl. -er*

pretend *v.* foregive *foregav, foregivet,* lade som om *lod, ladt som om*

pretty *adj.* smuk

prevent *v.* forhindre *-ede*

previously *adv.* før, tidligere

price *n.* pris *-en, pl. -er;* **price war** priskrig; **increase in price** prisstigning

priest *n.* præst *-en, pl. -er*

primary *adj.* primær

prince *n.* prins *-en, pl. -er*

princess *n.* prinsesse *-n, pl. -r*

prison *n.* fængsel *fængslet, pl. fængsler*

prisoner *n.* fange *-n, pl. -r*

pristine *adj.* uberørt

private *adj.* privat

prize *n.* præmie *-n, pl. -r*

probably *adv.* muligvis

problem *n.* problem *-et, pl. -er*

problematic *adj.* problematisk

procrastinate *v.* udsætte *udsatte, udsat*

prohibit *v.* forbyde *forbød, forbudt*

promise *v.* love *-ede*

pronounce *v.* udtale (a word) *-te;* erklære (declare) *-ede*

pronunciation *n.* udtale *-en*

proof *n.* bevis *-et, pl. -er*

proper *adj.* rigtig, passende

propose *v.* foreslå (suggest) *foreslog, foreslået;* fri (ask to marry) *-ede*

protect *v.* beskytte *-ede*

protection *n.* beskyttelse *-n, pl. -r;* **protective glasses** beskyttelsesbriller

protest *v.* protestere *-ede*
proud *adj.* stolt
prove *v.* bevise *-te*
provocative *adj.*
provokerende
puberty *n.* pubertet *-en*
public *adj.* offentlig; **public restrooms** offentlige toiletter; **open to the public** offentlig adgang
pull *v.* trække *trak, trukket*
pulse *n.* puls *-en*
pump *n.* pumpe *-n, pl. -r*; **bicycle pump** cykelpumpe
punctual *adj.* præcis
punish *v.* straffe *-ede*
purchase *v.* købe *-te*
pure *adj.* ren
push *v.* skubbe *-ede*

Q

qualification *n.* kvalifikation *-en, pl. -er*
qualified *adj.* kvalificeret
quality *n.* kvalitet *-en, pl. -er*
quarantine *n.* karantæne *-n, pl. -r*
quarrel *v.* skændes *skændtes*
quarter *n.* kvart (1/4) *-en, pl. -er*; kvarter (15 minutes) *-et, pl. -er*
queen *n.* dronning *-en, pl. -er*
quench *v.* slukke *-ede*
question *n.* spørgsmål *-et, pl. same*
questionnaire *n.* spørgeskema *-et, pl. -er*
quick *adj.* hurtig
quiet *adj.* stille, rolig
quit *v.* holde op *holdt, holdt op*
quite *adv.* temmelig; **not quite** ikke helt
quotation *n.* citat *-et, pl. -er*
quote *v.* citere *-ede*

R

rabies *n.* hundegalskab *-en*
race *n.* race *-n, pl. -r*
racism *n.* racisme *-n*
radio *n.* radio *-en, pl. -er*
rage *n.* vrede *-n*
railroad *n.* jernbane *-n, pl. -r*
rain *n.* regn *-en*
rain *v.* regne *-ede*
rainbow *n.* regnbue *-n, pl. -r*
raincoat *n.* regnfrakke *-n, pl. -r*
raise *v.* hæve (make higher) *-ede*
rambunctious *adj.* uregerlig
random *adj.* tilfældig
rape *n.* voldtægt *-en*
rapid *adj.* hurtig
rapist *n.* voldtægtsforbryder *-en, pl. -e*
rare *adj.* sjælden (infrequent); rødt (about meat)
rat *n.* rotte *-n, pl. -r*
rate *n.* takst *-en, pl. -er*
rather *adv.* hellere (preferably); temmelig (somewhat)
raw *adj.* rå
read *v.* læse *-te*
ready *adj.* parat, færdig
real *adj.* virkelig
realize *v.* indse (become aware of) *indså, indset*; realisere (accomplish) *-ede*
reason *n.* grund *-en, pl. -e*
reasonable *adj.* fornuftig
recall *v.* huske (remember) *-ede*
receipt *n.* kvittering *-en, pl. -er*
receive *v.* modtage *modtog, modtaget*
receiver *n.* modtager *-en, pl. -e*; rør (on telephone) *-et, pl. same*

recently *adv.* for nylig

reception *n.* reception *-en,*
pl. -er

recipe *n.* opskrift *-en, pl. -er*

reckless *adj.* uforsvarlig (irresponsible); hensynsløs
(inconsiderate)

recognize *v.* genkende
(know) *-te;* anerkende
(acknowledge) *-te*

recommend *v.* anbefale *-ede*

reconsider *v.* overveje igen
-ede igen

recover *v.* genvinde (get
something back)
genvandt, genvundet;
komme sig (from
sickness) *kom, kommet sig*

rectify *v.* rette *-ede*

recycle *v.* genbruge *-te;*
recycling center *n.*
genbrugsplads *-en, pl. -er*

rediscover *v.* genopdage *-ede*

redundant *adj.* overflødig
(superfluous); ordrig
(verbose)

reek *v.* stinke *stank, stinket*

reestablish *v.* genoprette *-ede*

refreshment *n.* forfriskning
-en, pl. -er

refrigerator *n.* køleskab *-et,*
pl. -e

refugee *n.* flygtning *-en, pl. -e*

refund *v.* refundere *-ede*

refuse (to do something) *v.*
nægte (at gøre noget) *-ede*
(at gøre noget)

regain *v.* genvinde *genvandt,*
genvundet

regarding *adv.* med hensyn
til

region *n.* område *-t, pl. -r*

register *v.* registrere *-ede*

regret *v.* fortryde *fortrød,*
fortrudt

regrettable *adj.* beklagelig

regular *adj.* regelmæssig

regulate *v.* regulere *-ede*

reimburse *v.* tilbagebetale *-te*

reinvest *v.* geninvestere *-ede*

related *adj.* beslægtet

relationship *n.* forhold *-et, pl.*
same

relative *n.* slægtning *-en,*
pl. -e

relative *adj.* relativ

relax *v.* slappe af *-ede af*

release *v.* frigive *frigav,*
frigivet, slippe løs *slap,*
sluppet løs; **press release**
n. pressemeddelelse *-n,*
pl. -r

relentless *adj.* ubarmhjertig

relevant *adj.* relevant

relieve *v.* lindre (pain) *-ede;* **to**
be relieved at være lettet

religious *adj.* religiøs

reluctant *adj.* modvillig

remain *v.* forblive *forblev,*
forblevet

remark *n.* bemærkning *-en,*
pl. -er

remarkable *adj.*
bemærkelsesværdig,
beundringsværdig

remarry *v.* gifte sig igen *-ede*
sig igen

remember *v.* huske *-ede*

remind *v.* minde om *-ede om*

remorse *n.* anger *-en*

remote *adj.* fjerntliggende

remote control *n.*
fjernbetjening *-en*

remove *v.* fjerne *-ede*

renew *v.* forny *-ede*

rent *n.* leje *-n*

rent *v.* leje *-ede*

repair *n.* reparation *-en, pl. -er*

repair *v.* reparere *-ede*

repeat *v.* gentage *gentog,*
gentaget

repercussion *n.* følge *-n, pl.*
-r, konsekvens *-en, pl. -er*
repetitious *adj.* fuld af
gentagelser
reply *n.* svar *-et, pl. same*
reply *v.* svare *-ede*
report *n.* rapport *-en, pl. -er*
repulsive *adj.* modbydelig,
afskyelig
reputation *n.* omdømme *-t*
request *n.* anmodning *-en,*
pl. -er
request *v.* anmode om *-ede*
om, bede om *bad, bedt om*
required *adj.* obligatorisk
requirement *n.* krav *-et, pl.*
same
rescue *v.* redde *-ede*
research *n.* forskning *-en*
resemble *v.* ligne *-ede*
reservation *n.* reservation
-en, pl. -er
reserve *v.* reservere *-ede*
reside *v.* bo *-ede*
residential area *n.*
beboelsesområde *-t, pl. -r*
resign *v.* trække sig tilbage
trak, trukket sig tilbage
resist *v.* modstå (temptation)
modstod, modstået; gøre
modstand (fight against)
gjorde, gjort modstand
resolve *v.* løse *-te*
resource *n.* ressource *-n, pl. -r*
respectable *adj.* respektabel
respond *v.* svare *-ede*
responsibility *n.* ansvar *-et*
responsible *adj.* ansvarlig
rest *n.* hvile *-n*
rest *v.* hvile sig *-ede sig*
restaurant *n.* restauration,
restaurant *-en, pl. -er*
result *n.* resultat *-et, pl. -er*
retell *v.* genfortælle
genfortalte, genfortalt

retire *v.* trække sig tilbage
trak, trukket sig tilbage
retrospective *adj.*
retrospektiv
return *v.* returnere *-ede,*
komme tilbage *kom,*
kommet tilbage
reveal *v.* afsløre *-ede*
revenge *n.* hævn *-en*
review *n.* anmeldelse (book
or film) *-n, pl. -r*
reward *n.* belønning *-en,*
pl. -er
rice *n.* ris *-en*
rich *adj.* rig, velhavende
ride *v.* ride *red, redet*
ridiculous *adj.* latterlig
right *adj.* rigtig, korrekt
right *n.* højre; **right-handed**
højrehåndet
ring *n.* ring *-en, pl. -e*
rinse *v.* skylle *-ede*
ripe *adj.* moden
road *n.* vej *-en, pl. -e*
road sign *n.* vejskilt *-et, pl. -e*
robbery *n.* røveri *-et, pl. -er*
roof *n.* tag *-et, pl. -e*
room *n.* værelse *-t, pl. -r*, rum
-met, pl. same
root *n.* rod *-en, pl. rødder*
root for *v.* holde med *holdt,*
holdt med
rot *v.* rådne *-ede*
rotten *adj.* rådden
round *adj.* rund
route *n.* rute *-n, pl. -r*
row *n.* række *-n, pl. -r*
row *v.* ro *-ede*
royal *adj.* kongelig; **the royal
family** kongefamilien
rubber *n.* gummi *-en*; **rubber
band** elastik; **rubber**
kondom (condom)
rude *adj.* uhøflig, ubehøvlet,
uforskammet

rug *n.* løst gulvtæppe *-t, pl. -r*
ruin *v.* ødelægge *ødelagde, ødelagt*
ruin *n.* ruin *-en, pl. -er*
rule *n.* regel *-en, pl. regler*
rumor *n.* rygte *-t, pl. -r*
run *v.* løbe *løb, løbet*
rush *v.* skynde sig *-te sig*
rush hour traffic *n.* myldretrafik *-ken*
rust *n.* rust *-en*
rust *v.* ruste *-ede*
rustic *adj.* rustik (style); landlig (country)
ruthless *adj.* ubarmhjertig, skånselsløs, nådesløs
rye *n.* rug *-en*

S

sacred *adj.* hellig
sad *adj.* sørgmodig, ked af det
safe *adj.* sikker, ufarlig
safety *n.* sikkerhed *-en*; **safety precautions** sikkerhedsforanstaltninger
sail *v.* sejle *-ede*
salary *n.* løn *-nen*
salt *n.* salt *-et*
same *adj.* samme; **the same as** *adv.* det/den/de samme som *(depending on noun gender and number)*
sand *n.* sand *-et*
satisfactory *adj.* tilfredsstillende
satisfied *adj.* tilfreds
Saturday *n.* lørdag
save *v.* redde *-ede*
say *v.* sige *sagde, sagt*
scan *v.* scanne *-ede*
scandal *n.* skandale *-n, pl. -r*
Scandinavian *adj.* skandinavisk
schedule *n.* køreplan (bus, train) *-en, pl. -er*; **on schedule** til tiden

school *n.* skole *-n, pl. -r*
science *n.* naturvidenskab *-en*
scientist *n.* videnskabsmand *-en, pl. videnskabsmænd*
scissors *n.* saks *-en, pl. -e*
scold *v.* skælde ud *-te ud*
score *n.* stilling (in game) *-en, pl. -er*
score *v.* score *-ede*
scream *n.* skrig *-et, pl. same*
scream *v.* skrige *skreg, skreget*
screw *n.* skrue *-n, pl. -r*
screwdriver *n.* skruetrækker *-en, pl. -e*
sculpture *n.* skulptur *-en, pl. -er*
sea *n.* hav *-et, pl. -e*
seafood *n.* fiskemad *-en*
search *v.* søge *-te*
season *n.* sæson *-en, pl. -er*
season *v.* krydre *-ede*
seasonal *adj.* sæsonbestemt
seat *n.* sæde *-t, pl. -r*; **reserved seat** reserveret siddeplads
seat belt *n.* sikkerhedssele (car) *-n, pl. -r*; sikkerheds- bælte (airplane) *-t, pl. -r*
secluded *adj.* ugenert (property); tilbagetrukken (isolated)
secondhand *adj.* brugt
secret *adj.* hemmelig
secret *n.* hemmelighed *-en, pl. -er*
secretary *n.* sekretær *-en, pl. -er*
secure *v.* sikre *-ede*
sedative *n.* beroligende middel
seduce *v.* forføre *-te*
see *v.* se *så, set*
seldom *adv.* sjældent
select *v.* vælge *valgte, valgt*

self-confident *adj.*
  selvbevidst, selvsikker
self-conscious *adj.* genert
self-defense *n.* selvforsvar *-et*;
  in self-defense i
  selvforsvar
self-esteem *n.* selvtillid *-en*
self-evident *adj.*
  selvindlysende
selfish *adj.* egoistisk,
  selvoptaget
sell *v.* sælge *solgte, solgt*
send *v.* sende *-te*
senior citizen *n.* pensionist
  -en, pl. -er
sensible *adj.* fornuftig
sentence *n.* sætning
  (grammar) *-en, pl. -er*
separate *adj.* separat, særskilt
September *n.* september
sequence *n.* rækkefølge *-n*
serious *adj.* alvorlig
serve *v.* servere (food) *-ede*
service *n.* betjening *-en*
service station *n.* tankstation
  -en, pl. -er
seven *num.* syv
seventeen *num.* sytten
seventy *num.* halvfjerds
several *pron., adj.* adskillige
sew *v.* sy *-ede*
sewer *n.* kloak *-ken, pl. -ker*
sex *n.* sex
sexual harrassment *n.*
  seksuel chikane
shade *n.* skygge *-n*
shadow *n.* skygge *-n, pl. -r*
shady *adj.* skyggefuld
shake *v.* ryste *-ede*
shallow *adj.* lavvandet
  (water); overfladisk
  (figurative use)
shame *n.* skam *-men*
share *v.* dele *-te*
sharp *adj.* skarp

sharpen *v.* skærpe *-ede*
shave *v.* barbere *-ede*
she *pron.* hun
shed *n.* skur *-et, pl. -e*
shed *v.* fælde (lose hair) *-ede*
shelf *n.* hylde *-n, pl. -r*
shell *n.* skal *-len, pl. -ler*; in a
  nutshell i en nøddeskal
shellfish *n.* skaldyr *-et, pl. same*
sherbet *n.* sorbet *-ten, pl. -ter*
shine *v.* skinne *-ede*
shoot *v.* skyde *skød, skudt*
shop *n.* butik *-ken, pl. -ker*,
  forretning *-en, pl. -er*
shop *v.* handle *-ede*
shore *n.* kyst *-en, pl. -er*
short *adj.* kort
shortage *n.* mangel *-en*
shortcut *n.* genvej *-en, pl. -e*;
  take a shortcut skyde
  genvej
shorten *v.* afkorte *-ede*
short-tempered *adj.* kort for
  hovedet, temperamentsfuld
should *v.* skulle *skulle, skullet*
  (pre. skal)
shout *v.* råbe *-te*
show *v.* vise *-te*
shower *n.* regnbyge (rain) *-n,*
  pl. -r; brusebad (bath) *-et,*
  pl. -e
shrink *v.* krympe *-ede*
shut *v.* lukke *-ede*
shy *adj.* genert
siblings *n.* søskende *(pl.)*
sick *adj.* syg
sickness *n.* sygdom *-men,*
  pl. -me
side *n.* side *-n, pl. -r*
sidewalk *n.* fortov *-et, pl. same*
sigh *n.* suk *-ket, pl. same*
sigh *v.* sukke *-ede*
sightsee *v.* se på
  seværdigheder *så, set på*
  seværdigheder

sign *n.* skilt (road, etc.) *-et, pl. -e*

sign *v.* skrive under *skrev, skrevet under*

signature *n.* underskrift *-en, pl. -er*

significant *adj.* vigtig

sign language *n.* tegnsprog *-et, pl. same*

silence *n.* stilhed *-en*

silver *n.* sølv *-et*

similar *adj.* lignende

simple *adj.* enkel (plain); simpel, ligetil, klar, indlysende (easily understood)

since *adv.* siden da

since *præp.* siden

since *conj.* eftersom (as)

sincere *adj.* oprigtig

sing *v.* synge *sang, sunget*

single *adj.* enlig (not married)

sink *v.* synke (ship) *sank, sunket*

sit *v.* sidde *sad, siddet*

six *num.* seks

sixteen *num.* seksten

sixty *num.* tres

size *n.* størrelse *-n, pl. -r*

skate *v.* stå på skøjter *stod, stået på skøjter*

skin *n.* skind *-et*, hud *-en*

sky *n.* himmel *-en* or *himlen, pl. himle*

sleep *v.* sove *sov, sovet;*
  sleeping bag *n.* sovepose *-n, pl. -r*

sleepless *adj.* søvnløs

sleepy *adj.* søvnig

slice *n.* skrive *-n, pl. -r*

slice *v.* skære i skiver *skar, skåret i skiver*

slide *v.* glide *gled, gledet*

slim *adj.* slank

slow *adj.* langsom

small *adj.* lille

smart *adj.* klog, intelligent

smell *n.* duft (pleasant) *-en, pl. -e*; lugt (unpleasant) *-en, pl. -e*

smell *v.* dufte (pleasant smell) *-ede*; lugte (unpleasant or neutral smell) *-ede*

smile *n.* smil *-et, pl. same*

smile *v.* smile *-ede*

smoke *n.* røg *-en*

smoke *v.* ryge *røg, røget*

smooth *adj.* glat

smuggle *v.* smugle *-ede*

snake *n.* slange *-n, pl. -r*

sneeze *v.* nyse *nøs, nyst*

snore *v.* snorke *-ede*

snow *n.* sne *-en*

snow *v.* sne *-ede*

snuff *n.* snustobak *-ken*

so *conj.* så

soap *n.* sæbe *-n*

sober *adj.* ædru

socialism *n.* socialisme *-n*

society *n.* samfund *-et, pl. same*

soda *n.* sodavand *-en, pl. same*

soft *adj.* blød

soldier *n.* soldat *-en, pl. -er*

some *adj.* nogen, noget, nogle (depending on noun gender and number)

somehow *adv.* på en eller anden måde

someone *pron.* en eller anden

something *pron.* et eller andet

sometime *adv.* på et eller andet tidspunkt

sometimes *adv.* undertiden, somme tider, til tider, nogle gange

somewhat *adv.* noget, temmelig, i nogen grad

somewhere *adv.* et eller andet sted

son n. søn -nen, pl. -ner

song n. sang -en, pl. -e

soon adv. snart

sore adj. øm

sorrow n. sorg -en, pl. -er

soul n. sjæl -en, pl. -e

sound n. lyd -en, pl. -e

sour adj. sur

south n. syd -en

spacious adj. rummelig, stor

speak v. tale -te

special adj. særlig, speciel

specific adj. specifik

specify v. specificere -ede

spectator n. tilskuer -en, pl. -e

speech n. tale -n, pl. -r

speed n. fart -en

spell v. stave -ede

spend v. bruge (money) -te;
tilbringe (time) tilbragte,
tilbragt

spice n. krydderi -et, pl. -er

spill v. spilde -te

spit v. spytte -ede

spoil v. forkæle (children)
-ede; blive fordærvet
(food) blev, blevet
fordærvet

spot n. plet (stain) -ten, pl.
-ter; plads (in line, etc.)
-en, pl. -er

spot v. få øje på fik, fået
øje på

spring n. forår (season) -et,
pl. same

spy n. spion -en, pl. -er

stain n. plet -ten, pl. -ter

stain v. plette -ede

staircase n. trappe -n, pl. -r

stamp n. stempel stemplet,
stempler; frimærke (mail)
-t, pl. -r; **stamped letter**
frankeret brev

stamp v. stemple -ede

stand v. stå stod, stået

standard of living n.
levestandard -en, pl. -er

stapler n. hæftemaskine -n,
pl. -r

star n. stjerne -n, pl. -r

starch n. stivelse -n; **starched
shirt** stivet skjorte

start v. begynde -te, starte
-ede

starve v. sulte -ede

stationery n. brevpapir -et

stay v. blive blev, blevet; **stay
overnight** blive natten over

steal v. stjæle stjal, stjålet

steam n. damp -en, pl. -e

steel n. stål -et; **stainless steel**
rustfrit stål

steep adj. stejl

stiff adj. stiv

still adv. endnu

sting v. stikke stak, stukket

stink v. stinke stank, stinket

stone n. sten -en, pl. -e

stop v. stoppe -ede, standse
-ede

store n. butik -ken, pl. -ker,
forretning -en, pl. -er

store v. opbevare -ede

storm n. stormvejr -et

story n. historie -n, pl. -r

straight adj. lige

strange adj. fremmed
(unknown); mærkelig
(weird)

straw n. strå -et, pl. same;
sugerør (for drinking) -et,
pl. same

strawberry n. jordbær -ret,
pl. same

stream n. å -en, pl. -er, bæk
-ken, pl. -ke

street n. gade -n, pl. -r

strength n. styrke -n, pl. -r

strengthen v. styrke -ede

stressful adj. stressende

strict adj. streng

strike *n.* strejke *-n, pl. -r*; **go on strike** gå i strejke

strike *v.* strejke *-ede*; slå (hit) *slog, slået*

string *n.* snor (for tying) *-en, pl. -e*; streng (for instrument) *-en, pl. -e*

strong *adj.* stærk

stubborn *adj.* stædig

student *n.* elev (grade school) *-en, pl. -er*; studerende (higher education)

study *v.* studere *-ede*, læse *-te*

stupid *adj.* dum

subconscious *adj.* underbevidst

subscription *n.* abonnement *-et, pl. -er*

suburb *n.* forstad *-en, pl. forstæder*

subway *n.* undergrundsbane *-n, pl. -r*; **Copenhagen subway** S-banen, S-toget

suddenly *adv.* pludselig

suffer *v.* lide *led, lidt*

sufficient *adj.* nok, tilstrækkelig

suggest *v.* foreslå *foreslog, foreslået*

suicide *n.* selvmord *-et, pl. same*

suitable *adj.* passende

suitcase *n.* kuffert *-en, pl. -er*

summer *n.* sommer *-en, pl. somre*

sun *n.* sol *-en, pl. -e*

sunbathe *v.* tage solbad *tog, taget solbad*

sunburned *adj.* solskoldet

Sunday *n.* søndag

sundown *n.* solnedgang *-en, pl. -e*

sunglasses *n.* solbriller *(pl.)*

sunny *adj.* solrig; **it is sunny** det er solskin

sunrise *n.* solopgang *-en, pl. -e*

sunscreen *n.* solcreme *-n*

sunstroke *n.* solstik

superficial *adj.* overfladisk

superfluous *adj.* overflødig

superglue *n.* kontaktlim *-en*

superstitious *adj.* overtroisk

supper *n.* aftensmad *-en*

support *v.* støtte *-ede*

suppose *v.* formode *-ede*

sure *adj.* sikker

surgeon *n.* kirurg *-en, pl. -er*

surname *n.* efternavn *-et, pl. -e*

surprise *n.* overraskelse *-n, pl. -r*

surprise *v.* overraske *-ede*

suspense *n.* spænding *-en*

suspicious *adj.* mistænksom, mistroisk

swallow *v.* synke *sank, sunket*

swear *v.* sværge (oath) *-ede* or *svor*; bande (curse) *-ede*

sweat *n.* sved *-en*

sweat *v.* svede *-te*

sweater *n.* trøje *-n, pl. -r*

sweep *v.* feje *-ede*

sweet *adj.* sød; **sweets** søde sager

swim *v.* svømme *-ede*

swimming pool *n.* svømmebassin *-et, pl. -er*

switch *n.* kontakt (electric) *-en, pl. -er*

switch *v.* skifte *-ede*

T

table *n.* bord *-et, pl. -e*

tailor *n.* skrædder *-en, pl. -e*

take *v.* tage *tog, taget*

talk *v.* tale *-te*, snakke *-ede*

talkative *adj.* snaksalig

tampon *n.* tampon *-en, pl. -er*

tanned *adj.* solbrændt, solbrun

tape *n.* bånd (cassette) -*et*,
  pl. same; tape (adhesive)
  -*en* (also called
  klæbestrimmel)
tape *v.* optage (on tape/film)
  optog, optaget
tart *adj.* syrlig
taste *v.* smage -*te*;
  taste/sample *n.*
  smagsprøve -*n, pl.* -*r*
tax *n.* skat -*ten, pl.* -*ter*
taxi *n.* taxi, taxa -*en, pl.* -*er*
taxpayer *n.* skatteyder -*en,*
  pl. -*e*
tea *n.* te -*en, pl.* -*er*
teach *v.* lære -*te*
teacher *n.* lærer -*en, pl.* -*e*
tear *n.* tåre -*n, pl.* -*r*
tear *v.* rive *rev, revet*
tease *v.* drille -*ede*
teaspoon *n.* teske -*en, pl.* -*er*
teetotaler *n.* afholdsmand
  -*en, pl. afholdsmænd*
telephone *n.* telefon -*en, pl.*
  -*er*; **phone book** *n.*
  telefonbog -*en,*
  pl. telefonbøger
telephone call *n.*
  telefonopringning -*en,*
  pl. -*er*, telefonopkald -*et,*
  pl. same
television *n.* fjernsyn -*et, pl.*
  same, tv *tv'et, pl. tv'er*
tell *v.* fortælle *fortalte, fortalt*;
  tell on *v.* sladre -*ede*
temperature *n.* temperatur
  -*en, pl.* -*er*
temporary *adj.* midlertidig
ten *num.* ti
tenant *n.* lejer -*en, pl.* -*e*
tent *n.* telt -*et, pl.* -*e*
terrible *adj.* forfærdelig,
  skrækkelig
tetanus *n.* stivkrampe -*n*;
  tetanus shot
  stivkrampevaccination

than *conj.* end
thankful *adj.* taknemmelig
thank you *n.* tak -*ken*
thatched roof *n.* stråtag -*et,*
  pl. -*e*
theater *n.* teater *teatret, pl.*
  teatre
theft *n.* tyveri -*et, pl.* -*er*
them *pron.* dem
themselves *pron.* dem selv
then *conj.* så; **back then**
  dengang
there *adv.* der
thereafter *adv.* derefter
therefore *adv.* derfor
thermometer *n.* termometer
  -*et, pl. termometre*
thermostat *n.* termostat -*en,*
  pl. -*er*
they *pron.* de
thick *adj.* tyk
thief *n.* tyv -*en, pl.* -*e*
thin *adj.* tynd
thing *n.* ting -*en, pl. same*
think *v.* tænke -*te*
thirst *n.* tørst -*en*
thirsty *adj.* tørstig
thirteen *num.* tretten
thirty *num.* tredive
this *pron.* denne/dette
  (common/nt. gender)
thorough *adj.* grundig
though *conj.* skønt
thought *n.* tanke -*n, pl.* -*r*
thoughtful *adj.* betænksom
thoughtless *adj.* ubetænksom
thousand *num.* tusind
thread *n.* tråd -*en, pl.* -*e*
threat *n.* trussel -*en* or
  truslen, pl. trusler
threaten *v.* true -*ede*
three *num.* tre
throne *n.* trone -*n, pl.* -*r*
through *prep.* gennem

throw *v.* kaste *-ede*

thumbtack *n.* tegnestift *-en,*
   pl. -er

thunder *n.* torden *-en*

Thursday *n.* torsdag

thus *adv.* således (in this
   manner); derfor
   (consequently)

ticket *n.* billet *-ten, pl. -ter*

tickle *v.* kildre *-ede*

ticklish *adj.* kilden

tide *n.* tidevand *-et*

tie *v.* binde *bandt, bundet*

tight *adj.* stram

time *n.* tid *-en, pl. -er*

tiny *adj.* lillebitte

to *prep.* til

today *adv.* i dag

together *adv.* sammen

toilet *n.* toilet *-tet, pl. -ter*, wc
   -'et, pl. -'er

toilet-trained *adj.* renlig

token *n.* polet *-ten, pl. -ter*

toll *n.* afgift *-en, pl. -er*

tomorrow *adv.* i morgen

tonight *adv.* i aften (evening);
   i nat (night)

too *adv.* også

toothbrush *n.* tandbørste *-n,*
   pl. -r

touch *v.* berøre *-te*

tough *adj.* hård, stærk

tourist *n.* turist *-en, pl. -er*

tournament *n.* stævne *-t,*
   pl. -r

toward *prep.* mod, imod

towel *n.* håndklæde *-t, pl. -r*

town *n.* by *-en, pl. -er*

tow truck *n.* kranbil *-en,*
   pl. -er

toy *n.* legetøj *-et*

traffic *n.* trafik *-ken*

traffic light *n.* trafiklys *-et,*
   pl. same

train *n.* tog *-et, pl. -e*

transfer *v.* overføre *-te*

translate *v.* oversætte
   oversatte, oversat

transparent *adj.*
   gennemsigtig

trash *n.* affald *-et*

trash can *n.* affaldsspand *-en,*
   pl. -e

travel *v.* rejse *-te*

travel agency *n.* rejsebureau
   -et, pl. -er

treat *v.* behandle *-ede*;
   treatment *n.* behandling
   -en, pl. -er

tree *n.* træ *-et, pl. -er*

tremble *v.* ryste *-ede*

trip *n.* tur *-en, pl. -e*

true *adj.* sand

try *v.* prøve *-ede*, forsøge *-te*

Tuesday *n.* tirsdag

tune *n.* melodi *-en, pl. -er*

tunnel *n.* tunnel *-en, pl. -er*

turkey *n.* kalkun *-en, pl. -er*

turn *n.* tur *-en, pl. -e*; your
   turn din tur; U-turn
   u-vending

turn *v.* vende *-te*

tweezers *n.* pincet *-ten,*
   pl. -ter

twelve *num.* tolv

twenty *num.* tyve

twice *adv.* to gange

twin *n.* tvilling *-en, pl. -er*

U

ugly *adj.* grim

umbrella *n.* paraply *-en, pl. -er*

unable *adj.* ude af stand til

unavoidable *adj.* uundgåelig

uncertain *adj.* usikker

unchanged *adj.* uforandret

unclog *v.* få luft i *fik, fået luft*
   i; rense *-ede*

uncomfortable *adj.*
   ubehagelig

uncommon *adj.* ualmindelig
unconscious *adj.* bevidstløs
unconstitutional *adj.*
    forfatningsstridig
undeniable *adj.* unægtelig
under *prep.* under
underage *adj.* mindreårig
underestimate *v.*
    undervurdere *-ede*
understand *v.* forstå *forstod,*
    forstået
underwear *n.* undertøj *-et*
undress *v.* tage tøjet af *tog,*
    taget tøjet af
unemployed *adj.* arbejdsløs
unexpected *adj.* uventet
unfair *adj.* uretfærdig
unfaithful *adj.* utro
unfeasible *adj.*
    uigennemførlig,
    uladsiggørlig
unforeseen *adj.* uforudset
unfortunately *adv.*
    uheldigvis
ungrateful *adj.*
    utaknemmelig
unhappy *adj.* ulykkelig
unharmed *adj.* uskadt
unhealthy *adj.* usund
unheard-of *adj.* uhørt
United States De forenede
    Stater
university *n.* universitet *-et,*
    pl. -er
unknown *adj.* ukendt
unlawful *adj.* ulovlig
unlimited *adj.* ubegrænset
unnecessary *adj.* unødvendig
unofficial *adj.* uofficiel
unpack *v.* pakke ud *-ede ud*
unpleasant *adj.* ubehagelig
unpopular *adj.* upopulær
unreasonable *adj.*
    fornuftstridig (against
    common sense); urimelig
    (not fair)

unreliable *adj.* upålidelig
unreserved *adj.* ikke
    reserveret (seat); ligefrem,
    åbenhjertig (frank, open)
unsafe *adj.* farlig
    (dangerous); upålidelig
    (unreliable); **unsafe sex**
    usikker sex
unsatisfactory *adj.*
    utilfredsstillende
unskilled labor *n.* ufaglært
    arbejdskraft
unstable *adj.* ustabil
untie *v.* binde op *bandt,*
    bundet op
until *conj.* indtil
unusual *adj.* unormal,
    påfaldende
up *prep.* op
upbringing *n.* opdragelse *-n*
update *v.* opdatere *-ede*
upgrade *v.* opgradere *-ede*
upset *adj.* rystet, chokeret,
    ophidset
upstairs *adv.* ovenpå
up-to-date *adj.* ajourført,
    tidssvarende
urban *adj.* bymæssig
urgent *adj.* pressende, som
    haster
use *v.* bruge *-te*
useful *adj.* gavnlig, praktisk,
    nyttig
useless *adj.* unyttig, nytteløs
usual *adj.* normal, almindelig
usually *adv.* normalt,
    almindeligvis

V

vacant *adj.* ledig
vacation *n.* ferie *-n, pl. -r*
vaccinate *v.* vaccinere *-ede*
vacuum cleaner *n.* støvsuger
    -en, pl. -e
valid *adj.* gyldig

valuable *adj.* værdifuld
vandalism *n.* hærværk *-et*
various *adj.* diverse, forskellige
vary *v.* variere *-ede*
vase *n.* vase *-n, pl. -r*
vegetable *n.* grøntsag *-en, pl. -er*
vegetarian *n.* vegetar *-en, pl. -er*, vegetarianer *-en, pl. -e*
vegetarian *adj.* vegetarisk, vegetariansk
vehicle *n.* køretøj *-et, pl. -er*
very *adv.* meget
veterinarian *n.* dyrlæge *-n, pl. -r*
vicinity *n.* nærhed *-en*; **in the vicinity of** i nærheden af
vicious *adj.* ondskabsfuld (evil); voldsom (strong)
victim *n.* offer *-et, pl. ofre*
victory *n.* sejr *-en, pl. -e*
view *n.* udsigt *-en*
village *n.* landsby *-en, pl. -er*
violence *n.* vold *-en*
violent *adj.* voldelig
virus *n.* virus *-sen, pl. -ser*
visibility *n.* sigtbarhed *-en*
visible *adj.* synlig
visit *n.* besøg *-et, pl. same*
visit *v.* besøge *-te*
visual *adj.* visuel
vocabulary *n.* ordforråd *-et, pl. same*
voice *n.* stemme *-n, pl. -r*
voluntary *adj.* frivillig
volunteer *n.* volontør *-en, pl. -er*
vomit *v.* kaste op *-ede op*
vote *n.* stemme *-n, pl. -r*; *v.* stemme *-te*
vulgar *adj.* vulgær

W

wages *n.* løn *-nen*
wait *n.* ventetid *-en*

wait *v.* vente *-ede*
waiter *n.* tjener *-en, pl. -e*
waiting room *n.* venteværelse *-t, pl. -r*
waitress *n.* servitrice *-n, pl. -r*
wake up *v.* vågne *-ede*; vække (someone else) *-ede*
walk *n.* gåtur *-en, pl. -e*
walk *v.* gå *gik, gået*
wall *n.* væg *-gen, pl. -ge*
wallet *n.* pung *-en, pl. -e*
want *v.* ønske *-ede*
war *n.* krig *-en, pl. -e*
warm *adj.* varm
warning *n.* advarsel *-en, pl. advarsler*
warranty *n.* garanti *-en, pl. -er*
wash *v.* vaske *-ede*
waste *n.* affald *-et*
waste *v.* spilde *-te*; **go to waste** gå til spilde
watch *n.* ur (wrist) *-et, pl. -e*
watch *v.* se (look at) *så, set* (på); holde øje med (keep an eye on) *holdt, holdt øje med*; **watch TV** se fjernsyn
water *n.* vand *-et*
waterfall *n.* vandfald *-et, pl. same*
watertight, waterproof *adj.* vandtæt
wave *n.* bølge *-n, pl. -r*
wave *v.* vinke *-ede*
we *pron.* vi
weak *adj.* svag
wealthy *adj.* rig, velhavende
weapon *n.* våben *-et, pl. same*
wear *v.* have på (clothes) *havde, haft på*
weather *n.* vejr *-et*
wedding *n.* bryllup *-pet, pl. -per*
Wednesday *n.* onsdag
week *n.* uge *-n, pl. -r*

weekend n. weekend -en, pl. -er

weep v. græde græd, grædt

weigh v. veje -ede

welcome v. byde velkommen bød, budt velkommen

welcome interj. velkommen

welfare state n. velfærdsstat -en, pl. -er

west n. vest

wet adj. våd

what pron., adv. hvad

wheel n. hjul -et, pl. same

wheelchair n. kørestol -en, pl. -e

when adv. hvornår (interrogative); conj. når (future); adv., conj. da (past)

whenever adv. når som helst

where pron., adv. hvor

whether conj. om

which pron. hvilken, hvilket, hvilke (depending on noun gender and number)

whine v. klynke (whimper) -ede; klage sig (complain) -ede sig

whisper v. hviske -ede

whistle v. fløjte -ede

who pron. hvem

whole adj. hel

whose pron. hvis

why pron. hvorfor

wide adj. bred

width n. bredde -n, pl. -r

wife n. kone -n, pl. -r

wild adj. vild

will v. ville ville, villet (pre. vil)

willing adj. villig

win v. vinde vandt, vundet

wind n. vind -en, pl. -e, blæst -en

window n. vindue -t, pl. -r

window-shop v. ose (slang) -ede, kigge vinduer -ede vinduer

wind up v. trække op trak, trukket op

windy adj. blæsende

wine n. vin -en, pl. -e

winter n. vinter -en, pl. vintre

wipe v. tørre -ede

wireless adj. trådløs

wise adj. klog

wish v. ønske -ede

wish n. ønske -t, pl. -r

with prep. med

withdraw v. trække tilbage trak, trukket tilbage

without prep. uden

witness n. vidne -t, pl. -r

woman n. kvinde -n, pl. -r

wonderful adj. vidunderlig

word n. ord -et, pl. same

work n. arbejde -t, pl. -r

work v. arbejde -ede

working class n. arbejderklasse -n

world n. verden -en, pl. verdner

worry n. bekymring -en, pl. -er

wrap v. pakke ind -ede ind

wring v. vride vred, vredet

wrinkled adj. rynket, krøllet

write v. skrive skrev, skrevet

writer n. forfatter -en, pl. -e

wrong adj. forkert

X

xenophobia n. fremmedhad -et

X ray n. røntgenbillede -t, pl. -r

x-ray v. røntgenfotografere -ede

Y

yacht n. lystbåd -en, pl. -e

yawn v. gabe -te

year n. år -et, pl. same

yearly *adv.* årligt
year-round *adj.* året rundt
yeast *n.* gær *-en*
yell *v.* råbe *-te*
yes *interj.* ja
yesterday *adv.* i går
yet *adv.* endnu
yield *v.* vige *veg, veget*
you *pron.* du; dig (when object)
young *adj.* ung
youth *n.* ungdom *-men*; ungt menneske (young person)
youthful *adj.* ungdommelig
youth hostel *n.* vandrerhjem *-met, pl. same*

Z

zebra *n.* zebra *-en, pl. -er*
zero *num.* nul
zip code *n.* postnummer *-et, pl. postnumre*
zipper *n.* lynlås *-en, pl. -e*
zoo *n.* zoologisk have

DANISH PHRASEBOOK

Arriving in Denmark

Emergencies

For police, ambulance, or fire fighters call: 112 (toll-free number)

Embassy of the United States of America
Dag Hammarskjölds Allé 24
2100 København Ø.
Tel. 35 55 31 44

Should your money get stolen, you may use the money transfer service offered by *BG Bank* in cooperation with Western Union to receive money from home. The service is available at Danish post offices and at any *BG Bank*.

Help!	**Hjælp!**
Hurry!	**Skynd jer!** (pl.)
	Skynd dig! (sing.)
Fire!	**Ildebrand!**
Run!	**Løb!**
Where is the emergency exit?	**Hvor er nødudgangen?**
Call the police!	**Ring efter politiet!**
Call an ambulance!	**Ring efter en ambulance!**
Call the firemen!	**Ring efter brandvæsenet!**
Send an ambulance.	**Send en ambulance.**
There was an accident.	**Der er sket en ulykke.**
There is a fire.	**Der er ildebrand.**
It's urgent.	**Det haster.**
Is there a doctor here?	**Er der en læge til stede?**
Thief!	**Tyv!**
I was mugged!	**Jeg er blevet overfaldet!**
I was raped!	**Jeg er blevet voldtaget!**
Someone stole my wallet and passport.	**Jeg har fået min pung og mit pas stjålet.**
I am innocent.	**Jeg er uskyldig.**
I did not see who did it.	**Jeg så ikke, hvem der gjorde det.**

Immigration

Under normal circumstances, an American tourist automatically gets a visa that is valid for three months.

Hello.
> **Goddag.**

What's your name?
> **Hvad hedder De/du?**

Where are you from?
> **Hvor kommer De/du fra?**

I am American.
> **Jeg er amerikaner.**

May I please see your passport?
> **Må jeg se Deres/dit pas?**

What is the purpose of your visit?
> **Hvad er formålet med Deres/dit ophold?**

I am here on vacation.
> **Jeg er på ferie.**

I am here on business.
> **Jeg er på forretningsrejse.**

How long will you be staying in Denmark?
> **Hvor længe agter De/du at blive i Danmark?**

immigration	**immigration** *n.: -en*
immigrant	**indvandrer** *n.: -en, pl. -e,* **immigrant** *n.: -en, pl. -er*
citizen	**statsborger** *n.: -en, pl. -e*
citizenship	**statsborgerskab** *n.: -et*
permanent residence	**fast bopæl** *(bopæl n.: -en, pl. -e)*
passport	**pas** *n.: -set, pl. same*
passport control	**paskontrol** *n.: -len*
EU citizens	**EU-borgere**
All nationalities	**Alle nationaliteter**
Schengen	**Schengen** (arriving from another EU country)
Non-Schengen	**Ikke Schengen** (arriving from outside the EU)
political asylum	**politisk asyl**

residence permit	**opholdstilladelse** *n.: -n, pl. -r*
tourist	**turist** *n.: -en, pl. -er*
tourist visa	**turistvisum** *n.: -met, pl.*
	turistvisa
work permit	**arbejdstilladelse** *n.: -n, pl. -r*

Customs

On entry from abroad, goods intended for personal use or consumption or as gifts may be brought into Denmark duty- and tax-free. Value, quantity, and age restrictions apply. The rules vary, depending on your country of departure (EU or non-EU country). The EU countries are: Austria, Belgium, Denmark, Finland, France, Germany, Great Britain, Greece, Holland, Ireland, Italy, Luxembourg, Portugal, Spain, and Sweden. Greenland and the Faeroe Islands are not considered EU territory. Details appear in *Excises: A Guide for Travelers*, available in English at duty-free shops, airports, etc.

When going through customs, you will see a red and a green lane, and sometimes a blue one. Use the red if you have goods to declare (or if you are not sure), the green if you have nothing to declare, and the blue if you are arriving from another EU country. If you bring too much, you may import the goods upon payment of duty and taxes; if you get caught smuggling, you will be fined.

Please open your suitcase / bag.
Åbn venligst Deres kuffert / taske.

It is for my personal use.
Det er til eget forbrug.

It is not new.
Det er ikke nyt.

customs officer	**toldembedsmand, tolder,**
	toldbetjent
customs check	**toldeftersyn**
customs declaration	**tolddeklaration**
customs duty	**toldafgift**
duty	**told**
duty-free	**toldfri**

pay duty on	**betale told af**
goods to declare	**varer at angive, varer at fortolde**
nothing to declare	**intet at angive, intet at fortolde**
tobacco	**tobak**
carton	**karton**
cigarettes	**cigaretter**
cigarillos	**cerutter**
cigars	**cigarer**
spirits	**spiritus** (alcoholic content above 22% vol.)
dessert wine	**hedvin** (alcoholic content of 22% vol. or less)
table wine	**bordvin** (red, white, and rosé)
sparkling wine	**mousserende vin**
coffee	**kaffe**
tea	**te**
perfume	**parfume**
cologne	**eau de cologne**
body search	**kropsvisitere** *v.: -ede*
smuggle	**smugle** *v.: -ede*
fine	**bøde** *n.: -n, pl. -r*

Basic Expressions

Yes.	**Ja.**
No.	**Nej.**
Hello.	**Goddag.**
Hi.	**Hej.** (informal)
Good morning.	**Godmorgen.**
Good evening.	**Godaften.**
Good-bye.	**Farvel.**
Good night.	**Godnat.**
See you later.	**Vi ses.**
Talk to you soon.	**Vi snakkes ved.**
Cheers!	**Skål!**
Congratulations!	**Tillykke!**
Sorry!	**Undskyld!**

I am sorry.
Det må De/du undskylde.

Excuse me, may I pass?
Undskyld, må jeg komme forbi?

Would you please repeat that?
Hvabehar?

Can you help me?
Kan De/du hjælpe mig?

Can you tell me …
Kan De/du sige mig …

I would like …
Jeg vil gerne have …

Thank you.
Tak.

Here you are.
Værsgo.

Thank you for the food.
Tak for mad. (Should always be said before leaving
the table)

You are welcome.
Velbekomme.

My pleasure.
Fornøjelsen er på min side.

How are you?
Hvordan går det?

Fine, thank you, how about you?
Fint tak, hvad med dig?

It's nice to see you.
Det er rart at se dig.

Say hi to those at home.
Hils hjemme.

The same to you.
I lige måde.

Does anyone here speak English?
Er der nogen her, der kan engelsk?

Do you speak English?
Kan De/du tale engelsk?

I don't speak Danish.
Jeg kan ikke tale dansk.

I speak a little Danish.
Jeg kan tale lidt dansk.

Please speak a little more slowly.
Tal venligst lidt langsommere.

How do you say ... in Danish?
Hvordan siger man ... på dansk?

What does ... mean?
Hvad betyder ...?

Please write it down.
Skriv det venligst ned for mig.

I will look it up in my dictionary.
Jeg slår det op i min ordbog.

I need an interpreter.
Jeg har brug for en tolk.

I am lost.
Jeg er faret vild.

May I have the bread, please?
Må jeg bede om brødet?

Can I use the phone, please?
Må jeg låne telefonen?

Hello.
Hallo. (telephone)

Is Mr. Jones there, please?
Træffer jeg hr. Jones?

May I leave a message please?
Må jeg lægge en besked?

Can you call back later?
Kan De/du ringe senere?

Could I ask you to take our picture?
Kan jeg få Dem til at tage et billede af os?

Is it OK if I take a picture?
Er det i orden, hvis jeg tager et billede?

Social Interaction

Social interaction in Denmark will seem mostly familiar to Americans, but differences do exist.

De is formal for "you"; *du* is informal. *De* is used extensively in formal correspondence and conversation. If you know people well you always use *du*. If you would like to suggest to someone that you say *du* to each other, you may ask, *Må jeg foreslå, at vi er dus?* (May I suggest that we say *du* to each other?)

Miss	**frøken**
Mr.	**hr.**
Mrs.	**fru**

The use of *hr.*, *fru*, and *frøken* is dwindling and seems overly formal in most situations.

The handshake is the most commonly used greeting. Good friends and family will hug. Kisses on the mouth are reserved for intimate relationships; even kisses on the cheek are quite rare. It is considered polite to maintain eye contact while talking.

For many Danes, swearing is part of everyday language use, and especially among young people, English swearwords have become widely used. Others find swearing unbecoming. People are generally very polite in terms of waiting in line, being considerate of the elderly, saying thank you, etc.

The Danish attitude toward sex and pornography differs drastically from the American. Pornographic magazines and videos are conspicuously displayed in many places, and pictures of nude people are common in advertisements, newspapers, and magazines. Sexual and even pornographic content is not uncommon on TV, and adult shops and services are numerous and widely advertised.

Generally, the Danes are less modest about displaying their bodies than Americans. Nudist beaches are common, being topless is acceptable at just about any beach, and people will typically sunbathe and walk around their houses and yards in their underwear. Children are usually allowed to run around naked at home, on beaches, and in parks until they turn six or seven. However, at public swimming pools, everyone must wear a bathing suit. Breastfeeding in public is fully acceptable.

Meals are important in Denmark. The Danes take great pride in setting the table nicely and preparing delicious meals. It is considered proper to use both knife and fork while eating, and although children are often excused, people generally stay at the table until everybody has finished eating. If you walk into a room where people are eating you should say *Velbekomme*. After a meal in a private home, you should always say *Tak for mad* (Thank you for the food) before leaving the table, and the parents or hostess will then say *Velbekomme*. The Danes often invite friends over for a meal rather than meeting out in town. Birthdays, weddings, anniversaries, etc. are typically celebrated with big parties at home, in a community house, or at an inn. Such a dinner may last three or four hours, and the guests will give speeches and bring songs they have written. After dinner, there is usually live music and dancing well into the night. If you are invited to someone's house or to a party you should arrive on time.

Electricity

The electrical current in Denmark is 230 volt AC in 50 cycles per second (50 hertz), but variations between 215 and 240 volt may occur. Plugs and outlets are different from those in the United States. Be prepared to bring or buy converters.

alternating current (AC)	**vekselstrøm** *n.: -men*
circuit breaker	**afbryder** *n.: -en, pl. -e*
converter, adaptor	**omformer** *n.: -en, pl. -e*
current	**strøm** *n.: -men*
direct current	**jævnstrøm** *n.: -men*
electrician	**elektriker** *n.: -en, pl. -e*
electricity	**elektricitet** *n.: -en*
extension cord	**forlængerledning** *n.: -en, pl. -er*

fuse	**sikring** *n.: -en, pl. -er*
grounding	**jordforbindelse** *n.: -n, pl. -r*
lightbulb	**pære** *n.: -n, pl. -r*
outlet	**stikkontakt** *n.: -en, pl. -er*
plug	**stik** *n.: -ket, pl. stik*
power outage	**strømsvigt** *n.: -et*
power surge	**strømstød** *n.: -et*

Public Signs

Avoid Pushing Door	**Undgå at skubbe på døren**
Back at 1 P.M.	**Tilbage kl. 13.**
Beware of Dog	**Pas på hunden**
Closed	**Lukket**
Do Not Touch	**Må ikke berøres**
Do Not Use	**Må ikke benyttes**
Downtown	**Centrum**
Elevator	**Elevator**
Emergency Exit	**Nødudgang**
Entrance	**Indgang**
Entrance (highway)	**Tilkørsel**
Exit	**Udgang**
Exit (highway)	**Afkørsel, Frakørsel**
Fire Door	**Branddør**
Fire Extinguisher	**Ildslukker**
Fire Hazard	**Brandfare**
For Rent	**Til leje**
For Sale	**Til salg**
Inflammable	**Brandfarlig**
Men	**Herrer**
Moved to ...	**Vi er flyttet til ...**
No Entrance	**Ingen adgang**
No Smoking	**Røgfrit område, Rygning forbudt**
No Trespassing	**Ingen adgang for uvedkommende.**
Opens automatically	**Åbner automatisk**
Personnel Only	**Kun adgang for personalet**
Pull	**Træk**

Push	**Tryk**
Reserved	**Forbeholdt ...,**
	Reserveret
Restroom	**Toilet**
Service	**Ekspedition**
Smoking area	**Rygeområde, Rygning**
	tilladt
Starts automatically	**Starter automatisk**
Stay Off Grass	**Græsset må ikke**
	betrædes
Tickets	**Billetsalg**
Tourist Information	**Turistbureau, Turist**
	information
Video Security	**Butikken er**
	videoovervåget,
	TV-overvågning
Watch out for pickpockets!	**Pas på lommetyve!**
With or without a	**Med/Uden**
reservation	**pladsbestilling** (for
	example at hairdresser)
Women	**Damer**

Money, Payment, and Tips

Unless the item is damaged, or you are buying a large quantity, you automatically pay the price on the price tag. The price is usually posted on the shelf, and at the cash register the price is scanned off a bar code. Some stores offer stations where the customers can check the price by scanning the bar code themselves. Bartering is not done. The Danes mostly pay with cash or debit cards. Checks are rarely used nowadays. Bills are typically paid through the postal service or banks via giro transfer or automatic withdrawal from bank accounts. Most stores, hotels, and restaurants also accept major credit cards and traveler's checks, but grocery stores do not, and small stores may not. The sales tax is usually included in the price. ATMs are readily available in most towns. Tips are included in the price, but if you would like to show your appreciation of good service, it is not unusual to leave a small tip at a restaurant or for a cab driver. You do not usually tip hairdressers or delivery men.

Denominations

1 krone = 100 øre

Coins: 25 øre, 50 øre, one krone, two kroner, five kroner
(femmer), 10 kroner (tier), 20 kroner (tyver)
Bills: 50 kroner, 100 kroner, 200 kroner, 500 kroner,
1000 kroner

ATM	**kontantautomat,** **kontantservice**
ATM card	**hævekort** *n.: -et, pl. same*
bank	**bank** *n.: -en, pl. -er*
	pengeinstitut *n.: -tet,* *pl. -ter*
bar code	**stregkode** *n.: -n, pl. -r*
bill	**seddel** *n.: -en* or *sedlen,* *pl. sedler*
cash	**kontanter, rede penge**
cash payment	**kontant betaling**
cash register	**kasse** *n.:. -n, pl. -r,* **kasseapparat** *n.: -et,* *pl. -er*
check	**check** *n.: -en, pl. -e*
coin	**mønt** *n.: -en, pl. -er*
credit card	**kreditkort** *n.: -et,* *pl. same*
debit card	**betalingskort** *n.: -et,* *pl. same*
deposit	**indsætte** *v.: indsatte,* *indsat*
exact change	**lige penge**
exchange rate	**valutakurs, vekselkurs** *n.: -en, pl. -er*
made out in Danish currency	**udstedt i dansk valuta**
money	**penge** *n. (pl.)*
money transfer	**pengeoverførsel** *n.: -en,* *pl. pengeoverførsler*
overdraw	**overtrække** *v.: overtrak,* *overtrukket*
pay	**betale** *v.: -te*
payment	**betaling** *n.: -en, pl. -er*
PIN number	**PIN-kode** *n.: -n, pl. -r*

price tag	**prismærke** *n.: -t, pl. -r*
receipt	**kvittering** *n.: -en, pl. -er*
sales tax	**moms** *n.: -en*
small change	**småpenge, småskillinger, ral**
spending limit	**beløbsgrænse** *n.: -n, pl. -r*
tip	**drikkepenge** *n. (pl.)*
traveler's check	**rejsecheck** *n.: -en, pl. -e*
withdraw	**hæve** *v.: -ede*

Pay at the cash register.
Betal ved kassen.

Can I please have a receipt?
Må jeg bede om en kvittering?

Do you accept credit cards?
Kan jeg betale med kreditkort?

Can you break a 500 kr. bill?
Kan De/du give tilbage på en 500-krone seddel?

Do you have exact change?
Har De/du lige penge?

How much is the dollar today?
Hvad står dollaren i i dag?

I'd like to change $300 to kroner.
Jeg vil gerne veksle $300 til kroner.

Where is the closest bank?
Hvor ligger den nærmeste bank?

When does the bank open?
Hvornår åbner banken?

Where do I find an ATM machine?
Hvor er der en kontantautomat?

Firsthand checks only.
Der modtages kun førstehåndschecks.

At the ATM
(Instructions will be in Danish and English.)

Open 24 hours	**Åben 24 timer i døgnet**
ATM fee	**Gebyr for udbetaling**

Free	**Gratis**
1% of the amount	**1% af beløbet**
Delete all	**Slet alt**
Error	**Fejl**
Approve	**Godkend**

Smoking

In general, Danes smoke more than Americans, and smoking is still widely accepted in public places. People usually allow guests to smoke in their homes. However, more places are now starting to prohibit smoking and make separate smoking areas available. On a train, for example, you will always have a choice. It is always polite to ask before you light up around other people. There is no age requirement for buying cigarettes.

to smoke	**at ryge**
No Smoking	**Røgfrit område, Rygning forbudt**
Smoking	**Rygeområde, Rygning tilladt**
Is it OK if I smoke?	**Er det i orden, hvis jeg ryger?**
tobacco	**tobak**
cigarettes	**cigaretter**
cigarillos	**cerutter**
cigars	**cigarer**
carton	**karton**

Alcohol

The legal age for buying and consuming alcohol in Denmark is 15. You must be 18 to legally purchase alcohol in bars and restaurants, but this rule is not strictly enforced. The legal drinking age is now under debate due to problems with addiction among teenagers. Beer, wine, and hard liquor can be purchased at liquor stores, food stores, and many gas stations. Drinking in public is allowed. The laws against drunk driving are very strict and widely enforced. The police can at any time ask a driver to take a Breathalyzer test (*udåndingsprøve*). Drunk driving is divided into two categories: *promillekørsel* (0.05–0.12%)

and *spirituskørsel* (over 0.12%), and punishment may, depending on blood content, include deferred or mandatory loss of license, moderate to severe fines, community service, rehabilitation, and jail sentences ranging from two weeks to three years.

Addresses

First Name, Last Name	Eva Madsen
Name of street, house number, apartment	Jernbanegade 17 ^{1. sal tv.}
Zip code, name of town	6000 Kolding

basement	**kælder**
ground floor, first floor	**stueetage, stuen (st.)**
second floor	**første sal**
third floor	**anden sal**
on the left	**til venstre (tv.)**
on the right	**til højre (th.)**

Family Relations

parent	**forælder** *n.: -en, pl. forældre*
father	**far** *n.: -en, pl. fædre*
mother	**mor** *n.: -en, pl. mødre*
child	**barn** *n.: -et, pl. børn*
daughter	**datter** *n.: -en, pl. døtre*
son	**søn** *n.: -nen, pl. -ner*
brother	**bror** *n.: -en, pl. brødre*
sister	**søster** *n.: -en, pl. søstre*
siblings	**søskende** *n. (pl.)*
half brother	**halvbroder** *n.: -en, pl. halvbrødre*
half sister	**halvsøster** *n.: -en, pl. halvsøstre*
twin	**tvilling** *n.: -en, pl. -er*
identical twins	**enæggede tvillinger**
uncle	**farbror** (father's brother) *n.: -en, pl. farbrødre*
	morbror (mother's brother) *n.: -en, pl. morbrødre*

	onkel (father's or mother's sister's husband)
aunt	**faster** (father's sister) *n.: -en, pl. fastre*
	moster (mother's sister) *n.: -en, pl. mostre*
	tante (father's or mother's brother's wife)
cousin	**fætter** (male) *n.: -en, pl. fætre*
	kusine (female) *n.: -n, pl. -r*
nephew	**nevø** *n.: -en, pl. -er*
niece	**niece** *n.: -n, pl. -r*
grandchild	**barnebarn** *n.: -et, pl. børnebørn* (no distinction for male and female)
grandparent	**bedsteforælder** *n.: -en, pl. bedsteforældre*
grandfather	**farfar** (father's father) *n.: -en*
	morfar (mother's father) *n.: -en*
	bedstefar *n.: -en, pl. bedstefædre*
grandmother	**farmor** (father's mother) *n.: -en*
	mormor (mother's mother) *n.: -en*
	bedstemor *n.: -en, pl. bedstemødre*
great grandfather	**oldefar** *n.: -en, pl. oldefædre*
great grandmother	**oldemor** *n.: -en, pl. oldemødre*
great grandchild	**oldebarn** *n.: -et, pl. oldebørn*
adopted child	**adoptivbarn** *n.: -et, pl. adoptivbørn*

adoptive parent	**adoptivforælder** *n.: -en,* *pl. adoptivforældre*
stepfather	**papfar** *n.: -en,* *pl. papfædre*
stepmother	**papmor** *n.: -en,* *pl. papmødre*
foster child	**plejebarn** *n.: -et,* *pl. plejebørn*
foster parent	**plejeforælder** *n.: -en,* *pl. plejeforældre*
spouse	**ægtefælle** *n.: -n, pl. -r*
wife	**hustru** *n.: -en, pl. -er,* **kone** *n.: -n, pl. -r* (**kone** is less formal)
husband	**ægtemand** *n.: -en,* *pl. ægtemænd,* **mand** *n.: -en,* *pl. mænd* (**mand** is less formal)
widow	**enke** *n.: -n, pl. -r*
widower	**enkemand** *n.: -en,* *pl. enkemænd*
married	**gift** *adj.*
not married	**ugift** *adj.*
single	**enlig** *adj.*

Asking Questions

How?	**Hvordan?**
How many?	**Hvor mange?**
How much?	**Hvor meget?**
What?	**Hvad?**
When?	**Hvornår?**
Where?	**Hvor?**
Which?	**Hvilken?**
Who?	**Hvem?**
Why?	**Hvorfor?**

Accommodations

A variety of lodging is available. The staff at hotels in major cities speaks English, and signs and other information are translated. Do not expect to have your luggage brought to your room unless you ask. Note! A Danish double room usually only sleeps two people (one double bed or two twin beds).

General Vocabulary

bed and breakfast	**Værelser Zimmer Rooms** (signs seen along roads)
campsite	**campingplads** *n.: -en, pl. -er* (camper **campingvogn**, tent **telt**)
farm holiday	**bondegårdsferie** *n.: -n, pl. -r* (The guests sleep, eat, and help out on the farm.)
holiday apartment	**ferielejlighed** *n.: -en, pl. -er*
hotel	**hotel** *n.: -let, pl. -ler*
cabin	**hytte** *n.: -n, pl. -r*
inn	**kro** *n.: -en, pl. -er*
motel	**motel** *n.: -let, pl. -ler*
pension	**pensionat** *n.: -et, pl. -er*
private visit	**privatbesøg** *n.: -et, pl. same*
vacation home	**sommerhus** *n.: -et, pl. -e*
youth hostel	**vandrerhjem** *n.: -met, pl. same*
time-share apartment	**timeshare-lejlighed** *n.: -en, pl. -er*

* * * * * *

all meals included	**fuld forplejning**
arrival	**ankomst**
at the reception desk	**i receptionen**
bathroom sink	**håndvask** *n.: -en, pl. -e*
bathtub	**badekar** *n.: -ret, pl. same*
bed	**seng** *n.: -en, pl. -e*
bedding	**sengetøj** *n.: -et*

Accommodations

bed linen	**sengelinned** *n.: -et*
bedspread	**sengetæppe** *n.: -t, pl. -r*
bellhop	**piccolo** *n.: -en, pl. -er*
bill	**regning** *n.: -en, pl. -er*
blanket	**tæppe** *n.: -t, pl. -r*
breakfast	**morgenmad** *n.: -en*
bunk bed	**køje** *n.: -n, pl. -r*
business center	**forretningscenter** *n.: forretningscentret, pl. forretningscentre*
cancel	**afbestille** *v.: -te*
check in	**checke ind** *v.: -ede ind*
check out	**checke ud** *v.: -ede ud*
clean	**ren** *adj.*
cleaning	**rengøring** *n.: -en*
complimentary breakfast	**morgenmad inkl.**
confirmation letter	**bekræftelse** *n.: -n, pl. -r*
cover for down comforter	**dynebetræk** *n.: -ket, pl. same*
dirty	**beskidt, snavset** *adj.*
double bed	**dobbeltseng** *n.: -en, pl. -e*
double room	**dobbeltværelse** *n.: -t, pl. -r*
down comforter	**dyne** *n.: -n, pl. -r*
excluded	**eksklusive (ekskl.)**
exercise room	**motionscenter** *n.: motionscentret, pl. motionscentre*
facial tissue	**papirlommetørklæde** *n.: -t, pl. -r*
fully booked	**fuldt optaget, fuldt belagt**
hair dryer	**hårtørrer, føntørrer** *n.: -en, pl. -e*
honeymoon suite	**brudesuite** *n.: -n, pl. -r*
included	**inklusive (inkl.)**
in the hall	**på gangen**
in the room	**på værelset**
iron	**strygejern** *n.: -et, pl. same*
ironing board	**strygebræt** *n.: -tet, pl. -ter*
leaving	**med afrejse**
maid	**stuepige** *n.: -n, pl. -r*
mattress (too hard/soft)	**madras (for hård/blød)** *n.: -sen, pl. -ser*
newspaper	**avis** *n.: -en, pl. -er*
no smoking room	**ikke-rygerværelse** *n.: -t, pl. -r*

no vacancy	**alt optaget**
number of nights	**antal overnatninger**
order	**bestille** *v.: -te*
overnight stay	**overnatning** *n.: -en,* *pl. -er*
pillow	**hovedpude** *n.: -n, pl. -r*
pillowcase	**hovedpudebetræk** *n.: -ket, pl. same*
price per night	**pris pr. nat**
private bath	**privat bad**
receptionist	**portier** *n.: -en, pl. -er*
reserve	**reservere** *v.: -ede*
rent	**leje** *v.: -ede*
rollout bed	**ekstra opredning** *(opredning n.: -en,* *pl. -er)*
room	**værelse** *n.: -t, pl. -r*
room for people w/allergies	**allergikerværelse** *n.: -t,* *pl. -r*
room service	**room service, servering** **på værelset**
shower	**brusebad** *n.: -et*
shower stall	**brusekabine** *n.: -n, pl. -r*
single bed	**enkeltseng** *n.: -en, pl. -e*
single room	**enkeltværelse** *n.: -t, pl. -r*
sleeping bag	**sovepose** *n.: -n, pl. -r*
telephone	**telefon** *n.: -en, pl. -er*
television	**fjernsyn** *n.: -et, pl. same,* **tv** *n.: tv'et, pl. tv'er*
toilet	**toilet** *n.: -tet, pl. -ter*
toilet paper	**toiletpapir** *n.: -et*
towel	**håndklæde** *n.: -t, pl. -r*
unacceptable	**uacceptabel** *adj.*
unsatisfactory	**utilfredsstillende** *adj.*
vacant	**ledig** *adj.*
washcloth	**vaskeklud** *n.: -en, pl. -e*
wake-up call	**vækning** *n.: -en, pl. -er*

Vacation Homes

During peak season, vacation homes are usually rented out for at least one week at a time, starting on Saturdays or Sundays.

account to be settled after departure	**afregnes efter afrejse**
annex (not necessarily heated)	**anneks** *n.: -et, pl. -er*
bedroom wing	**soveafdeling** *n.: -en, pl. -er*, **værelsesfløj** *n.: -en, pl. -e*
built from bricks	**bygget af mursten**
built from wood	**bygget af træ**
cancellation insurance	**afbestillingsforsikring** *n.: -en, pl. -er*
changeover day	**skiftedag** *n.: -en, pl. -e*
check-in between 3 P.M. and 6 P.M.	**indflytning mellem kl. 15.00 og 18.00**
cleaning materials	**rengøringsartikler** *n. (pl.)*
cleanup before departure	**slutrengøring** (The house and grounds must be left tidy and clean, including fridge, freezer, stove, oven, grill, bathrooms, and windows [in and outside].)
date of arrival	**ankomstdato** *n.: -en, pl. -er*
date of departure	**afrejsedato** *n.: -en, pl. -er*
deposit	**depositum** *n.: -met, pl. -mer*
fee	**gebyr** *n.: -et, pl. -er*
heating expenses	**varmeforbrug** *n.: -et*
house and furnishings	**hus og inventar**
location	**beliggenhed** *n.: -en*
loft	**hems** *n.: -en, pl. -e*
lot (slightly hilly)	**grund (kuperet)** *n.: -en, pl. -e*
made out in Danish currency	**udstedt i dansk valuta**
meter (gas/electricity/water)	**måler (gas/el/vand)** *n.: -en, pl. -e*
normal electricity expenses	**normalt strømforbrug**
number of adults	**antal voksne**
number of bedrooms	**antal soverum**
number of children	**antal børn**
no later than 10 A.M.	**senest kl. 10**
ocean view	**havudsigt** *n.: -en*
partly remodeled	**delvist moderniseret**
payment	**betaling** *n.: -en*

pet	**husdyr** *n.: -et, pl. same*
possible damage	**eventuelle skader**
private lot	**ugenert grund**
protected nature area	**fredet naturområde**
rate	**rate** *n.: -n, pl. -r*
rental agreement	**lejemål** *n.: -et, pl. same*
renters to bring	**medbringes** (bed linen **sengelinned,** tablecloths **bordduge,** dish towels **viskestykker,** sink rags **karklude,** towels **håndklæder,** toiletries **toiletartikler)**
room	**værelse** *n.: -t, pl. -r*
sewer	**kloak** *n.: -ken, pl. -ker*
skylight	**ovenlysvindue** *n.: -t, pl. -r*
smoke detector	**røgalarm** *n.: -en, pl. -er*
square meter	**m²** **(kvadratmeter)**
standard equipment	**standardudstyr** *n.: -et*
sun porch	**solstue** *n.: -n, pl. -r*
telephone expenses	**telefonforbrug** *n.: -et*
thatched roof	**stråtag** *n.: -et, pl. -e*
thermostat	**termostat** *n.: -en, pl. -er*
to report defects and deficiencies, call ...	**for at anmelde fejl og mangler, kontakt ...**
total rental price	**samlet lejepris**
type of beach	**strandens beskaffenhed**
unlimited use of	**fri afbenyttelse af ...**
water expenses	**vandforbrug** *n.: -et*
water pipe	**vandrør** *n.: -et, pl. same*

Repairs

bricklayer	**murer** *n.: -en, pl. -e*
carpenter	**tømrer** *n.: -en, pl. -e* (framing), **snedker** *n.: -en, pl. -e* (indoor trim and furniture)
craftsman	**håndværker** *n.: -en, pl. -e*
electrician	**elektriker** *n.: -en, pl. -e*
painter	**maler** *n.: -en, pl. -e*
plumber	**VVS-mand** *n.: -en, pl. VVS-mænd* (heating, ventilation, and plumbing)

repair	**reparere** *v.: -ede*
roofer	**taglægger** *n.: -en, pl. -e*
sewer cleaning service	**slamsugning** *n.: -en*
sewer contractor	**kloakmester** *n.: -en,* *pl. kloakmestre*

Furniture and Appliances

bathroom sink	**håndvask** *n.: -en, pl. -e*
bathtub	**badekar** *n.: -ret, pl. same*
bed	**seng** *n.: -en, pl. -e*
carpet	**gulvtæppe** *n.: -t, pl. -r*
chair	**stol** *n.: -en, pl. -e*
closet	**skab** *n.: -et, pl. -e*
clothes dryer	**tørretumbler** *n.: -en, pl. -e*
coffee table	**sofabord** *n.: -et, pl. -e*
couch	**sofa** *n.: -en, pl. -er*
desk	**skrivebord** *n.: -et, pl. -e*
dishwasher	**opvaskemaskine** *n.: -n,* *pl. -r*
fireplace	**pejs** *n.: -en, pl. -e*
freezer	**fryser** *n.: -en, pl. -e*
furnace	**fyr** *n.: -et, pl. same*
garden furniture	**havemøbler** *n. (pl.)*
hot-water tank	**varmtvandsbeholder** *n.: -en, pl. -e*
Jacuzzi	**spabad** *n.: -et, pl. -e*
kitchen sink	**køkkenvask** *n.: -en, pl. -e*
lamp	**lampe** *n.: -n, pl. -r*
microwave	**mikrobølgeovn** *n.: -en,* *pl. -e*
night table	**natbord** *n.: -et, pl. -e*
oven	**ovn** *n.: -en, pl. -e*
radiator	**radiator** *n.: -en, pl. -er*
radio	**radio** *n.: -en, pl. -er*
refrigerator	**køleskab** *n.: -et, pl. -e*
sandbox	**sandkasse** *n.: -n, pl. -r*
satellite dish	**parabolantenne** *n.: -n,* *pl. -r*
sauna	**sauna** *n.: -en, pl. -er*
shower	**brusebad** *n.: -et, pl. -e*
stereo	**stereoanlæg** *n.: -get,* *pl. same*
stove	**komfur** *n.: -et, pl. -er*
swimming pool	**svømmebassin** *n.: -et,* *pl. -er*

swing	**gynge** *n.: -n, pl. -r*
table	**bord** *n.: -et, pl. -e*
television	**fjernsyn** *n.: -et, pl. same,* **tv** *n.: tv'et. pl. tv'er*
tile floor	**klinkegulv** *n.: -et, pl. -e*
toilet	**toilet** *n.: -tet, pl. -ter*
washing machine	**vaskemaskine** *n.: -n, pl. -r*
wooden floor	**trægulv** *n.: -et, pl. -e*
wood stove	**brændeovn** *n.: -en, pl. -e*

Using the Washing Machine

In many parts of Denmark, the water contains a lot of calcium, so the detergent does not work equally well everywhere. In areas with high calcium levels, people use *Calgon mod kalk* or *Minus Kalk* (powder or tablets) to protect their washing machines.

washing machine	**vaskemaskine**
door	**dør** or **lugeåbning**
ready	**klar**
start	**start**
pause	**pause**
delayed start	**forvalg time**
time remaining	**resttid**
finished	**slut, færdig**
too much soap	**overdosering**
stain remover	**pletfjerner**
laundry detergent	**vaskemiddel, vaskepulver**
fabric softener	**skyllemiddel**
presoak/stained clothes	**iblødsætning/plettet tøj**
pre-wash	**forvask**
main wash	**vask**
rinse	**skyl**
delayed rinse	**skyllestop**
spin	**centrifugering**
drain	**udpumpning**
extra rinse	**ekstra skyl**
short program	**kort program**
reduced spin	**reduceret centrifugering**
high water level	**højt vandniveau**
energy saver program	**energispare, spareprogram**
starch	**stivning**
white cottons	**kogevask** (90–95° C/195° F)

colorfast cottons	**kulørtvask, farveægte bomuld** (60° C/140° F)
permanent press	**strygefrit, strygelet** (60° C/105° F)
delicates	**finvask** (30° C/85° F)
wool	**uldprogram**
gentle spin	**skånsom centrifugering**
Laundromat	**møntvask** *n.: -en, pl. -e*
coin	**mønt** *n.: -en, pl. -er*
token	**polet** *n.: -ten, pl. -ter*

Using the Dryer

dryer	**tørretumbler**
time dry	**tidsprogram**
extra dry	**ekstra tørt**
dry	**skabstørt**
slightly damp	**let fugtigt**
ready for ironing	**strygetørt**
cool down	**afkøling**
cottons	**bomuld**
linen	**linned**
synthetics, permanent press	**strygefrit, strygelet**
on	**tænd**
off	**sluk**

Using the Dishwasher

dishwasher	**opvaskemaskine**
rinse only	**forskyl**
normal	**normal**
short wash, light wash	**kvikvask, kort program**
soak and scrub	**intensiv**
energy saver program	**energispare, økonomiprogram**
dry	**tørring**
dishwasher detergent	**opvaskemiddel til maskinopvask**
rinse agent	**afspændingsmiddel**
salt for filter	**filtersalt**

Kitchen Items

| aluminum foil | **aluminiumsfolie** *n.: -n* |
| bottle opener | **oplukker** *n.: -en, pl. -e* |

bowl	**skål** *n.: -en, pl. -e*
can opener	**dåseåbner** *n.: -en, pl. -e*
coffeepot	**kaffekande** *n.: -n, pl. -r*
colander	**dørslag** *n.: -et, pl. same*
corkscrew	**proptrækker** *n.: -en, pl. -e*
cutting board	**skærebræt** *n.: -tet, pl. -ter*
dish towel	**viskestykke** *n.: -t, pl. -r*
fork	**gaffel** *n.: -en or gaflen, pl. gafler*
frying pan	**stegepande** *n.: -n, pl. -r*
glass	**glas** *n.: -set, pl. same*
grater	**rivejern** *n.: -et, pl. same*
handmixer	**håndmikser** *n.: -en, pl. -e*
kettle	**kedel** *n.: -en, pl. kedler*
kitchen towel	**køkkenrulle** *n.: -n*
knife	**kniv** *n.: -en, pl. -e*
measuring cup	**målebæger** *n.: -et, pl. -e*
measuring spoon	**måleske** *n.: -en, pl. -er*
pan	**gryde** *n.: -n, pl. -r*
plastic bag	**plastikpose** *n.: -n, pl. -r*
plastic wrap	**husholdningsfilm** *n.: -en*
plate	**tallerken** *n.: -en or tallerknen, pl. -er or tallerkner*
pot cover	**grydelåg** *n.: -et, pl. same*
pot holder	**grydelap** *n.: -pen, pl. -per*
scales	**vægt** *n.: -en, pl. -e*
serving dish	**fad** *n.: -et, pl. -e*
sieve	**si** *n.: -en, pl. -er*
sink rag	**karklud** *n.: -en, pl. -e*
spoon	**ske** *n.: -en, pl. -er*
teapot	**tepotte** *n.: -n, pl. -r*
teaspoon	**teske** *n.: -en, pl. -er*
toaster	**brødrister** *n.: -en, pl. -e*
waffle iron	**vaffeljern** *n.: -et, pl. same*
whisk	**piskeris** *n.: -et, pl. same*
wine glass	**vinglas** *n.: -set, pl. same*
wooden spoon	**grydeske** *n.: -en, pl. -er*

Cleaning

all-purpose cleaner	**universalrengørings-middel**
broom	**kost** *n.: -en, pl. -e*
brush	**fejekost** *n.: -en, pl. -e*
bucket	**spand** *n.: -en, pl. -e*

calcium remover	**kalkfjerner, afkalker**
dishbrush	**opvaskebørste** *n.: -n, pl. -r*
dish detergent	**opvaskemiddel** *n.: -et* or *opvaskemidlet*
drain opener	**afløbsrens**
dustpan	**fejeblad** *n.: -et, pl. -e*
glass cleaner	**glasklar, spejl og rude puds**
oil soap	**brun sæbe** (for wooden floors)
plunger	**vaskesuger** *n.: -en, pl. -e,* **svuppert** *n.: -en, pl. -er*
rag	**klud** *n.: -en, pl. -e*
scouring detergent	**skurecreme, skurepulver**
soap	**sæbe** *n.: -n*
soap pad	**rensesvamp, Rens-let**
sponge	**svamp** *n.: -en, pl. -e*
toilet bowl cleaner	**WC-rens**
toilet paper	**toiletpapir** *n.: -et*
unscented	**uparfumeret** *adj.*
vacuum cleaner	**støvsuger** *n.: -en, pl. -e*

Common Phrases

Hello, my name is …
Goddag, jeg hedder …

I'd like a room for one night / … nights.
Jeg vil gerne reservere et værelse til en nat / … nætter.

Do you have a double room available Monday, September 3?
Har I et ledigt dobbeltværelse mandag d. 3. september?

I'm sorry, but everything is booked.
Jeg beklager, men alt er desværre optaget.

I would like to reserve a double room with a private bath.
Jeg vil gerne reservere et dobbeltværelse med eget bad.

Smoking or non-smoking?
Ryger eller ikke-ryger?

How much is a double room with a rollout bed?
Hvor meget koster et dobbeltværelse med en ekstra opredning?

Accommodations

Could we please see the room?
Kan vi få lov til at se værelset?

The room is too cold / hot / dark / small.
Værelset er for koldt / varmt / mørkt / lille.

Do you have something bigger / cheaper / on a lower floor?
Har De noget, der er større / billigere / beliggende på en lavere etage?

Do you have a room with a view of the ocean?
Har De et værelse med havudsigt?

I would like help with my luggage.
Jeg vil gerne have hjælp med min bagage.

I would like a wake-up call at 7 A.M., please.
Jeg vil gerne bestille vækning til kl. 7.

Is breakfast included?
Er det med morgenmad?

You have reserved a single room for two nights, arriving June 12 and leaving June 14.
De har reserveret to overnatninger på enkeltværelse med ankomst d. 12. juni og afrejse d. 14. juni.

Does the room have two single beds or a double?
Har værelset to enkeltsenge eller en dobbeltseng?

Is there a shuttle bus from your hotel to the airport?
Går der lufthavnsbus fra hotellet til lufthavnen?

It is a free service.
Det er gratis.

Does the room have a telephone and television?
Er der telefon og fjernsyn på værelset?

Does your hotel have a business center?
Er der forretningscenter på hotellet?

You have a message.
Der er en besked til Dem.

Who is it?
Hvem er det?

Just a moment.
Lige et øjeblik.

Please come in.
Kom ind.

Could I please have two extra towels?
Må jeg bede om to ekstra håndklæder?

What is your cancellation policy?
Kan værelset afbestilles?

At the latest 24 hours prior to your scheduled arrival.
Senest 24 timer inden den planlagte ankomst.

What time is checkout?
Hvornår skal vi være ude af værelset?

May I please have the bill?
Må jeg bede om regningen?

We accept cash and credit cards.
Vi tager imod kontant betaling og kreditkort.

How many does the vacation home sleep?
Hvor mange sovepladser er der i sommerhuset?

How far is it from the beach?
Hvor langt er der til stranden?

The toilet / sink in our bathroom is clogged.
Toilettet / vasken i vores badeværelse er tilstoppet.

Our television does not work.
Fjernsynet virker ikke.

There is no hot water.
Der er ingen varmt vand.

The bulb is burned out.
Pæren er sprunget.

Transportation

Schedules

When using public transportation in Denmark read the schedule carefully and be on time. Generally, buses, trains, and ferries run like clockwork and will not wait for you if you are half a block away.

Note! In Danish, the month and date are reversed, so February fifth would be 05/02.

When is the next bus?
Hvornår kører næste bus?

I missed the bus.
Jeg kom for sent til bussen.

The train is three minutes late.
Toget er tre minutter forsinket.

schedule (buses and trains)	**køreplan** *n.: -en, pl. -er*
schedule (ferries)	**sejlplan** *n.: -en, pl. -er*
every day	**alle dage**
weekday	**hverdag** *n.: -en, pl. -e*
weekdays except Saturdays	**hverdage undt. lørdage**
Sundays and religious holidays	**søn- og helligdage**
Fridays only	**kun fredag**
not Mondays	**ikke mandag**
school days	**skoledage**
not on school days	**ikke skoledage**
No service on this route Dec. 24	**Turen køres ikke 24/12**
departure	**afgang (afg.)**
arrival	**ankomst (ank.)**
valid	**gyldig**
valid from 11/26/02 until 05/31/03	**gyldig fra 26.11.02 til 31.05.03**
during daytime hours	**i dagtimerne**
during rush hour	**i myldretiden**

Traveling By Airplane

airport	**lufthavn** *n.: -en, pl. -e*
airplane	**flyvemaskine** *n.: -n, pl. -r,* **flyver** *n.: -en, pl. -e*
airplane ticket	**flybillet** *n.: -ten, pl. -ter*
aisle	**midtergang** *n.: -en, pl. -e*
aisle seat	**gangplads** *n.: -en, pl. -er*
board	**gå om bord** *v.: gik, gået om bord*
boarding card	**boardingkort, boardingpas**
business class	**business-klasse**
cancelled	**aflyst**
carry-on	**håndbagage** *n.: -n*
check in	**checke ind** *v.: -ede ind*
delayed	**forsinket**
domestic flight	**indenrigsfly** *n.: -et, pl. same*
economy, tourist	**turistklasse**
emergency landing	**nødlanding** *n.: -en, pl. -er*
first class	**første klasse**
gate	**gate** *n.: -n*
international flight	**udenrigsfly** *n.: -et, pl. same*
land	**lande** *v.: -ede*
landed	**landet**
life jacket	**redningsvest** *n.: -en, pl. -e*
oxygen mask	**iltmaske** *n.: -n, pl. -r*
pilot	**pilot** *n.: -en, pl. -er*
row	**række** *n.: -n, pl. -r*
runway	**landingsbane** *n.: -n, pl. -r*
seat belt	**sikkerhedsbælte** *n.: -t, pl. -r*
stewardess	**stewardesse** *n.: -n, pl. -r*
take off	**lette** *v.: -ede*
turbulence	**turbulens** *n.: -en, pl. -er*
window seat	**vinduesplads** *n.: -en, pl. -er*

Prepare for landing.
Gør klar til landing.

Transportation

Traveling By Train

Traveling by train in Denmark is quick, easy, comfortable, good for the environment and reliable. In 1999, 92 percent of the trains ran according to schedule. There is hourly service between major cities from early morning until late at night, and your train ticket extends to using the bus to and from the train station. Familiarity with basic Danish geography is useful as only major stops and end destinations appear on electronic screens and platform signs at the stations. If in doubt whether it is the right train, ask a conductor or a fellow traveler.

Types of Trains

InterCity (*IC*) trains run on the main routes every hour and offer *Business* and *Standard* seating. *InterCityLyn* (*ICL*) trains run Monday–Friday during the day; they are aimed at business people and thus offer only *Business* and *Business Plus* seating. *Interregionaltog* (*IR*) run as a supplement to the *InterCity* trains on Fridays and Sundays. *Regionaltog* (*Re*) operate on regional and local routes. In addition, train service is available through Sweden to the island of Bornholm. Copenhagen has an efficient subway system called *S-tog* (S-trains). They run every 5 to 10 minutes during the day and at longer intervals during the evenings. Train connections are available directly from *Kastrup*, the Copenhagen airport, to downtown Copenhagen as well as to the rest of Denmark.

Types of Seating

To be guaranteed a seat, a reservation (*pladsbillet*) is necessary. On *Business* and *Business Plus* the reservation is included in the ticket; on *Standard* it is extra. You can reserve a seat as far as two months in advance. The seat number is displayed above the seat on the luggage shelf. You have a choice between smoking (*Ryger*) or non-smoking (*Ikke-ryger*). Furthermore, *Familiepladser* (family seats) are available where children can play freely, and for real peace and quiet you can order *Hvileplads* (resting seat) where no cell phones are allowed.

Sleeping cars are available on international trains. A *Sovevogn* has 2–4 bunks with privacy and real bedding; a *liggevogn* has 4–6 bunks with less privacy and consequently, the expectation that people sleep in their clothes. Beer, soft drinks, tea and coffee, magazines, newspapers, candy, and snacks are available on *IC* and *ICL* trains; on *Business* and *Business Plus,* drinks, snacks, and newspapers are included. It is possible to bring pets, bicycles, and baby carriages on trains. Bikes are not allowed on *InterCityLyn* and rush-hour *S-trains*. Sometimes a reservation is necessary for a bike. Telephones, fax, plugs for headphones, and 220 V outlets are available on the trains. When boarding the train, pay close attention to the information on your ticket. Find the exact platform section (*perronafsnit*), car (*vogn*), and seat (*siddeplads*). This is important as not all parts of the train will go to the same destination. If you do not have a seat reservation you may sit where it says *Kan være reserveret* above the seat.

Ordering Tickets

To order tickets from home, call 70 13 14 15 for domestic tickets or 70 13 14 16 for international tickets. You can also order tickets on www.dsb.dk (English link available). At stations and on trains you can pay with cash, checks, and *Dankort* (Danish debit card). At major stations and over the phone you can also pay with major credit cards. Children under 15 are half price, and an adult can bring two children under 10 for free. Certain discount tickets are available, for example for seniors. Most train stations have a ticket office. At smaller stations and outside normal business hours, you use a vending machine that takes coins or debit cards. Tickets are also available on the train for a surcharge of 25 kr.; however, on S-trains and certain other trains this is not the case. Here you must have a valid ticket before getting on the train, otherwise you may be fined 500 kr. Some train tickets need to be punched (red machines are located at all stations) prior to boarding the train; otherwise you may be asked to pay 25 kr.

Special Tickets

An S-train ticket enables you to go by bus or train in the greater Copenhagen area. You can also buy a ticket valid for 24 hours, a punch card valid for 10 journeys, or the Copenhagen Card—a special tourist card that allows unlimited travel on buses and subways as well as free visits to over 60 sights and museums in and around Copenhagen and in southern Sweden. The Copenhagen Card is available on a one-, two-, or three-day basis. A three-day adult ticket runs about $50. The card is available at tourist information centers, some hotels, and train stations.

Price Zones

Fares for buses and S-trains are based on the "zones" you travel through. In the greater Copenhagen area, you can use the same ticket for buses and trains. Maps are located at bus stops and S-train stations to help you decide how much the journey will cost. Tourists will typically use individual tickets or punch cards and thus travel based on *ringzoner* (ring zones). There are 7 *ringzoner* in Copenhagen and northeastern Sjælland, each with a different color. Study the maps carefully and count the number of zones you will be in, including your start and end zones. Pay or punch your card accordingly. You always pay for at least two zones. When using the night bus (*natbus*) you must pay double. If in doubt, ask for assistance at the ticket office, from the bus driver or a fellow traveler.

locker	**bagageboks** *n.: -en, pl. -e*
lost and found	**hittegodskontor** *n.: -et, pl. -er*
luggage storage (supervised)	**garderobe (betjent)** *n.: -n, pl. -r*
newsstand	**kiosk** *n.: -en, pl. -er*
price 15 kr.	**pris 15 kr.**
restroom	**WC** *n.: -'et, pl. -'er*, **toilet** *n.: -tet, pl. -ter*
shower	**brusebad** *n.: -et, pl. -e*
shower time 20 minutes	**badetid 20 minutter**
ticket	**billet** *n.: -ten, pl. -ter*
ticket office	**billetkontor** *n.: -et, pl. -er*
ticket vending machine	**billetautomat** (cash or debit card only)
train	**tog** *n.: -et, pl. same*
train station	**banegård** *n.: -en, pl. -e*

travel agency	**rejsebureau** *n.: -et, pl. -er*
travel center	**rejsecenter** *n.: -et* or *rejsecentret, pl. rejsecentre*
waiting room	**venterum** *n.: -met, pl. same*

✼ ✼ ✼ ✼ ✼ ✼

additional charge	**tillæg** *n.: -get, pl. same*
adult	**voksen** *n.: pl. voksne*
arrival	**ankomst** *n.: -en, pl. -er*
arrive	**ankomme** *v.: ankom, ankommet*
bicycle ticket	**cykelbillet** *n.: -ten, pl. -ter*
change trains	**skifte tog** *v.: -ede tog*
child	**barn** *n.: -et, pl. børn*
children accompanied by an adult	**børn i følge med voksen**
conductor	**konduktør** *n.: -en, pl. -er*
day of departure	**udrejsedag** *n.: -en, pl. -e*
day of return	**hjemrejsedag** *n.: -en, pl. -e*
delayed	**forsinket**
depart	**afgå** *v.: afgik, afgået*
departure	**afgang** *n.: -en, pl. -e*
engine	**lokomotiv** *n.: -et, pl. -er*
family seating	**familieplads** *n.: -en, pl. -er*
freight train	**godstog** *n.: -et, pl. same* or *-e*
from	**fra**
help for handicapped passengers	**handicapassistance**
non-smoking	**ikke-ryger**
no stops	**uden stop**
number of people traveling	**antal rejsende**
one person at a time	**Én person ad gangen**
one-way ticket	**enkeltbillet** *n.: -ten, pl. -ter*
passenger train	**passagertog** *n.: -et, pl. same* or *-e*
place of ticket purchase	**solgt** (+ geographical name)

platform	**perron** *n.: -en, pl. -er*
platform section	**perronafsnit** *n.: -tet,* *pl. same (A, B, C, etc.)*
punch card	**klippekort** *n.: -et,* *pl. same*
quiet seating	**hvileplads** *n.: -en,* *pl. -er*
reserved seat	**pladsbillet** *n.: -ten,* *pl. -ter*
return ticket	**returbillet** *n.: -ten,* *pl. -ter*
schedule	**køreplan** *n.: -en, pl. -er*
seat reservation	**pladsreservation** *n.: -en,* *pl. -er*
sleeping car	**sovevogn, liggevogn** *n.: -en, pl. -e*
smoking	**ryger**
stops upon request	**standser på forlangende**
supervision of children traveling alone (ages 4–15)	**børneguideplads** *n.: -en,* *pl. -er*
to	**til**
track	**spor** *n.: -et, pl. same*
train	**tog** *n.: -et, pl. -e or same*
train car	**vogn** *n.: -en, pl. -e*

Watch for through trains!
PAS PÅ! Gennemgående tog.

The train leaves from track no. 3.
Toget afgår fra spor 3.

The train is five minutes late.
Toget er fem minutter forsinket.

Safety Zone
Sikkerhedszone

Do not cross yellow dots when no train is present.
**De gule prikker må kun overskrides, når der
holder tog.**

✱ ✱ ✱ ✱ ✱ ✱

additional ticket	**tillægsbillet** (more than six zones)

choice of ticket	**billetvalg** *n.: -et, pl. same*
price zone	**takstzone** *n.: -n, pl. -r*
punch card valid for 10 journeys	**10-turskort** *n.: -et, pl. same*
subway/metro	**S-tog** *n.: -et, pl. -e*
subway station	**S-togsstation** *n.: -en, pl. -er*
ticket for two zones	**billet til to zoner**
ticket for all zones	**billet til alle zoner**
ticket vending machine	**billetautomat** (cash or debit cards only)

✻ ✻ ✻ ✻ ✻ ✻

When is the next train to …?
Hvornår afgår næste tog til …?

When does the train arrive in …?
Hvornår ankommer toget til …?

I would like a one-way ticket.
Jeg vil gerne købe en enkeltbillet.

Do you have special student / senior citizen rates?
Får studerende / pensionister rabat?

Does this train stop in Kolding?
Standser toget i Kolding?

Do I change anywhere?
Skal jeg skifte nogen steder?

Yes, you change in Fredericia.
Ja, De skal skifte i Fredericia.

to get on a train
at stå på et tog

to get off a train
at stå af et tog

New passengers?
Nye rejsende?

The train arrives in Kolding in a few minutes.
Om få minutter ankommer toget til Kolding.

Next station: Køge 1:35 P.M.
Næste station: Køge 13.35.

Car no. 12 continues to Aarhus.
Vogn 12 kører videre mod Aarhus.

The two front cars continue to Aalborg.
De to forreste vogne kører videre mod Aalborg.

The last two cars continue to Esbjerg.
De to bagerste vogne kører videre mod Esbjerg.

Please exit through the doors on the right.
Der er udstigning i højre side.

Please exit through the doors on the left.
Der er udstigning i venstre side.

(This seat) may be reserved.
Kan være reserveret.

Traveling By Bus

Where is the closest bus stop?
Hvor er det nærmeste busstoppested?

Which bus goes to …?
Hvilken bus kører til …?

I would like to get off at …
Jeg vil gerne af ved …

Would you please tell me where to get off?
Sig venligst, hvor jeg skal af.

airport shuttle	**lufthavnsbus** *n.: -sen, pl. -ser*
bus	**bus** *n.: -sen, pl. -ser*
bus (countryside)	**rutebil** *n.: -en, pl. -er*
bus driver	**buschauffør** *n.: -en, pl. -er*
bus station (countryside)	**rutebilstation** *n.: -en, pl. -er*
bus stop	**busstoppested** *n.: -et, pl. -er*
bus terminal	**busterminal** *n.: -en, pl. -er*, **busstation** *n.: -en, pl. -er*
bus ticket	**busbillet** *n.: -ten, pl. -ter*
city bus	**bus, bybus** *n.: -sen, pl. -ser*

fare zone	**takstzone** *n.: -n, pl. -r* (fare according to length of trip— see train section)
get a discount	**få rabat**
get off	**stå af** *v.: stod, stået af*
get on	**stå på** *v.: stod, stået på*
night bus	**natbus** *n.: -sen, pl. -ser*
one-way ticket	**enkeltbillet** *n.: -ten, pl. -ter*
return ticket	**returbillet** *n.: -ten, pl. -ter*
tourist bus	**turistbus** *n.: -sen, pl. -ser*
Not in service	**Ikke i rute**

Car Rental

I would like to rent a car.
Jeg vil gerne leje en bil.

car	**bil** *n.: -en, pl. -er*
car rental company	**biludlejningsfirma** *n.: -et, pl. -er*
rent	**leje** *v.: -ede*
rental car	**udlejningsbil** *n.: -en, pl. -er*

What kind?
Hvilken slags?

camper	**campingvogn** *n.: -en, pl. -e*
convertible	**cabriolet** *n.: -en, pl. -er*
four-person/six-person	**firepersoners/ sekspersoners**
four-door	**firedørs**
Jeep/SUV	**Jeep** *n.: -en, pl. -er* or *-s*
minivan	**minibus** *n.: -sen, pl. -ser*
sedan	**personbil** *n.: -en, pl. -er*, **sedan** *n.: -en, pl. -er*
sports car	**sportsvogn** *n.: -en, pl. -e*
station wagon	**stationcar** *n.: -en, pl. -s*
two-door	**todørs**

Transportation

How much does it cost?
Hvor meget koster det?

auto-theft insurance	**biltyveriforsikring** *n.: -en*
collision insurance	**kaskoforsikring** *n.: -en*
deductible	**selvrisiko** *n.: -en*
gas expenses	**benzinafregning**
liability insurance	**ansvarsforsikring** *n.: -en*
payment for used gas upon return	**betaling af brugt benzin ved afleveringen**
price per 24 hours	**pris pr. døgn**
price per kilometer	**pris pr. kilometer**
required liability insurance	**standard ansvarsforsikring**
return with full gas tank	**aflevering af bilen fuldt tanket**
unlimited mileage	**fri kilometer**

Does the car have ...?
Har bilen ...?

airbag	**airbag** *n.: -en, pl. -s*
air-conditioning	**klimaautomatik** *n.: -ken*
automatic transmission	**automatgear** *n.: -et, pl. same*
CD player	**cd-afspiller** *n.: -en, pl. -e*
child locks	**børnesikring** *n.: -en*
cruise control	**fartpilot** *n.: -en*
four-wheel drive	**firehjulstræk, 4-hjulstræk** *n.: -ket*
front wheel drive	**forhjulstræk** *n.: -ket*
heated seat	**elsæde** *n.: -t, pl. -r*
hookup for camper or trailer	**anhængertræk** *n.: -ket*
power locks (remote)	**centrallås** *n.: -en, pl. -e* (fjernbetjent)
power mirror	**elspejl** *n.: -et, pl. -e*
power steering	**servostyring** *n.: -en*
power window	**elrude** *n.: -n, pl. -r*
radio	**radio** *n.: -en, pl. -er*
rear wheel drive	**baghjulstræk** *n.: -ket*
roof box	**tagboks** *n.: -en, pl. -e*
roof rack	**tagbagagebærer** *n.: -en, pl. -e*

safety seat (for child)	**barnestol** *n.: -en, pl. -e,* **autostol** *n.: -en, pl. -e*
seat belt	**sikkerhedssele** *n.: -n, pl. -r*
snow tire	**vinterdæk** *n.: -ket, pl. same*
stick shift	**almindeligt gearskift**
studded snow tire	**pigdæk** *n.: -ket, pl. same* (only legal between Oct. 1 and April 30)
sun roof	**soltag** *n.: -et, pl. -e*
tape deck	**kassetteafspiller** *n.: -en, pl. -e*
trunk	**bagagerum** *n.: -met, pl. same*

Traveling By Car or Motorcycle

You must be 18 to drive in Denmark, and have your driver's license, registration papers, and proof of insurance with you. Your American license is fully acceptable for a normal tourist visit. Cars and motorcycles must have at least their low beams (*nærlys*) on at all times. General speed limits have replaced most speed limit signs; unless otherwise posted, they are as follows: 50 km/hour within town limits, 80 km/hour on normal country roads (*landeveje*), 90 km/hour on certain bigger country roads (*motortrafikveje*), and 110 km/hour on highways (*motorveje*). Many towns have so-called *miljøveje*—roads with speed bumps and lane obstructions to make people slow down. In addition, the number of zones with a 30 or 40 km/hour speed limit (*stilleområder*) is growing, especially as school zones. The speed limits may be subject to change. There are fewer police cars on the roads in Denmark than in the U.S., but if you are caught speeding, the fines can easily be $300 or more. You are not allowed to turn right on a red light anywhere in Denmark. In the countryside, many intersections are roundabouts. Children under three are only allowed in the front seat if they are in a safety seat. Smaller children in the back seat must be in age-appropriate safety equipment. It is illegal to drive without safety belts.

accident	**trafikulykke** *n.: -n, pl. -r*
car	**bil** *n.: -en, pl. -er*

city limit	**bygrænse** *n.: -n, pl. -r*
driver's license	**kørekort** *n.: -et, pl. same*
duty to yield	**vigepligt** *n.: -en*
green light	**grønt lys**
highway (110 km/hour)	**motorvej** *n.: -en, pl. -e*
inspection/emission report	**synsrapport** *n.: -en, pl. -er*
intersection	**vejkryds** *n.: -et, pl. same*
license plate	**nummerplade** *n.: -n, pl. -r*
motorcycle	**motorcykel** *n.: motorcyklen, pl. motorcykler*
proof of insurance	**forsikringsbevis** *n.: -et, pl. same*
red light	**rødt lys**
registration papers	**registreringsattest** *n.: -en, pl. -er*
right of way	**forkørselsret** *n.: -ten*
road with speed bumps	**miljøvej** *n.: -en, pl. -e*
roundabout	**rundkørsel** *n.: -en or rundkørslen, pl. rundkørsler*
rush hour	**myldretid** *n.: -en*
speed limit	**hastighedsbegrænsning, fartbegrænsning** *n.: -en*
speeding ticket	**fartbøde** *n.: -n, pl. -r*
stop sign	**stopskilt** *n.: -et, pl. -e*
traffic jam	**trafikprop** *n.: -pen, pl. -per*
truck	**lastbil** *n.: -en, pl. -er*
yellow light	**gult lys**

Speed Limits

town/city (50 km/hour)	**by** *n.: -en, pl. -er*
country road (80 km/hour)	**landevej** *n.: -en, pl. -e*
large country road (90 km/hour)	**motortrafikvej** *n.: -en, pl. -e*
highway (110 km/hour)	**motorvej** *n.: -en, pl. -e*

Tourists should be aware that they could be asked to pay any traffic violation ticket on the spot. If unable to do so, the consequences could be quite unpleasant. If they are driving their own car the police have the right to confiscate it until the ticket has been paid. If they are driving a rental car the police have the right to take them into custody until the ticket has been paid.

Parking

The parking conditions in Denmark are similar to those in the United States—the bigger the city, the harder it is to find a spot. You can park along the streets in designated areas, in parking lots, and in garages. Most parking spots are free, for others you pay. Parking meters are not standard. If you pay for parking it is usually in a private garage, or automatic ticket machines are used. Instead, the Danes use *parkeringsskiver* (parking discs), a clock that you put on the inside of your front windshield. When you park the car you set it for the correct time, and depending on the lot, you have one, two, or sometimes three hours of free parking. It is basically an honor system, but you are ticketed if caught exceeding the time limit. All rental cars should have a *P-skive*, or you can get one at a gas station. The sign for parking spots reserved for the disabled is the same as in the U.S. When coming into a large town, signs will indicate if a certain parking lot is full or not.

Where can I park?
Hvor kan jeg parkere?

Where is the closest parking lot?
Hvor ligger den nærmeste parkeringsplads?

Am I allowed to park here?
Er det tilladt at parkere her?

Is parking free here?
Er det gratis at parkere her?

Parking for visitors only.
Parkeringspladser er forbeholdt gæster.

area where *P-skive* is required	**P-zone** *n.: -n, pl. -r*
automatic ticket machine	**billetautomat** *n.: -en, pl. -er*

fee	**afgift** *n.: -en, pl. -er*
full	**optaget**
long-term parking	**langtidsparkering/langtid**
marked stall	**parkeringsbås** *n.: -en, pl. -e*
park	**parkere** *v.: -ede*
parking in marked spots	**P i afmærkede områder**
parking lot	**parkeringsplads, P-plads** *n.: -en, pl. -er*
parking ticket (fine)	**parkeringsbøde** *n.: -n, pl. -r*
parking ticket (ticket to park)	**P-billet** *n.: -ten, pl. -ter*
short-term parking	**korttidsparkering/korttid**
reserved for ...	**forbeholdt ...**
vacancy	**Fri**
Amount includes sales tax.	**Afgift inkl. moms.**
Fee required.	**Der betales afgift.**
Four kroner per hour.	**Fire kr. pr. time.**
Help	**Hjælp**
Maximum three hours.	**Max. tre timer.**
Monday–Friday 8 A.M. until 6 P.M.	**mandag–fredag 8–18.00**
No coins	**Ingen mønter**
No parking	**Parkering forbudt**
Pay for parking here.	**Betal Deres p-billet her.**
Push here	**Tryk her**

The ticket is valid in all parking lots.
P-billetten er gyldig på alle P-pladser.

The vending machine does not give change.
Automaten veksler ikke og kan ikke give tilbage.

Road Signs

Delays possible	**Risiko for kø**
Deliveries allowed 7–11 A.M.	**Varekørsel / Ærindekørsel tilladt 7–11.**
Detour	**Omkørsel**
Except bicycles	**Cykler undtaget**

Icy road	**Glat føre**
Loading zone (stopping/ standing allowed)	**Af- og pålæsning tilladt/Ind- og udstigning tilladt**
No motor vehicles	**Ingen motorkøretøjer**
No parking	**Parkering forbudt**
No parking of bikes and mopeds.	**Henstillen af cykler og knallerter forbudt.**
No passing	**Overhaling forbudt**
No through traffic	**Gennemkørsel forbudt**
One way	**Ensrettet**
Pedestrian street	**Gågade**
road sign	**vejskilt** *n.: -et, pl. -e*
Soft shoulder	**Blød rabat**

Getting Help on the Road

If your car breaks down on the road, you can get quick help from *Dansk Autohjælp* by dialing 70 10 80 90. The service is nationwide and staffed around the clock. The mechanics will either repair your car on the spot or tow you to the closest repair shop. If necessary, they will also help you arrange for overnight lodging. They accept cash and major credit cards. When dialing the number, you get the following voice prompt, *De har nu tre muligheder. Ved behov for assistance, tast 3.* (You now have three options. If you need help, push 3.) After pushing 3, you will hear, *Vent venligst.* (Please wait.)

warning triangle	**advarselstrekant**
jumper cables	**startkabler**

I have run out of gas.
    Jeg er kørt tør for benzin.

I have a flat tire.
    Jeg er punkteret.

I have locked the key in my car.
    Jeg har låst nøglen inde i bilen.

My car won't start.
    Min bil vil ikke starte.

I need a tow truck.
Jeg har brug for en kranvogn.

My front windshield is broken.
Min forrude er smadret.

Car Parts and Repairs

The car needs brake fluid / oil.
Bilen mangler bremsevæske / olie.

There is a broken belt.
Der er sprunget en rem.

The battery is flat.
Batteriet er afladet. / Der er ingen strøm på batteriet.

The car makes a funny noise.
Bilen laver en mærkelig lyd.

antifreeze	**frostvæske** *n.: -en*
antilock brake	**ABS-bremse** *n.: -n, pl. -r*
battery	**batteri** *n.: -et, pl. -er*
belt	**rem** *n.: -men, pl. -me*
blinker	**blinklygte** *n.: -n, pl. -r*
brake fluid	**bremsevæske** *n.: -n*
brake lights	**stoplys** *n.: -et, pl. same*
bumper	**kofanger** *n.: -en, pl. -e*
car part	**reservedel** *n.: -en, pl. -e*
change the oil	**skifte olie** *v.: -ede olie*
charge	**oplade, lade op** *v.: -ede, -ede op*
check	**checke** *v.: -ede*
choke	**choker** *n.: -en, pl. -e*
clutch	**kobling** *n.: -en, pl. -er*
coolant	**kølervæske** *n.: -n*
cylinder	**cylinder** *n.: -en, pl. -e*
dashboard	**instrumentbræt** *n.: -tet, pl. -ter*
emergency brake	**nødbremse, parkeringsbremse** *n.: -n, pl. -er*
engine	**motor** *n.: -en, pl. -er*
exhaust/emission pipe	**udstødningsrør** *n.: -et, pl. same*

fender	**skærm** *n.: -en, pl. -e*
fog light	**tågelygte** *n.: -n, pl. -r*
front light	**forlys** *n.: -et, pl. same*
front wheel drive	**forhjulstræk** *n.: -ket*
front windshield	**forrude** *n.: -n, pl. -r*
high beam (brights)	**fjernlys** *n.: -et, pl. same* (also called *langt lys*)
hood	**motorhjelm** *n.: -en, pl. -e*
hub cap	**hjulkapsel** *n.: hjulkapslen, pl. hjulkapsler*
jack	**donkraft** *n.: -en, pl. -e*
lightbulb	**lyspære** *n.: -n, pl. -r*
low beams	**nærlys** *n.: -et, pl. same*
mechanic	**mekaniker** *n.: -en, pl. -e*
mirror	**spejl** *n.: -et, pl. -e*
mudguard	**stænkklap** *n.: -pen, pl. -per*
muffler	**lydpotte** *n.: -n, pl. -r*
odometer	**kilometertæller** *n.: -en, pl. -e*
oil	**olie** *n.: -n*
parking light	**positionslys** *n.: -et, pl. same*
patch, fix a flat	**lappe** *v.: -ede*
rearview mirror	**bakspejl** *n.: -et, pl. -e*
rear wheel drive	**baghjulstræk** *n.: -ket*
rear window	**bagrude** *n.: -n, pl. -r*
repair, fix	**reparere** *v.: -ede*
repair shop	**autoværksted** *n.: -et, pl. -er*
seal, gasket	**pakning** *n.: -en, pl. -er*
seat belt	**sikkerhedssele** *n.: -n, pl. -r*
shock absorber	**støddæmper** *n.: -en, pl. -e*
side mirror	**sidespejl** *n.: -et, pl. -e*
spare tire	**reservehjul** *n.: -et, pl. same*
spark plug	**tændrør** *n.: -et, pl. same*
speedometer	**speedometer** *n.: -et,* **hastighedsmåler** *n.: -en*
steering gear	**styretøj** *n.: -et*

steering wheel	**rat** *n.: -tet, pl. same*
tail lights	**baglys** *n.: -et, pl. same*
tire	**dæk** *n.: -ket, pl. same*
tire pressure	**dæktryk** *n.: -ket*
transmission	**gearkasse** *n.: -n, pl. -r*
trunk	**bagagerum** *n.: -met, pl. same*
tube	**slange** *n.: -n, pl. -r*
valve	**ventil** *n.: -en, pl. -er*
windshield washer fluid	**sprinklervæske** *n.: -n*
windshield wiper	**vinduesvisker** *n.: -en, pl. -e*
work, function	**virke** *v.: -ede*

Buying Gas

Danish gas stations almost exclusively have self-serve pumps.

Where is the closest gas station?
   Hvor ligger den nærmeste tankstation?

buy	**købe** *v.: -te*
car wash	**bilvask** *n.: -en*
diesel	**diesel**
gas	**benzin** *n.: -en*
gas station	**benzinstation, tankstation, servicestation** *n.: -en, pl. -er*
gas with cleaning agent	**Shell V-Power**
octane number	**oktantal (oktan 92, 95, or 98)**
oil	**olie** *n.: -n*
price per liter	**pris pr. liter**
reserve tank	**reservetank** *n.: -en, pl. -e*
unleaded	**blyfri**
windshield washer fluid	**sprinklervæske** *n.: -n*

Biking and Repairs

Denmark has a filigree of bike paths that are separated from the road for safety. Drivers are used to watching out for bikes, but be careful. The bike must be equipped with a bell, and when riding in the dark, both a yellow/white front light and a red rear light must be clearly visible at all times. Helmets are optional. Bike rentals are readily available. In Copenhagen, city-owned bikes are available free of charge.

bell	**cykelklokke** *n.: -n, pl. -r*
bicycle	**cykel** *n.: -en* or *cyklen, pl. cykler*
	cykle *v.: -ede*
bicycle helmet	**cykelhjelm** *n.: -en, pl. -e*
bicycle pump	**cykelpumpe** *n.: -n, pl. -r*
bicycle valve	**cykelventil** *n.: -en, pl. -er*
bike path	**cykelsti** *n.: -en, pl. -er*
carrier	**bagagebærer** *n.: -en, pl. -e*
chain	**kæde** *n.: -n, pl. -r*
chain guard	**kædeskærm** *n.: -en, pl. -e*
change gears	**skifte gear** *v.: -ede gear*
city bike	**almindelig cykel, city bike**
fender	**skærm** *n.: -en, pl. -e*
fix a flat tire	**lappe** *v.: -ede*
foot brake	**fodbremse** *n.: -n, pl. -r*
front brake	**forbremse** *n.: -n, pl. -r*
front fork	**forgaffel** *n.: -en* or *forgaflen, pl. forgafler*
front light	**forlygte** *n.: -n, pl. -r*
front wheel	**forhjul** *n.: -et, pl. same*
gear	**gear** *n.: -et, pl. same*
hand brake	**håndbremse** *n.: -n, pl. -r*
handlebars	**styr** *n.: -et, pl. same*
have a flat tire	**punktere** *v.: -ede*
lower the seat	**sætte sadlen ned** *v.: satte, sat sadlen ned*
mountain bike	**mountain bike, bjergcykel** *n.: bjergcyklen, pl. bjergcykler*
pedal	**pedal** *n.: -en, pl. -er*
raise the seat	**sætte sadlen op** *v.: satte, sat sadlen op*
rear brake	**bagbremse** *n.: -n, pl. -r*
rear light	**baglygte** *n.: -n, pl. -r*
rear wheel	**baghjul** *n.: -et, pl. same*

road bike	**racercykel,**
	landevejscykel
	n.: ... cyklen,
	pl. ...cykler
saddle	**sadel** *n.: sadlen, pl. sadler*
shock absorber	**støddæmper** *n.: -en, pl. -e*
spoke	**eger** *n.: -en, pl. -e*
sprocket	**tandhjul** *n.: -et, pl. same*
tandem bicycle	**tandemcykel**
	n.: tandemcyklen,
	pl. tandemcykler
tire	**dæk** *n.: -ket, pl. same*
tube	**slange** *n.: -n, pl. -r*

The chain slipped off.
  Kæden sprang af.

The chain snapped.
  Kæden sprang.

The chain is too loose / too tight.
  Kæden er for løs / for stram.

I have a flat tire.
  Jeg er punkteret.

Walking

Use sidewalks and pedestrian crossings as much as possible. Jaywalking is generally frowned upon. Actually, the Danish word for "jaywalker" is quite telling—*fumlegænger* means an inept pedestrian, implying that the person is foolish. Danes generally wait for the walk sign before crossing the street, even if traffic is sparse. If walking along bike paths or country roads, walk on the left side, facing oncoming traffic.

cross the street	**gå over gaden** *v.: gik,*
	gået over gaden
crosswalk	**fodgængerovergang**
	n.: -en, pl. -e
jaywalker	**fumlegænger** *n.: -en, pl. -e*
pedestrian	**fodgænger** *n.: -en, pl. -e*
pedestrian street	**gågade** *n.: -n, pl. -r*
sidewalk	**fortov** *n.: -et, pl. -e*
walk	**gå** *v.: gik, gået*

Ferries and Bridges

Jutland and the main islands are now connected by bridges, but ferries are still a necessity to reach the smaller islands. *Storebæltsbroen* is a toll bridge (cash and credit cards accepted); all other bridges are free except *Øresundsbroen* between Copenhagen and Sweden.

Ferry information is available in English at http://www.europe-today.com/denmark/public-transportation2.html.

bridge	**bro** *n.: -en, pl. -er*
bridge toll	**broafgift** *n.: -en, pl. -er,* **bropenge** *n. (pl.)*
car deck	**vogndæk** *n.: -ket, pl. same*
car ferry	**bilfærge** *n.: -n, pl. -r* (takes cars and people)
deck	**dæk** *n.: -ket, pl. same*
ferry	**færge** *n.: -n, pl. -r*
ferry connection	**færgeforbindelse** *n.: -n, pl. -r*
ferry port, berth	**færgehavn** *n.: -en, pl. -e,* **færgeleje** *n.: -t, pl. -r*
ferry service	**færgeoverfart** *n.: -en*
ferry ticket	**færgebillet** *n.: -ten, pl. -ter*
hovercraft	**flyvebåd** *n.: -en, pl. -e*
life belt	**redningsbælte** *n.: -t, pl. -r*
lifeboat	**redningsbåd** *n.: -en, pl. -e*
life jacket	**redningsvest** *n.: -en, pl. -e*
lighthouse	**fyrtårn** *n.: -et, pl. same*
minivan	**minibus** *n.: -sen, pl. -ser*
passenger	**passager** *n.: -en, pl. -er*
passenger car	**personbil** *n.: -en, pl. -er*
passenger ferry	**personfærge** *n.: -n, pl. -r* (only transports people and bicycles)
pay	**betale** *v.: -te*
pier, dock	**kaj** *n.: -en, pl. -er*
reservations	**pladsbestilling** *n.: -en, pl. -er*
sail	**sejle** *v.: -ede*
schedule	**sejlplan** *n.: -en*

I would like to make a reservation.
Jeg vil gerne bestille plads.

I have a reservation.
Jeg har en pladsreservation.

When does the ferry leave?
Hvornår sejler færgen?

The ferry leaves at 2 P.M.
Færgen sejler kl. 14.

When is the ferry expected to dock?
Hvornår forventes færgen i havn?

The ferry will dock shortly.
Færgen er i havn om få minutter.

I am seasick.
Jeg er søsyg.

I am nauseous.
Jeg har kvalme.

I need to throw up.
Jeg skal kaste op.

During the crossing, all passengers must leave their cars and the car deck.
Ophold på vogndæk samt i biler under overfarten er ikke tilladt.

Please wait as long as possible to start your cars.
Bilisterne bedes venligst starte motorerne så sent som muligt.

Please go to your cars now.
Vi beder Dem venligst indtage Deres pladser på vogndækket.

Maps

If you have access to the Internet, private addresses can be looked up at http://www.kraks.dk. The website will automatically provide a map.

airport	**lufthavn** *n.: -en, pl. -e*
beltway	**ringvej** *n.: -en, pl. -e*
campsite	**campingplads** *n.: -en, pl. -er* (for tents and campers)

car ferry	**bilfærge** *n.: -n, pl. -r*
castle/manor	**slot** *n.: -tet, pl. -te*; **herregård** *n.: -en, pl. -e*
city map	**bykort** *n.: -et, pl. same*
dead end	**blind vej** *(vej n.: -n, pl. -e)*
dirt road	**grusvej** *n.: -n, pl. -e*
entrance ramp	**tilkørsel** *n.: tilkørslen, pl. tilkørsler*
exit ramp	**frakørsel** *n.: frakørslen, pl. frakørsler*
golf course	**golfbane** *n.: -n, pl. -r*
highway	**motorvej** *n.: -en, pl. -e*; **Europavej** *n.: -en, pl. -e*
hostel	**vandrerhjem** *n.: -met, pl. same*
international border	**statsgrænse** *n.: -n, pl. -r*
legend	**signaturforklaring** *n.: -en, pl. -er*
map	**kort** *n.: -et, pl. same*
main road	**primærvej** *n.: -en, pl. -e*, **hovedvej** *n.: -en, pl. -e*
Marguerite Route	**Marguerit-ruten** (see p. 183)
minor road	**bivej** *n.: -en, pl. -e*, **anden vej**
passenger ferry	**personfærge** *n.: -n, pl. -r*
railroad	**jernbane** *n.: -n, pl. -r*
scale	**målestoksforhold** *n.: -et, pl. same*
secondary road	**sekundærvej** *n.: -en, pl. -e*
top-quality beach	**blå badestrand/godt badevand** (marked on map with blue along the coast)
tourist information	**turistinformation** *n.: -en*

Asking For Directions

north	**nord**
south	**syd**
east	**øst**
west	**vest**
to the south of	**syd for**

Transportation

right	**højre**
left	**venstre**
straight	**lige ud**
on your left	**på venstre hånd**
on your right	**på højre hånd**
turn left	**drej til venstre**
turn right	**drej til højre**
go straight	**kør ligeud**

* * * * * *

after	**efter**
at	**ved**
behind	**bagved**
next to	**ved siden af**
opposite	**overfor**
after the church	**efter kirken**
at the first traffic light	**i det første lyskryds**
at the second intersection	**i det andet vejkryds**
at the next corner	**på næste hjørne**
third street on your left	**tredje vej på venstre hånd**

* * * * * *

athletic field	**sportsplads** *n.: -en, pl. -er*
bridge	**bro** *n.: -en, pl. -er*
church	**kirke** *n.: -n, pl. -r*
city hall	**rådhus** *n.: -et, pl. -e*
cul-de-sac	**lukket vej**
dead end	**blind vej**
fork in the road	**vejgaffel**
gas station	**tankstation** *n.: -en, pl. -er*
hospital	**hospital** *n.: -et, pl. -er*
park	**park** *n.: -en, pl. -er*
road	**vej** *n.: -en, pl. -e*
school	**skole** *n.: -n, pl. -r*
street	**gade** *n.: -n, pl. -r*

* * * * * *

Could you please show me the way to …?
  Kan De/du vise mig vej til …?

How do I find …?
  Hvordan finder jeg …?

How far is … from here?
  Hvor langt er der til …?

Would you please show me on the map where we are?
Kan De/du vise mig på kortet, hvor vi er?

How long does it take to drive to …?
Hvor lang tid tager det at køre til …?

You can walk there in 10 minutes.
De/du kan gå derhen på 10 minutter.

Follow the signs that say …
Følg skiltene, hvorpå der står …

Go east.
Kør mod øst / østpå.

I am lost.
Jeg er faret vild.

You need to turn around.
De/du er nødt til at vende.

Make a U-turn.
Lav en U-vending.

You are going the right way.
De/du er på rette vej.

You are going the wrong way.
De/du er kørt forkert.

Look for a white church.
Kig efter en hvid kirke.

Scenic Routes

Most country roads in Denmark would be considered
scenic routes, but certain roads have been designated as
such. They are called *Marguerit-ruten* (The daisy route)
and are marked on maps and along the roads by square
brown signs with a white and yellow daisy.

Taking a Cab

Cabs are readily available in the streets in major cities. In
smaller towns and the countryside you should order one
ahead of time. They are listed under *Taxi* or *Taxa* in the
phone book. Rates are similar to those in the U.S. Tips are
not necessary, but greatly appreciated. The law requires
that passengers wear seat belts.

address	**adresse** *n.: -n, pl. -r*
cab	**taxi** *n.: -en, pl. -er,*
	taxa *n.: -en, pl. -er,*
	hyrevogn *n.: -en,*
	pl. -e
cab driver	**taxachauffør** *n.: -en,*
	pl. -er
limousine	**limousine** *n.: -n, pl. -r*
tip	**drikkepenge** *n. (pl.)*

I would like to order a cab.
Jeg vil gerne bestille en taxi.

I am going to Svalevej 13.
Jeg skal til Svalevej 13.

How much do I owe?
Hvor meget skylder jeg?

Travel Distances

Esbjerg–Lillebæltsbroen	92 km
(bridge between Jutland and Fynen)	
Greenå–Struer	160 km
Kolding–Ålborg	206 km
København–Gedser	155 km
København–Helsingør	45 km
København–Korsør	114 km
København–Lillebæltsbroen	211 km
København–Odense	169 km
Ringkøbing–Århus	129 km
Skagen–Frøslev (German border)	391 km
Svendborg–Lillebæltsbroen	87 km
Thisted–Frøslev (German border)	277 km

Shopping

The Customer

You generally get excellent service in Danish stores. Many salespeople have completed an apprenticeship that includes classes at a commercial school as well as practical experience, so they provide valuable information about the products. However, as malls and discount stores proliferate, the level of personal service is decreasing. In many places, you must take a number to be served (*et kø-nummer*). Gift wrapping is usually free.

store	**forretning** *n.: -en, pl. -er,* **butik** *n.: -ken, pl. -ker*
Entrance	**Indgang**
Exit	**Udgang**
Push	**Tryk**
Pull	**Træk**
Opening hours	**Åbningstider**
We have moved to ...	**Flyttet til ...**
Will return at ...	**Tilbage kl. ...**
customer	**kunde** *n.: -n, pl. -r*
customer restroom	**kundetoilet** *n.: -tet, pl. -ter*
customer friendly	**kundevenlig**
customer service	**kundebetjening, kundeservice**
personal service	**personlig betjening**
sales clerk	**ekspedient** (male) / **ekspeditrice** (female)
shop	**handle** *v.: -ede*
buy	**købe** *v.: -te*
shopping cart	**indkøbsvogn** *n.: -en, pl. -e*
grocery bag	**bærepose** *n.: -n, pl. -r*
bottle deposit	**pant** *n.: -en*
payment	**betaling** *n.: -en*
sales tax	**moms** *n.: -en*
bar code	**stregkode** *n.: -n, pl. -r*
rules for accepting checks	**checkregler**
valid identification	**gyldig legitimation**
identification card	**ID-kort**
Danish debit card	**Dankort**
size	**størrelse** *n.: -n, pl. -r*

Only firsthand checks accepted.
Der modtages kun førstehåndschecks.

Would you like it wrapped as a present?
Skal den/det/de pakkes ind som gave?

Yes, please.
Ja tak.

No, thank you.
Nej tak.

Could I please see the manager?
Kan jeg få lov at tale med en supervisor?

May I help you?
Hvad kan jeg hjælpe med? / Hvad skulle det være?

I would like to look at …
Jeg vil gerne se på en/et …

I am just looking.
Jeg kigger bare.

What size do you take?
Hvilken størrelse bruger De/du?

I take size …
Jeg bruger størrelse …

May I try on this dress?
Må jeg prøve den her kjole?

Where is the fitting room?
Hvor er prøveværelset?

I need one size smaller / bigger.
Jeg skal bruge en størrelse mindre / større.

Does it come in other colors?
Fås den/det/de i andre farver?

How many / much do you need?
Hvor mange / meget skal De/du bruge?

How much does … cost?
Hvor meget koster …?

How much do they cost apiece?
Hvor meget koster de stykket?

How much is it altogether?
Hvor meget bliver det i alt?

The item has been discontinued.
Varen er udgået.

We do not have the item in stock.
Vi har ikke varen på lager.

Is the item exchangeable?
Kan varen byttes?

No exit through cash register without purchase.
Ingen udgang gennem kasselinien uden varekøb.

Please contact customer service.
Henvend Dem venligst i informationen.

Please take a number. (for waiting in line)
Tryk / Tag venligst et nummer. (kø-nummer)

Store Hours

Danish law regulates when the stores can be open, and on Sundays and religious holidays opening hours are quite limited. Typical opening hours are 9:30 A.M. to 5:30 P.M. Monday through Friday, 9:30 A.M. to 1:00 P.M. on Saturdays and closed on Sundays. Small grocery stores, kiosks, and gas stations are allowed to sell food in the evenings and on Sundays, but grocery stores with an annual income above a certain amount cannot. Each store can choose four Sundays a year to be open, and stores within a certain distance from a harbor are allotted additional hours.

Shopping Carts

Shopping carts are available at supermarkets, but a coin (10 or 20 kr.) must be inserted. When the cart is returned, you get your coin back. Always use a shopping cart or basket while shopping, never your own bag until after you have paid.

Grocery Bags

In most stores, you will be offered a bag for free at the cash register, but at supermarkets you must either bring your own or pay for plastic bags. You usually bag your own groceries.

Bottle Deposit

Because of the Danish *returflaskesystem* (returnable bottle system), most soda and beer bottles are returnable and require a deposit.

Payment

See Money, Payment, and Tips, p. 139.

Exchange Policies

Returned items are readily accepted in Denmark if you have saved the receipt. Many stores put a special sticker on the item (*et byttemærke*), so you do not even need the receipt. If you wish to be able to return compact discs and DVDs, ask to have them *plomberet*, see below. If a store will not refund your money for a returned item, you will get a credit slip. Sale items may not be returnable.

credit slip	**tilgodeseddel** *n.:* *tilgodesedlen,* pl. *tilgodesedler*
exchange	**bytte** *v.:* *-ede*
exchangeable within two weeks	**14 dages bytteret**
exchange policy	**bytteordning** *n.:* *-en,* pl. *-er*
"exchange sticker"	**byttemærke** *n.:* *-t,* pl. *-r*
final sale	**kan ikke byttes**
full refund	**pengene tilbage**
proof of warranty	**garantibevis** *n.:* *-et,* pl. *-er*
receipt	**kvittering** *n.:* *-en,* pl. *-er,* **bon** *n.:* *-en,* pl. *-er*
reduced	**nedsat**
return	**returnere** *v.:* *-ede,* **levere tilbage** *v.:* *-ede tilbage*
sale	**udsalg** *n.:* *-et*
wrap in plastic and seal with a special sticker	**plombere** *v.:* *-ede*

Sales Tax

In Denmark, the sales tax is usually included in the price (20%). If the price excludes sales tax, twenty-five percent is

added. This is usually the case with professional services.
However, as a visitor from outside the EU, you are
entitled to a refund for the taxes you pay on purchases
you bring out of the EU within three months after
purchase/delivery. This is done through Global Refund
Tax Free Shopping, a service offered by major retailers.
When shopping, ask for Global Refund Cheques and
cash them at the last customs authority in the EU. In Denmark, offices (*Told og Skat*) are located at the airports in
Billund and Copenhagen (Kastrup Airport) as well as at
certain ferry berths. Remember that to qualify for a tax
refund, each purchase must exceed 300 kr., including tax.
The shops are not obligated to help you get a refund, but
most willingly do so. You will be asked to document your
residence abroad, usually by showing your passport.
Make sure you get a detailed receipt with the date, a
detailed description of the bought items, the price before
and after taxes, and the seller's name, address, and tax ID
number. If you ask the store to ship your purchase
directly out of Denmark, you should not need to pay the
sales tax.

Types of Stores

Where can I find a/an ...?
Hvor ligger der en/et ...?

antiquarian bookstore	**antikvariat** *n.: -et, pl. -er*
antiques	**antikvitetshandler** *n.: -en, pl. -e*
bakery	**bager** *n.: -en, pl. -e*
bookstore	**boghandler** *n.: -en, pl. -e*
butcher	**slagter** *n.: -en, pl. -e*
candy and ice cream store	**slik- og isbutik** *n.: -ken, pl. -ker*
cheese store	**osteforretning** *n.: -en, pl. -er*
clothing store	**tøjforretning** *n.: -en, pl. -er*
computer store	**edb-forretning** *n.: -en, pl. -er*
discount store	**lavprisvarehus** *n.: -et, pl. -e*

Shopping

drugstore	**materialhandler** *n.: -en, pl. -e*
fish dealer	**fiskehandler** *n.: -en, pl. -e*
florist	**blomsterhandler** *n.: -en, pl. -e*
gas station	**tankstation** *n.: -en, pl. -er*, **benzinstation** *n.: -en, pl. -er*
greengrocer	**grønthandler** *n.: -en, pl. -e*
hardware store	**isenkræmmerbutik** *n.: -ken, pl. -ker*
health food store	**helsekostforretning** *n.: -en, pl. -er*
hobby store	**hobbyforretning** *n.: -en, pl. -er*
home center	**trælast** *n.: -en, pl. -er*, **byggecenter** *n.: byggecentret, pl. byggecentre*
jeweler	**guld- og sølvsmed** *n.: -en, pl. -e*
kiosk	**kiosk** *n.: -en, pl. -er*
optician	**optiker** *n.: -en, pl. -e*
pedestrian street	**gågade** *n.: -n, pl. -r* (called *Strøget* in Copenhagen)
pharmacy	**apotek** *n.: -et, pl. -er*
shoe store	**skotøjsforretning** *n.: -en, pl. -er*
shopping mall	**storcenter** *n.: storcentret, pl. storcentre* (indoor mall)
souvenir shop	**souvenirforretning** *n.: -en, pl. -er*
sports store	**sportsforretning** *n.: -en, pl. -er*
supermarket	**supermarked** *n.: -et, pl. -er*
thrift store	**genbrugsforretning** *n.: -en, pl. -er*
toy store	**legetøjsforretning** *n.: -en, pl. -er*
wine store	**vinhandler** *n.: -en, pl. -e*

In addition, many towns have a farmer's market with fruit, vegetables, fish, cheese, and flowers. Many people set up stands by the road, offering fruit, vegetables, eggs, and honey. Customers typically help themselves and leave payment in a container.

farmer's market	**torv, torvedag**

Advertising

½ price	**½ pris, halv pris**
3 pairs	**3 par**
3 for the price of 2	**Ta' 3 for 2**
5 pieces/items	**5 stk.**
advertisement	**reklame** *n.: -n, pl. -r*
before	**før**
coupon	**rabatkupon, rabatmærke**
discount	**rabat**
everyday price	**normalpris**
from ... and up	**fra ... og opefter**
now	**nu**
price for set	**sætpris**
reduced	**nedsat**
sale	**udsalg** (Usually all stores have huges sales in January and July.)
special	**tilbud**
surplus stock	**restlager**
take your pick	**frit valg**
weekly special	**ugens tilbud**
you save	**du sparer**

Clothes and Shoes

bathrobe	**badekåbe** *n.: -n, pl. -r,* **slåbrok** *n.: -ken, pl. -ker*
belt	**livrem** *n.: -men, pl. -me* (men's), **bælte** *n.: -t, pl. -r* (women's)
bikini	**bikini** *n.: -en, pl. -er*
blouse	**bluse** *n.: -n, pl. -r*

boot (leather)	**læderstøvle** *n.: -n, pl. -r*
boot (rubber or rain)	**gummistøvle** *n.: -n, pl. -r*
bra	**bh** *n.: -'en, pl. -'er*, **brystholder** *n.: -en, pl. -e* (C cup = C-skål)
cap	**hue** *n.: -n, pl. -r*, **kasket** *n.: -ten, pl. -ter*
clam diggers	**stumpebukser** *n. (pl.)*
clog(s)	**træsko** *n.: -en, pl. same*
coat	**frakke** *n.: -n, pl. -r*
down jacket	**dynejakke** *n.: -n, pl. -r*
dress	**kjole** *n.: -n, pl. -r*
dress shirt	**manchetskjorte** *n.: -n, pl. -r*
evening gown	**balkjole** *n.: -n, pl. -r*
glove	**handske** *n.: -n, pl. -r*
G-string	**g-streng** *n.: -en, pl. -e*
hat	**hat** *n.: -ten, pl. -te*
headband	**pandebånd** *n.: -et, pl. same*
jacket	**jakke** *n.: -n, pl. -r*
jacket and skirt (matching)	**spadseredragt** *n.: -en, pl. -er*
jeans	**cowboybukser** *n. (pl.)*, **jeans** *n. (pl.)*
mitten	**vante** *n.: -n, pl. -r*
nightgown	**natkjole** *n.: -n, pl. -r*
overalls	**overalls** *n. (pl.)*
pajamas	**pyjamas** *n.: -sen, pl. -ser*
pants, trousers	**bukser** *n. (pl.)*
pantyhose, tights	**nylonstrømpe** *n.: -n, pl. -r*
raincoat	**regnjakke** *n.: -n, pl. -r*
raingear	**regntøj** *n.: -et, pl. same*
rain pants	**regnbukser** *n. (pl.)*
sandal	**sandal** *n.: -en, pl. -er*
scarf	**halstørklæde** *n.: -t, pl. -r*, **tørklæde** *n.: -t, pl. -r*
shirt	**skjorte** *n.: -n, pl. -r* (men's), **skjortebluse** *n.: -n, pl. -r* (women's)
shoe	**sko** *n.: -en, pl. same*
shoe laces	**snørebånd** *n.: -et, pl. same*
shoe polish	**skosværte** *n.: -n*

shorts	**shorts** n. (pl.)
skirt	**nederdel** n.: -en, pl. -e
slip	**underkjole** n.: -n, pl. -r, **underskørt** n.: -et, pl. -er
slippers	**hjemmesko** n.: -en, pl. same, **indesko** n.: -en, pl. same
sock	**sok** n.: -ken, pl. -ker, **strømpe** n.: -n, pl. -r
suit	**jakkesæt** n.: -tet, pl. same
sweater	**trøje** n.: -n, pl. -r, **sweater** n.: -en, pl. -e
sweat suit	**træningsdragt** n.: -en, pl. -er
swimsuit	**badedragt** n.: -en, pl. -er (women's), **badebukser** n. (pl.) (men's)
tank top	**ærmeløs T-shirt, bluse** n.: -n, pl. -r
tie	**slips** n.: -et, pl. same
T-shirt	**T-shirt** n.: -en, pl. -s
turtleneck sweater	**rullekravesweater** n.: -en, pl. -e
tuxedo	**smoking** n.: -en, pl. -er
underpants	**underbukser** n. (pl.) (women's and men's), **trusser** n. (pl.) (women's)
undershirt	**undertrøje** n.: -n, pl. -r
underwear	**undertøj** n.: -et
windbreaker	**vindjakke** n.: -n, pl. -r

In the Fitting Room

I need one size smaller / bigger.
Jeg skal bruge en størrelse mindre / større.

fitting room	**prøveværelse** n.: -t, pl. -r
try on	**prøve** v.: -ede
with underwear	**med undertøj på**
measure	**måle** v.: -te

measuring tape	**målebånd** *n.: -et, pl. same*, **centimetermål** *v.: -et, pl. same*
shorten	**lægge op** *v.: lagde, lagt op*
take in	**lægge ind** *v.: lagde, lagt ind*
let out	**lægge ud** *v.: lagde, lagt ud*
too big	**for stor**
too long	**for lang**
too short	**for kort**
too small	**for lille**
too tight	**for stram**

Sizes

Sock sizes follow shoe sizes. Pantyhose sizes follow dress sizes. Men's pants follow waist measurements (*taljemål*), and men's dress shirts follow clothes sizes plus collar measurements in centimeters.

Clothes for Men—Herretøj

U.S.	Denmark
Small	37–38
Medium	39–40
Large	41–42
X Large	43–44
XX Large	45–46
XXX Large	47–48

Clothes for Women—Dametøj

U.S.	Denmark
Petite	34–36
Small	38
Medium	40
Large	42
X Large	44
XX Large	46–48

Clothes for Children—Børne- og babytøj

U.S.	Denmark	
preemie	**44 cm**	**kuvøsestørrelse**
newborn	**50 cm**	**nyfødt**
1 month	**56 cm**	**1 måned**
2–3 months	**62 cm**	**2–3 måneder**
4–6 months	**68 cm**	**4–6 måneder**
6–9 months	**74 cm**	**6–9 måneder**
12 months	**80 cm**	**1 år**
18 months	**86 cm**	**1½ år**
2 years	**92 cm**	**2 år**
3 years	**98 cm**	**3 år**
16 years	**176 cm**	**16 år**

Shoe Sizes

The smallest shoe size is 17 for babies/toddlers (*begynder-størrelse*). For men's sizes add 33 to the U.S. equivalent, for women's add 31. A men's 9 in the U.S. is thus a size 42. A women's 8 is a size 39. Some shoes are available in half sizes.

Colors

color	**farve** *n.: -n, pl. -r*
black	**sort**
blue	**blå**
brown	**brun**
dark blue	**mørkeblå**
dark yellow	**mørkegul**
gray	**grå**
green	**grøn**
light blue	**lyseblå**
light brown	**lysebrun**
orange	**orange**
pink	**pink, lyserød**
purple	**lilla**
red	**rød**
teal	**turkisgrøn**
turquoise	**turkisblå**
unbleached	**ubleget**
white	**hvid**
yellow	**gul**

Materials

pattern	**mønster**
with a pattern	**med mønster**
monochromatic	**ensfarvet**
plaid	**ternet**
striped	**stribet**

❋ ❋ ❋ ❋ ❋ ❋

corduroy	**jernbanefløjl**
cotton	**bomuld**
fur	**pels**
leather	**læder**
nylon	**nylon**
silk	**silke**
suede	**ruskind**
synthetic	**kunststof**
velour	**velour**
velvet	**fløjl**
washable	**vaskeægte**
waterproof, rainproof	**vandtæt**
water resistant	**vandskyende**
wicking	**svedtransporterende**
windproof	**vindtæt**
wool	**uld**

Dry Cleaning

dry-clean	**rense** *v.: -ede*
dry cleaner	**renseri** *n.: -et, pl. -er*
dry cleaning	**rensning** *n.: -en, pl. -er*
iron	**stryge** *v.: strøg, strøget*
press	**presse** *v.: -ede*

Remember to empty all pockets.
   Husk at tømme alle lommerne.

buckle	**spænde** *n.: -t, pl. -r*
button	**knap** *n.: -pen, pl. -per*
shoulder pad	**skulderpude** *n.: -n, pl. -r*
zipper	**lynlås** *n.: -en, pl. -e*

We do not guarantee …
   Vi garanterer ikke for …

Note! We do not guarantee against shrinkage.
Bemærk! For evt. krympning garanteres ikke.

Is this dress dry-cleanable?
Er det muligt at rense den her kjole?

I need my clothes by Saturday morning.
Jeg skal bruge tøjet senest lørdag morgen.

Washing Instructions

washing instructions	**vaskeanvisninger**
clothes line	**tørresnor** *n.: -en, pl. -e,* **tørrestativ** *n.: -et, pl. -er*
clothespin	**tøjklemme** *n.: -n, pl. -r*
coat hanger	**bøjle** *n.: -n, pl. -r*
colorfast	**farveægte**
dry flat	**liggetørres**
iron	**strygejern** *n.: -et, pl. same*
ironing board	**strygebræt** *n.: -tet, pl. -ter*
line-dry	**hængetørres**
machine washable	**kan maskinvaskes**
permanent press	**strygefri**
preshrunk	**krympefri**
Do not soak.	**Undgå iblødsætning.**
Do not use bleach.	**Brug ikke blegemidler.**
Dry cleaning recommended.	**Rensning anbefales.**
Iron as needed.	**Stryges efter behov.**
Shape while wet.	**Strækkes i facon i våd tilstand.**
Use detergent for delicates.	**Brug uldvaskemiddel.**
Use only detergent without optical white.	**Brug kun vaskemiddel uden optisk hvidt.**
Wash by hand.	**Vask i hånden.**
Wash separately with like colors.	**Vask separat med lignende farver.**
Wash inside out.	**Vask med vrangsiden ud.**
Will shrink 20%.	**Krymper 20%.**

Jewelry / Piercing / Tattoos

A lot of beautiful jewelry is available in Denmark. Tattoos and body piercing are becoming increasingly popular in Denmark. Those under 15 must obtain parental permission.

Branding, scarification, implantation, etc. are also gaining ground.

jewelry	**smykker**
amber	**rav** *n.: -et*
ankle bracelet	**ankelkæde** *n.: -n, pl. -r*
barrette	**hårspænde** *n.: -t, pl. -r*
bracelet	**armbånd** *n.: -et, pl. same*
brooch	**broche** *n.: -n, pl. -r*
diamond	**diamant** *n.: -en, pl. -er*
earring	**ørenring** *n.: -en, pl. -e*
garnet	**granat** *n.: -en, pl. -er*
gold	**guld** *n.: -et*
jade	**jade** *n.: -n*
karat	**karat** *n.: -en*
necklace	**halskæde** *n.: -n, pl. -r*
opal	**opal** *n.: -en, pl. -er*
pearl	**perle** *n.: -n, pl. -r*
ring	**ring** *n.: -en, pl. -e*
sapphire	**safir** *n.: -en, pl. -er*
silver	**sølv** *n.: -et*
white gold	**hvidguld** *n.: -et*
wristwatch	**armbåndsur, ur** *n.: -et, pl. -e*

❋ ❋ ❋ ❋ ❋ ❋

tattoo	**tatovering** *n.: -en, pl. -er*

❋ ❋ ❋ ❋ ❋ ❋

bellybutton	**navle** *n.: -n, pl. -r*
ear	**øre** *n.: -t, pl. -r*
eyebrow	**øjenbryn** *n.: -et, pl. same*
genital piercing	**intimpiercing** *n.: -en, pl. -er*
gold (14 or 18 karat)	**guld (14 eller 18 karat)**
lip	**læbe** *n.: -n, pl. -r*
niobium	**niobium**
nipple	**brystvorte** *n.: -n, pl. -r*
nose	**næse** *n.: -n, pl. -r*
pierce	**pierce** *v.: -ede*
piercing	**piercing** *n.: -en, pl. -er*
piercing of body	**kropspiercing** *n.: -en, pl. -er*

piercing of ears	**ørepiercing** n.: -en, pl. -er
piercing of face	**ansigtspiercing** n.: -en, pl. -er
ring	**ring** n.: -en, pl. -e
stud, stud earring	**stikker, ørestikker** n.: -en, pl. -e
surgical steel	**kirurgisk stål**
titanium	**titanium**
tongue	**tunge** n.: -n, pl. -r

At the Photography Store

When can I pick up the pictures?
Hvornår kan jeg hente billederne?

200 ASA	**ISO 200**
battery	**batteri** n.: -et, pl. -er
best if developed before ...	**filmen bør fremkaldes inden ...**
black and white film	**sort-hvid film** (*film* n.: -en, pl. same)
cable release	**trådudløser** n.: -en, pl. -e
camera	**kamera** n.: -et, pl. -er, **fotografiapparat** n.: -et, pl. -er
camera shop	**fotoforretning** n.: -en, pl. -er
charge (battery)	**oplade** v.: -ede
color film	**farvefilm** n.: -en, pl. same
develop	**fremkalde** v.: -te
development	**fremkaldelse** n.: -n
digital	**digital** adj.
enlarge	**forstørre** v.: -ede
film speed	**filmhastighed** n.: -en, pl. -er
flash	**blitz** n.: -en
glossy	**blank** adj.
lens	**linse** n.: -n, pl. -r
light meter	**lysmåler** n.: -en, pl. -e
mat	**mat** adj.
number of copies	**antal kopier**
number of exposures	**antal billeder**
one-hour photo	**inden for en time**

Shopping

overexpose	**overeksponere** *v.: -ede*
photograph	**fotografi** *n.: -et, pl. -er*
photographer	**fotograf** *n.: -en, pl. -er*
photography store	**fotoforretning** *n.: -en, pl. -er*
pick up	**afhente** *v.: -ede*
picture	**billede** *n.: -t, pl. -r*
playing time	**spilletid** *n.: -en*
ready for pickup	**færdig til afhentning**
reorder	**genbestille** *v.: -te*
size	**størrelse** (9x13 cm, 10x15 cm, 13x18 cm, 15x21 cm, 18x24 cm, 20x30 cm)
slide	**lysbillede** *n.: -t, pl. -r, dias n.: -et, pl. same*
underexpose	**undereksponere** *v.: -ede*
video camera	**videokamera** *n.: -et, pl. -er*
videotape	**videobånd** *n.: -et, pl. same*

Photocopying

photocopying	**fotokopiering**
ready to copy	**klar til kopiering**
select paper	**vælg papir**
up	**op**
down	**ned**
zoom	**zoom**
justification	**centrering**
number of copies	**Antal kopier**

Food

Meat	**Kød**
beef	**oksekød** *n.: -et*
cold cuts	**afskåret pålæg** (slice = skive *n.: -n, pl. -r*)
ground beef	**hakket oksekød**
ham	**skinke** *n.: -n, pl. -r*
lamb	**lammekød** *n.: -et*

mincemeat	**hakkekød** *n.: -et*
pork	**svinekød** *n.: -et*, **grisekød** *n.: -et*
veal	**kalvekød** *n.: -et*

Poultry	**Fjerkræ**
chicken	**kylling** *n.: -en, pl. -er*
duck	**and** *n.: -en, pl. ænder*
goose	**gås** *n.: -en, pl. gæs*
ostrich	**struds** *n.: -en, pl. -er*
pheasant	**fasan** *n.: -en, pl. -er*
quail	**agerhøne** *n.: -n, pl. agerhøns*
turkey	**kalkun** *n.: -en, pl. -er*

Game	**Vildt**
deer	**dyrekød** *n.: -et*
hare, rabbit	**hare** *n.: -n, pl. -r*

Fish	**Fisk**
calamari	**blæksprutte** *n.: -n, pl. -r*
cod	**torsk** *n.: -en, pl. same*
flounder	**rødspætte** *n.: -n, pl. -r*
herring	**sild** *n.: -en, pl. same*
lobster	**hummer** *n.: -en, pl. -e*
mussel	**musling** *n.: -en, pl. -er*
oyster	**østers** *n.: -en, pl. same*
salmon	**laks** *n.: -en, pl. same*
shellfish	**skaldyr** *n.: -et, pl. same*
shrimp	**reje** *n.: -n, pl. -r*
trout	**ørred** *n.: -en, pl. -er*
tuna	**tun** *n.: -en, pl. same*

Dairy Products	**Mælkeprodukter**
skim milk	**skummetmælk** *n.: -en*
2% milk	**letmælk** *n.: -en*
whole milk	**sødmælk** *n.: -en*
buttermilk	**kærnemælk** *n.: -en*
chocolate milk	**kakaomælk** *n.: -en*
homogenized	**homogeniseret** *adj.*
pasteurized	**pasteuriseret** *adj.*

lactic acid	**mælkesyre** *n.: -n*
lactose	**mælkesukker** *n.: -et*
heavy whipping cream	**piskefløde** *n.: -n*
half and half	**fløde** *n.: -n* (13%)

* * * * * *

butter	**smør** *n.: -ret*
margarine	**Kærgården** (75% milkfat and 25% rapeseed oil)
for baking	**bagemargarine** *n.: -n*
for frying	**stegemargarine** *n.: -n*
egg	**æg** *n.: -get, pl. same*
ice cream	**is** *n.: -en, pl. is*
junket	**tykmælk** *n.: -en/*
	ymer *n.: -en /*
	ylette *n.: -en*
sour cream	**cremefraiche** *n.: -n*
yogurt	**yoghurt** *n.: -en, pl. -er*

* * * * * *

cheese	**ost** *n.: -en, pl. -e* (collective n. ost)
cheese (for slicing)	**skæreost** *n.: -en*
blue cheese	**danablu** *n.: -en,* **roquefort** *n.: -en*
cottage cheese	**hytteost** *n.: -en*
cream cheese	**smøreost** *n.: -en*
feta	**fetaost** *n.: -en*
goat cheese	**gedeost** *n.: -en*
parmesan	**parmesanost** *n.: -en*

* * * * * *

mild	**mild** *adj.*
medium ripe	**mellemlagret** *adj.*
very ripe	**lagret** *adj.*
extremely ripe and smelly cheese	**Gamle Ole**

Note! When you buy fruit and vegetables in a Danish supermarket you usually need to weigh the produce yourself before going to the cash register. Scales are located in the fresh produce area.

Weigh-It-Yourself Service
Vej selv service

Place the item on the scale.
Læg varen på vejeplan.

Push the corresponding button.
Tryk på den ønskede vejetast.

Remember the price label.
Husk etiket.

Fruit	Frugt
apple	**æble** *n.: -t, pl. -r*
apricot	**abrikos** *n.: -en, pl. -r*
banana	**banan** *n.: -en, pl. -er*
blackcurrant	**solbær** *n.: -ret, pl. same*
blueberry	**blåbær** *n.: -ret, pl. same*
cherry	**kirsebær** *n.: -ret, pl. same*
coconut	**kokosnød** *n.: -den, pl. -der*
cranberry	**tranebær** *n.: -ret, pl. same*
date	**daddel** *n.: -en or dadlen, pl. dadler*
elderberry	**hyldebær** *n.: -ret, pl. same*
fig	**figen** *n.: -en or fignen, pl. figner*
gooseberry	**stikkelsbær** *n.: -ret, pl. same*
grape	**vindrue** *n.: -n, pl. -r*
grapefruit	**grapefrugt** *n.: -en, pl. -er*
kiwi	**kiwifrugt** *n.: -en, pl. -er*
lemon	**citron** *n.: -en, pl. -er*
nectarine	**nektarin** *n.: -en, pl. -er*
olive	**oliven** *n.: -en, pl. same*
orange	**appelsin** *n.: -en, pl. -er*
peach	**fersken** *n.: -en or fersknen, pl. ferskner*
pear	**pære** *n.: -n, pl. -r*
pineapple	**ananas** *n.: -en, pl. -er*
plum	**blomme** *n.: -n, pl. -r*
prune	**sveske** *n.: -n, pl. -r*
raisin	**rosin** *n.: -en, pl. -er*
raspberry	**hindbær** *n.: -ret, pl. same*
red currant	**ribs** *n.: -et, pl. same*
rhubarb	**rabarber** *n.: -en, pl. same*
rose hip	**hyben** *n.: -et, pl. same or -er*

strawberry	**jordbær** *n.: -ret, pl. same*
tangerine	**mandarin** *n.: -en, pl. -er*
watermelon	**vandmelon** *n.: -en, pl. -er*

Vegetables	**Grøntsager**

artichoke	**artiskok** *n.: -ken, pl. -ker*
asparagus	**asparges** *n.: -en, pl. -er* or *asparges*
avocado	**avokado** *n.: -en, pl. -er*
bean	**bønne** *n.: -n, pl. -r*
beet	**rødbede** *n.: -n, pl. -r*
bell pepper	**peberfrugt** *n.: -en, pl. -er*
Brussels sprout	**rosenkål** *n.: -en, pl. same*
cabbage	**kål** *n.: -en*
carrot	**gulerod** *n.: -en, pl. gulerødder*
cauliflower	**blomkål** *n.: -en, pl. same*
celery	**bladselleri** *n.: -en, pl. -er* or *same*
Chinese cabbage	**kinakål** *n.: -en, pl. same*
corn	**majs** *n.: -en, pl. same*
cucumber	**agurk** *n.: -en, pl. -er*
eggplant	**aubergine** *n.: -n, pl. -r*
garden cress	**havekarse** *n.: -en*
garlic	**hvidløg** *n.: -et, pl. same*
green onions	**forårsløg** *n.: -et, pl. same*
horseradish	**peberrod** *n.: -en, pl. same*
leek	**porre** *n.: -n, pl. -r*
lettuce	**salat** *n.: -en*
mushroom	**champignon** *n.: -en, pl. -er*
onion	**løg** *n.: -et, pl. same*
pea	**ært** *n.: -en, pl. -er*
potato	**kartoffel** *n.: -en* or *kartoflen, pl. kartofler*
radish	**radise** *n.: -n, pl. -r*
red cabbage	**rødkål** *n.: -en, pl. same*
soybean	**sojabønne** *n.: -n, pl. -r*
spinach	**spinat** *n.: -en*
tomato	**tomat** *n.: -en, pl. -er*
watercress	**brøndkarse** *n.: -n*
white cabbage	**hvidkål** *n.: -en, pl. same*
zucchini	**courgette** *n.: -n, pl. -r*

Nuts and Seeds	**Nødder og kerner**
almond	**mandel** *n.: -en* or *mandlen, pl. mandler*
Brazil nut	**paranød** *n.: -den, pl. -der*
Hazelnut	**hasselnød** *n.: -den, pl. -der*
pine nut	**pinjekerne** *n.: -n, pl. -r*
poppy seed	**valmuefrø** *n.: -et, pl. same*, **birkes** *n.: -et, pl. same*
sesame seed	**sesamfrø** *n.: -et, pl. same*
sunflower seed	**solsikkefrø** *n.: -et, pl. same*
walnut	**valnød** *n.: -den, pl. -der*

Herbs and Spices	**Urter og krydderier**
allspice	**allehånde**
anise	**anis**
basil	**basilikum**
bay leaf	**laurbærblad**
caraway seeds	**kommen**
cardamom	**kardemomme**
cayenne pepper	**cayenne**
chamomile	**kamille**
chervil	**kørvel**
chili pepper	**chili**
chives	**purløg**
cinnamon	**kanel**
cloves	**nelliker**
coriander	**koriander**
curry	**karry**
dill	**dild**
fennel	**fennikel**
garlic	**hvidløg**
marjoram	**merian**
mint	**mynte**
nutmeg	**muskat**
oregano	**oregano**
paprika	**paprika**
parsley	**persille**
pepper	**peber**

purslane	**portulak**
rosemary	**rosmarin**
saffron	**safran**
sage	**salvie**
salt	**salt**
tarragon	**estragon**
thyme	**timian**
turmeric	**gurkemeje**
vanilla	**vanille**

Baked Goods — Bagværk

baguette	**baguette** *n.: -n, pl. -r,* **flute** *n.: -n, pl. -s*
bread	**brød** *n.: -et, pl. same*
bread in square slices (white or whole wheat)	**toastbrød** *n.: -et, pl. same* (fits into toaster)
bread with kernels and seeds	**fuldkornsbrød** *n.: -et, pl. same*
breakfast roll	**rundstykke** *n.: -t, pl. -r*
cake	**kage** *n.: -n, pl. -r*
cake shaped as a pretzel	**kringle** *n.: -n, pl. -r*
cake with whipped cream	**flødeskumskage** *n.: -n, pl. -r*
cookie	**småkage** *n.: -n, pl. -r*
cracker	**kiks** *n.: -n, pl. same*
crisp	**sprød** *adj.*
crust	**skorpe** *n.: -n, pl. -r*
custard	**creme** *n.: -n, pl. -r*
French bread	**franskbrød** *n.: -et, pl. same*
gluten (gluten-free)	**gluten (glutenfri)**
layer cake	**lagkage** *n.: -n, pl. -r*
muffin	**muffin** *n.: -en, pl. -s*
roll	**bolle** *n.: -n, pl. -r*
rye bread	**rugbrød** *n.: -et, pl. same*
rye flour	**rugmel** *n.: -et*
soft	**blød** *adj.*
sourdough	**surdej** *n.: -en*
spelt bread	**speltbrød** *n.: -et, pl. same*
wheat flour	**hvedemel** *n.: -et*
yeast	**gær** *n.: -en*

Miscellaneous	**Diverse**
apple juice	**æblejuice** *n.: -n*
beer	**øl** *n.: -len, pl. -ler;* **øl** *n.: -let (collective noun)*
bran	**klid** *n.: -det*
candle	**stearinlys** *n.: -et, pl. same*
carbonated water, club soda	**danskvand** *n.: -en, pl. same*
cocoa	**kakao** *n.: -en*
coffee	**kaffe** *n.: -n*
dish soap	**opvaskemiddel** *n.: -et* or *opvaskemidlet*
facial tissue	**papirlommetørklæde** *n.: -t, pl. -r*
flour	**mel** *n.: -et*
honey	**honning** *n.: -en*
instant coffee	**pulverkaffe** *n.: -n*
jam/jelly	**syltetøj** *n.: -et /* **gelé** *n.: -en, pl. -er*
juice	**saft** *n.: -en,* **saftevand** *n.: -et,* **juice** *n,: -en, pl. -r*
ketchup	**ketchup** *n.: -pen*
kitchen towel	**køkkenrulle** *n.: -n, pl. -r*
margarine	**margarine** *n.: -n*
mayonnaise	**mayonnaise** *n.: -n*
mustard	**sennep** *n.: -pen*
napkin	**serviet** *n.: -ten, pl. -ter*
oil	**olie** *n.: -n*
orange juice	**appelsinjuice** *n.: -n*
potato starch	**kartoffelmel** *n.: -et*
powdered sugar	**flormelis** *n.: -en*
rice	**ris** *n.: -en*
rolled oats	**havregryn** *n. (pl.)*
sauce	**sauce** *n.: -n, pl. -r,* **sovs** *n.: -en, pl. -er* or *-e*
soda	**sodavand** *n.: -en, pl. same*
soup	**suppe** *n.: -n, pl. -r*
sugar	**sukker** *n.: -et*
tartar sauce	**remoulade** *n.: -n*
tea	**te** *n.: -en*
vinegar	**eddike** *n.: -n*

Food Labels

The labels on Danish food items can be hard to decipher as many of the ingredients are described with "E-numbers." For people with allergies it may be advisable to invest in an "E-number Book" (*E-nummerbog*). They are available at bookstores for about US$30.

antioxidant	**antioxidant**
Best if served chilled	**Bør nydes afkølet**
Best if used before ...	**Mindst holdbar til ...**
biodegradable	**biologisk nedbrydelig**
calcium	**calcium** or **kalcium**
calories	**kalorier**
canned goods	**helkonserves**
carbohydrates	**kulhydrater**
cholesterol	**kolesterol**
color	**farvestof**
contains no artificial color	**indeholder ingen farvestoffer**
decaffeinated	**koffeinfri**
dietary fibers	**kostfibre**
energy	**energi**
fat	**fedt**
folic acid	**folinsyre**
food label	**varedeklaration**
gelatin	**gelatine**
ingredients	**ingredienser**
iron	**jern**
lactic acid	**mælkesyre**
lactose	**mælkesukker**
nutrition facts	**næringsindhold**
opened and refrigerated	**åbnet i køleskab**
organic	**økologisk**
packed on ...	**pakkedato**
perishables	**halvkonserves**
pitted	**udstenet**
preservative	**konserveringsmiddel**
protein	**protein**
ready to serve	**serveringsklar, klar til servering**
saturated fat	**mættede fedtsyrer**
see dates	**se datomærkning**

serving	**portion**
shake well	**omrystes før brug**
spice	**krydderi**
starch	**stivelse**
storage below +5°	**opbevaring ved højst +5°**
sugars	**sukkerarter**
two weeks refrigerated	**14 dage i køleskab**
unopened at room temperature	**uåbnet ved stuetemperatur**
unsaturated fat	**umættede fedtsyrer**
vitamins	**vitaminer**
water	**vand**

Liquor

Alcoholic beverages are available at liquor and grocery stores as well as at many gas stations. The legal drinking age in Denmark is 15, so teenagers have easy access to alcohol. At bars, patrons must be 18 to buy alcohol. Drunk driving is punished very harshly in Denmark (see pages 142–43). Beer is taxed according to alcohol content, with a higher content meaning higher tax and therefore higher price.

beer	**øl** (4.4–4.6% alcohol)
household beer	**hvidtøl**
beer on tap	**fadøl**
lager	**pilsner**
stout	**porter**
light beer	**lys øl** (2.6–2.7% alcohol)
gold beer	**guldøl** (5% alcohol)
elephant beer	**elefantøl** (7.2% alcohol)
Easter beer	**påskebryg** (7.4% alcohol—only sold around Easter)
Christmas beer	**julebryg** (7.4% alcohol—only sold around Christmas)
"P-day"	**P-dag** (the day *påskebryggen* becomes available in stores)
"J-day"	**J-dag** (the day *julebryggen* becomes available in stores)

Shopping

champagne	**champagne** *n.: -n, pl. -r*
cognac	**cognac** *n.: -en, pl. -er,*
	konjak *n.: -ken, pl. -ker*
gin	**gin** *n.: -nen, pl. -ner*
port	**portvin** *n.: -en, pl. -e*
red wine	**rødvin** *n.: -en, pl. -e*
rosé	**rosé** *n.: -en, pl. -er*
rum	**rom** *n.: -men*
schnapps, aquavit	**snaps** *n.: -en, pl. -e,*
	akvavit *n.: -ten, pl. -ter*
sherry	**sherry** *n.: -en, pl. -er*
sparkling wine	**mousserende vin** *n.: -en,*
	pl. -e
wine	**vin** *n.: -en, pl. -e*
whisky	**whisky** *n.: -en, pl. -er*
white wine	**hvidvin** *n.: -en, pl. -e*

✳ ✳ ✳ ✳ ✳ ✳

bottle opener	**oplukker** *n.: -en, pl. -e*
corkscrew	**proptrækker** *n.: -en, pl. -e*
one drink/one shot	**genstand** *n.: -en, pl. -e*
chilled	**afkølet, kold**
deep-flavored	**fyldig**
dry	**tør**
on the rocks	**med isterninger**
room temperature	**tempereret**
straight up	**uden isterninger**
sweet	**sød**

Personal Hygiene

aftershave lotion	**barbersprit** *n.: -ten*
brush	**børste** *n.: -n, pl. -r*
chapstick, lip balm	**læbepomade** *n.: -n, pl. -r*
cologne	**eau de cologne** *n.: -n, pl. -r*
comb	**kam** *n.: -men, pl. -me*
conditioner	**balsam** *n.: -men, pl. -mer*
condom	**kondom** *n.: -et, pl. -er*
contact lens	**kontaktlinse** *n.: -n, pl. -r*
cotton-tipped swab	**vatpind** *n.: -en, pl. -e*
dental floss	**tandtråd** *n.: -en*
deodorant	**deodorant** *n.: -en, pl. -er*
diaphragm	**pessar** *n.: -et, pl. -er*

durable	**holdbar** *adj.*
electric razor	**barbermaskine** *n.: -n,* *pl. -r*
eyeglasses	**briller** *n. (pl.)*
eyeliner	**eyeliner** *n.: -en, pl. -e*
eye shadow	**øjenskygge** *n.: -n*
IUD	**spiral** *n.: -en, pl. -er*
lipliner	**lipliner** *n.: -en, pl. -e*
lipstick	**læbestift** *n.: -en, pl. -er*
liquid	**flydende** *adj.*
lotion	**lotion** *n.: -en, pl. -er* or *-s*
mascara	**mascara** *n.: -en, pl. -er*
(the) morning after pill	**fortrydelsespille,** **hovsapille** *n.: -n, pl. -r*
mouthwash	**mundskyllevand** *n.: -et*
nail polish	**neglelak** *n.: -ken*
nail polish remover	**acetone** *n.: -n, pl. -r,* **neglelakfjerner**
panty shields/liners	**trusseindlæg** *n.: -get,* *pl. same*
perfume	**parfume** *n.: -n, pl. -r*
(the) pill	**p-pille** *n.: -n, pl. -r*
powder	**pudder** *n.: -et, pl. -e*
quick dry	**hurtigttørende** *adj.*
razor blade	**barberblad** *n.: -et, pl. -e*
sanitary napkin	**hygiejnebind** *n.: -et,* *pl. same*
shampoo	**shampoo, shampo** *n.: -en,* *pl. -er*
shaving cream	**barberskum** *n.: -met*
tampon	**tampon** *n.: -en, pl. -er* (Tampax and OB readily available)
toothbrush	**tandbørste** *n.: -n, pl. -r*
toothpaste	**tandpasta** *n.: -en*
toothpick	**tandstikker** *n.: -en, pl. -e*
without perfume	**uparfumeret** *adj.*

At the Hairdresser/Salon

I would like to make an appointment for a haircut.
Jeg vil gerne bestille tid til klipning.

I would like to get highlights.
Jeg vil gerne have lavet reflekser.

I would like my hair short.
Jeg vil gerne klippes kort.

bald	**skaldet**
bleach *v.*	**afblege**
blow-dry	**føntørre**
bodifying	**giver fylde**
brush *n./v.*	**børste**
comb *n.*	**kam**
conditioner	**balsam**
contain	**indeholde**
curly hair	**krøllet hår**
cut *v.*	**klippe**
dandruff	**skæl**
dry hair	**tørt hår**
dry scalp	**tør hårbund**
dye *v.*	**farve**
fine hair	**fint hår**
gel	**gelé**
hair	**hår**
haircut	**klipning**
hairdresser	**frisør**
hairspray	**hårspray**
highlights	**reflekser**
long hair	**langt hår**
manicure	**manicure**
mousse *n.*	**mousse**
normal hair	**normalt hår**
oily hair	**fedtet hår**
perm, permanent wave	**permanent**
shampoo	**shampoo**
short hair	**kort hår**
sideburns	**bakkenbarter**
split (about ends)	**spalte**
straighten	**glatte**
straight hair	**glat hår**
streaks	**striber**
tanning center	**solcenter/solarierum/ solarium**
thick hair	**tykt hår**

thin hair	**tyndt hår**
wash *v.*	**vaske**
wax *n.*	**voks**

Kids' Items

baby blanket	**svøb** *n.: -et, pl. same,* **tæppe** *n.: -t, pl. -r*
baby bottle	**sutteflaske** *n.: -n, pl. -r*
baby carriage	**barnevogn** *n.: -en, pl. -e*
baby carrier	**bæresele** *n.: -n, pl. -r*
baby monitor	**babyalarm** *n.: -en, pl. -er,* **lytteanlæg** *n.: -get, pl. same*
baby powder	**børnepudder** *n.: -et, pl. -e*
baby wipe	**baby vaskeserviet** *n.: -ten, pl. -ter,* **baby vådserviet** *n.: -ten, pl. -ter*
bassinet	**kurvevugge** *n.: -n, pl. -r*
bathtub	**badekar** *n.: -ret, pl. same*
bib	**hagesmæk** *n.: -ken, pl. -ke*
booster seat	**stoleforhøjer** *n.: -en, pl. -e*
bottle nipple	**flaskesut** *n.: -ten, pl. -ter*
bouncer seat	**skråstol med gyngefunktion** *(skråstol n.: -en, pl. -e)*
car seat	**barnestol** *n.: -en, pl. -e,* **autostol** *n.: -en, pl. -e*
car seat (booster)	**selepude** *n.: -n, pl. -r*
car seat (infant)	**baby-autostol** *n.: -en, pl. -e*
changing table	**puslebord** *n.: -et, pl. -e,* **puslekommode** *n.: -n, pl. -r*
childproof	**børnesikret** *adj.*
cloth diaper	**stofble** *n.: -en, pl. -er*
cradle	**vugge** *n.: -n, pl. -r*
crib, bed	**barneseng** *n.: -en, pl. -e*
diaper bag	**pusletaske** *n.: -n, pl. -r*
diaper bucket	**blespand** *n.: -en, pl. -e*
diaper pants	**blebukser** *n. (pl.)*
diaper rash ointment	See pages 284–85.

disposable diaper	**éngangsble** *n.: -en, pl. -er*
disposable washcloth	**engangsvaskeklud** *n.: -en, pl. -e*
formula	**modermælkserstatning** *n.: -en*
highchair	**højstol** *n.: -en, pl. -e*
insect net	**insektnet** *n.: -tet, pl. same*
nursing bra	**ammebh** *n.: -'en, pl. -'er*
nursing pads	**ammeindlæg** *n.: -get, pl. same*
pacifier	**narresut** *n.: -ten, pl. -ter*
playpen	**kravlegård** *n.: -en, pl. -e*
portable crib, playpen	**rejseseng** *n.: -en, pl. -e*
potty-chair	**pottestol** *n.: -en, pl. -e*
rain cover	**regnslag** *n.: -et, pl. same*
rice cereal	**risvælling** *n.: -en, pl. -er*
safety seat for bike	**cykelstol** *n.: -en, pl. -e*
stepping stool	**skammel** *n.: -en* or *skamlen, pl. skamler*
stroller	**klapvogn** *n.: -en, pl. -e,* **kalecheklapvogn** *n.: -en, pl. -e*
toilet seat	**toiletsæde** *n.: -t, pl. -r*
walker	**gåstol** *n.: -en, pl. -e*

At the Florist

The Danes adore flowers and enjoy gardening. Potted plants and cut flowers are cheap and readily available. Guests often bring the hostess flowers. Bouquets of fresh flowers are regularly brought to graveyards.

Do you deliver?
Bringer De ud?

What's the address?
Hvad er adressen?

annual	**etårig plante, sommerblomst**
bouquet	**buket** *n.: -ten, pl. -ter*
cut flowers	**afskårne blomster**
flower	**blomst** *n.: -en, pl. -er*

perennial	**staude, flerårig plante**
plant	**plante** *n.: -n, pl. -r*
potted plant	**potteplante** *n.: -n, pl. -r*
spray	**bårebuket** *n.: -ten, pl. -ter*
wreath	**krans** *n.: -en, pl. -e*

❋ ❋ ❋ ❋ ❋ ❋

Common Cut Flowers

carnation	**nellike** *n.: -n, pl. -r*
chrysanthemum	**krysantemum** *n.: -men, pl. -mer*
daffodil	**påskelilje** *n.: -n, pl. -r*
freesia	**fresia** *n.: -en, pl. -er* or *fresier*
gerbera	**gerbera** *n.: -en, pl. same*
lily	**lilje** *n.: -n, pl. -r*
rose	**rose** *n.: -n, pl. -r*
tulip	**tulipan** *n.: -en, pl. -er*

Eating Out

Eating establishments in Denmark are similar to those in the U.S., and meals are served about the same time of the day. The Danes also treasure their coffee breaks, when they drink tea or coffee and may eat one of those famous pastries. Trying the specialty-filled Danish lunch menu (*smørrebrød/det kolde bord*) accompanied by beer and schnapps is an absolute must. Unless otherwise noted, a fifteen percent tip is included in your bill. You may choose to leave an additional small tip (usually 20–40 kr.).

Places to Eat

bar (serving snacks)	**bar** *n.: -en, pl. -er*
bar (serving light meals)	**værtshus** *n.: -et, pl. -e,* **bodega** *n.: -en, pl. -er*
café (serving light meals)	**café** *n.: -en, pl. -er*
cafeteria (serving buffet-style meals)	**cafeteria** *n.: cafeteriet, pl. cafeterier*
catering service	**mad ud af huset**
coffee shop	**kaffebar** *n.: -en, pl. -er*
discotheque (serving snacks)	**diskotek** *n.: -et, pl. -er*
hotdog stand	**pølsevogn** *n.: -en, pl. -e*
inn (with full menu and bar)	**kro** *n.: -en, pl. -er*
pastry shop (serving cake, coffee, and tea)	**konditori** *n.: -et, pl. -er*
pizza place	**pizzaria** *n.: -et, pl. -er*
pub (serving snacks)	**pub** *n.: -ben, pl. -ber*
restaurant (with full menu and full bar)	**restaurant** *n.: -en, pl. -er*
vegetarian restaurant	**vegetarrestaurant** *n.: -en, pl. -er*

Meals

meal	**måltid** *n.: -et, pl. -er*
breakfast	**morgenmad** *n.: -en,* **morgencomplet**
brunch	**brunch** *n.: -en, pl. -er*
coffee (mid-morning)	**formiddagskaffe** *n.: -n*
coffee (mid-afternoon)	**eftermiddagskaffe** *n.: -n*

coffee (mid-evening)	**aftenkaffe** *n.: -n*
coffee and cake	**kaffe og kage**
lunch	**frokost** *n.: -en, pl. -er*
dinner	**aftensmad** *n.: -en,* **middag** *n.: -en, pl. -e*

General Vocabulary and Phrases

address	**adresse** *n.: -n, pl. -r*
à la carte	**a la carte**
buffet	**buffet** *n.: -en, pl. -er,* **tagselvbord** *n.: -et*
cancel	**afbestille** *v.: -te*
chopstick	**spisepind** *n.: -en, pl. -e*
coffee cup	**kaffekop** *n.: -pen, pl. -per*
deliver	**bringe (ud)** *v.: bragte, bragt (ud)*
fast food	**fast food**
fork	**gaffel** *n.: -en or gaflen, pl. gafler*
glass	**glas** *n.: -set, pl. same*
knife	**kniv** *n.: -en, pl. -e*
large	**stor** *adj.*
market price	**markedspris** *n.: -en, pl. -er*
medium	**mellem** *adj.*
mug (for tea)	**tekrus** *n.: -et, pl. same*
napkin	**serviet** *n.: -ten, pl. -ter*
order	**bestille** *v.: -te*
order a table	**bestille bord** *(bord n.: -et, pl. -e)*
overdone	**stegt** (fried) / **kogt** (boiled) **for meget**
phone number	**telefonnummer** *n.: -et, pl. telefonnumre*
plate	**tallerken** *n.: -en or tallerknen, pl. tallerkner*
reservation (for four people)	**reservation (til fire personer)** *n.: -en, pl. -er*
salt and pepper	**salt og peber** *(salt n.: -et, peber n.: -et)*

served with (served w/ ...)	**serveres med (serveres m/ ...)**
small	**lille** *adj.*
soup of the day	**dagens suppe** *(suppe n.: -n, pl. -r)*
spoon	**ske** *n.: -en, pl. -er*
teaspoon	**teske** *n.: -en, pl. -er*
too raw	**for råt**
too salty	**for salt**
too sweet	**for sødt**
too tough	**for sejt**
underdone	**stegt** (fried) / **kogt** (boiled) **for lidt**
wineglass	**vinglas** *n.: -set, pl. same*

Here you are.
> **Værsgo.**

Please start.
> **Værsgo at begynde.**

Thank you!
> **Tak!**

Thank you very much!
> **Mange tak!**

I would like to reserve a table for four.
> **Jeg vil gerne bestille bord til fire personer.**

What time?
> **Hvad tid?**

How long a wait for a table for two?
> **Hvor lang ventetid er der på et bord til to?**

Do you deliver?
> **Bringer I mad ud af huset?**

You call, we bring!
> **De ringer, vi bringer!**

Could I please have a menu?
> **Må jeg bede om et menukort?**

Could I please see the wine list?
> **Må jeg bede om et vinkort?**

Do you serve vegetarian food?
Serverer De vegetarmad?

What would you like to eat / drink?
Hvad kunne De tænke Dem at spise / drikke?
(formal)
Hvad kunne du tænke dig at spise / drikke?
(informal)

What can you recommend?
Hvad kan De/du anbefale?

I would like …
Jeg vil gerne have …

That's not what I ordered. I asked for …
Det har jeg ikke bestilt. Jeg bad om …

All main courses served with bread.
Alle hovedretter serveres med brød.

Could I please have the bill?
Må jeg bede om regningen?

The kitchen closes at 11 P.M.
Køkkenet lukker kl. 23.00.

Wine

See pages 209–10. (Shopping)

champagne	**champagne** *n.: -n, pl. -r*
chilled/cold	**afkølet** *adj.* **/ kold** *adj.*
decanter	**karaffel** *n.: -en* or *karaflen, pl. karafler*
deep-flavored, full-bodied	**fyldig** *adj.*
dessert wine	**dessertvin, hedvin**
dry	**tør** *adj.*
house wine	**husets vin**
light	**let** *adj.*
liqueur	**likør** *n.: -en, pl. -er*
on the rocks	**med isterninger**
red wine	**rødvin** *n.: -en, pl. -e*
rosé	**rosé** *n.: -en, pl. -er*
room temperature	**tempereret** *adj.*
schnapps	**snaps** *n.: -en, pl. -e,* **brændevin** *n.: -en*

Eating Out

sparkling wine	**mousserende vin**
straight up	**uden isterninger**
sweet	**sød** *adj.*
vintage wine	**årgangsvin** *n.: -en, pl. -e*
wine	**vin** *n.: -en, pl. -e*
wine list	**vinkort** *n.: -et, pl. same*
white wine	**hvidvin** *n.: -en, pl. -e*

Hot Drinks

coffee	**kaffe** *n.: -n*
hot chocolate	**varm chokolade**
(w/ whipped cream)	**(m/ flødeskum)**
	(chokolade n.: -n)
hot drinks	**varme drikke**
tea	**te** *n.: -en*

Cold Drinks

apple juice	**æblejuice** *n.: -n*
beer (see page 209)	**øl** *n.: -len, pl. -ler; øl*
	n.: -let (collective noun)
beer and soda	**øl og vand**
beer on tap	**fadøl**
bottled beer	**flaskeøl**
bottled water	**kildevand på flaske**
	(kildevand n.: -et)
club soda, mineral water	**danskvand** *n.: -en,*
	pl. same, **mineralvand**
	n.: -en, pl. same
cold drinks	**kolde drikke**
foreign beer	**udenlandsk øl**
orange juice	**appelsinsaft**
(freshly squeezed)	**(friskpresset)** *n.: -en*
soda	**sodavand** *n.: -en, pl. same*

Food

appetizer	**forret** *n.: -ten, pl. -ter*
assorted lunch foods	**frokostplatte** *n.: -n, pl. -r,*
	frokosttallerken
cheese plate/board	**osteanretning** *n.: -en,*
	pl. -er

children's menu	**børnemenu** *n.: -en, pl. -er*
dessert	**dessert** *n.: -en, pl. -er*
fish dish	**fiskeret** *n.: -ten, pl. -ter*
light warm dish	**lun ret** *(ret n.: -ten, pl. -ter)*
luxury assorted lunch menu	**det store kolde bord**
main course	**hovedret** *n.: -ten, pl. -ter*
meat dish	**kødret** *n.: -ten, pl. -ter*
menu	**spisekort** *n.: -et, pl. same,* **menukort** *n.: -et, pl. same*
pasta dish	**pastaret** *n.: -ten, pl. -ter*
pizza	**pizza** *n.: -en, pl. -er*
salad	**salat** *n.: -en, pl. -er*
sandwich/open-faced sandwiches	**sandwich** *n.: -en, pl. -er /* **smørrebrød** *n.: -et*
soup	**suppe** *n.: -n, pl. -r*

Preparation

al dente	**al dente**
au gratin	**gratineret**
baked	**bagt**
baked in aluminum foil	**ovnstegt i folie**
boiled	**kogt**
braised	**braiseret, grydestegt**
breaded and fried	**paneret**
broiled	**grilleret**
cured	**gravad**
deep-fried	**friturestegt**
flambéed	**flamberet**
golden brown	**gyldenbrun**
grilled	**grillet, grillstegt, grilleret**
hard-boiled	**hårdkogt**
in puff pastry	**indbagt i butterdej**
marinated	**marineret**
medium	**medium**
oven-baked	**ovnbagt, stegt i ovn**
pan-fried	**pandestegt**
poached	**pocheret**
prepare	**tilberede** *v.: -te*
rare	**rødt**
raw	**rå, råt**

roasted	**ovnstegt**
sautéed	**sauteret, brunet i smør**
skewered	**på spyd**
smoked	**røget**
soft-boiled	**blødkogt**
steamed	**dampet, dampkogt**
stewed	**stuvet**
stuffed with meat	**farseret**
thickened	**jævnet**
thickened with eggs	**legeret**
well-done	**gennemstegt**
with dressing /	**med dressing /**
sauce on the side	**sauce ved siden af**
without dressing / sauce	**uden dressing / sauce**

Breakfast

bacon	**bacon** *n.: -en* or *-et*
bread	**brød** *n.: -et, pl. same* (see page 206)
breakfast	**morgenmad** *n.: -en*
breakfast roll	**rundstykke** *n.: -t, pl. -r*
butter	**smør** *n.: -ret*
cheese	**ost** *n.: -en, pl. -e*
coffee	**kaffe** *n.: -n*
croissant	**croissant** *n.: -en, pl. -er*
dark rye bread	**rugbrød** *n.: -et, pl. same*
egg (hard-boiled/soft-boiled)	**æg (hårdkogt/blødkogt)** *n.: -get, pl. same*
fresh fruit	**frisk frugt** (*frugt n.: -en, pl. -er* or *pl. same* [*collective noun*])
fried eggs	**spejlæg** *n.: -get, pl. same*
grapefruit	**grapefrugt** *n.: -en, pl. -er*
ham	**skinke** *n.: -n, pl. -r*
hot oatmeal	**havregrød** *n.: -en*
marmalade	**marmelade** *n.: -en*
milk	**mælk** *n.: -en* (see page 201)
muffin	**muffin** *n.: -en, pl. -s*
oatmeal	**havregryn** *n. (pl.)*
omelet	**omelet** *n.: -ten, pl. -ter*
orange juice	**appelsinjuice** *n.: -n*

scrambled eggs	**røræg** *n. (pl.)*
tea	**te** *n.: -en*
toast	**ristet brød**
yogurt w/ muesli	**yoghurt m/ müesli** *(yoghurt n.: -en, pl. -er)*
white bread	**franskbrød** *n.: -et,* *pl. same*

Lunch

anchovy	**ansjos** *n.: -en, pl. -er*
apples fried with bacon	**æbleflæsk** *n.: -et or -en*
baguette	**flute** *n.: -n, pl. -s*
beet	**rødbede** *n.: -n, pl. -r*
caper	**kapers** *n.: -en, pl. same*
caviar	**kaviar** *n.: -en*
cheese	**ost** *n.: -en, pl. -e*
cod roe	**torskerogn** *n.: -en*
cucumber salad	**agurkesalat** *n.: -en*
cured salmon	**gravad laks** *(laks n.: -en,* *pl. same)*
curried herring	**karrysild** *n.: -en, pl. same*
dark rye bread	**rugbrød** *n.: -et, pl. same*
eel	**ål** *n.: -en, pl. same*
egg	**æg** *n.: -get, pl. same*
French fry	**pomfrit** *n.: -ten, pl. -ter*
fruit salad	**frugtsalat** *n.: -en, pl. -er*
green salad	**grøn salat** *(salat n.: -en,* *pl. -er)*
ham	**skinke** *n.: -n, pl. -r*
hash browns	**brasede kartofler** *n. (pl.)*
horseradish salad	**peberrodssalat** *n.: -en*
Italian salad	**italiensk salat**
liver pâté	**leverpostej** *n.: -en, pl. -e*
lobster	**hummer** *n.: -en, pl. -e*
lunch	**frokost** *n.: -en*
mackerel salad	**makrelsalat** *n.: -en, pl. -er*
meatball	**frikadelle** *n.: -n, pl. -r* (panfried) **kødbolle** *n.: -n, pl. -r* (boiled in soup or sauce)
pickled cucumber	**asie** *n.: -n, pl. -r*

pickled herring	**marinerede sild** *(sild n.: -en, pl. same)*
plaice w/ tartar sauce	**rødspættefilet m/ remoulade** *(filet n.: -en, pl. -er)*
potato salad	**kartoffelsalat** *n.: -en, pl. -er*
red cabbage	**rødkål** *n.: -en*
roast beef	**roastbeef** *n.: -en*
roast pork	**flæskesteg** *n.: -en, pl. -e*
salami	**spegepølse** *n.: -n, pl. -r*
sardine	**sardin** *n.: -en, pl. -er*
sausage	**pølse** *n.: -n, pl. -r*
sausage (pork)	**medisterpølse** *n.: -n*
shrimp	**reje** *n.: -n, pl. -r*
smoked herring	**røget sild** *(sild n.: -en, pl. same)*
smoked salmon	**røget laks** *(laks n.: -en, pl. same)*
steak tartare	**bøf tatar** *n.: -en*
tuna fish salad	**tunsalat** *n.: -en, pl. -er*
white bread	**franskbrød** *n.: -et, pl. same*

Dinner

beef	**oksekød** *n.: -et*
chicken	**kylling** *n.: -en*
dinner	**middag** *n.: -en, pl. -e*
duck	**andesteg** *n.: -en*
filet of beef	**oksefilet** *n.: -en*
garlic bread	**hvidløgsbrød** *n.: -et, pl. same*
hamburger and onions	**hakkebøf med løg** *(bøf n.: -fen, pl. -fer)*
lamb	**lammekølle** *n.: -n*
lightly smoked, boiled pork	**hamburggerryg** *n.: -gen*
pasta	**pasta** *n.: -en*
pork	**svinekød** *n.: -et*
pork chop	**svinekotelet** *n.: -ten, pl. -ter*
potato	**kartoffel** *n.: -en or kartoflen, pl. kartofler*
rice	**ris** *n.: -en*

roast pork	**flæskesteg** *n.: -en, pl. -e*
salmon steak	**laksekotelet** *n.: -ten,* *pl. -ter*
steak	**bøf** *n.: -fen, pl. -fer*
tenderloin	**mørbrad** *n.: -en, pl. -er*
turkey roast	**kalkunsteg** *n.: -en, pl. -e*
veal	**kalvekød** *n.: -et*
venison	**vildt** *n.: -et*

✳ ✳ ✳ ✳ ✳ ✳

brown gravy	**brun sovs** *(sovs n.: -en,* *pl. -e)*
cream sauce	**flødesauce** *n.: -n, pl. -r*
red wine sauce	**rødvinssauce** *n.: -n, pl. -r*
tomato sauce	**tomatsauce** *n.: -n, pl. -r*
white wine sauce	**hvidvinssauce** *n.: -n, pl. -r*

Dessert

apple cake	**æblekage** *n.: -en*
cake	**kage** *n.: -n, pl. -r*
cookie	**småkage** *n.: -n, pl. -r*
crepe	**pandekage** *n.: -n, pl. -r*
dessert	**dessert** *n.: -en, pl. -er*
fruit	**frugt** *n.: -en, pl. -er* or *pl. same*
fruit compote w/ cream	**rødgrød m/ fløde**
heavy cream	**fløde** *n.: -n*
ice cream	**is** *n.: -en*
pie	**tærte** *n.: -n, pl. -r*
puff pastry	**butterdej** *n.: -en*
rice pudding	**risalamande** *n.: -n* (traditional Christmas dessert)
sorbet	**sorbet** *n.: -ten, pl. -ter*
soufflé	**fromage** *n.: -n, pl. -r*
whipped cream	**flødeskum** *n.: -met* or *-men*

Communications

Telephone Usage

Almost every Danish home has a telephone, pay phones are readily available, and cell phones are used freely in public, too freely some claim, as many Danes seem to use them without much thought for discreetness. It is illegal to use a handheld phone while driving; headsets, microphones, and speakers must be used instead. Some pay phones are still coin-operated, but for most you need a phone card. Phone cards are available at post offices, telecommunication stores, and many kiosks. To make international calls, dial 00 + country code (1 for the U.S.) + area code + number. All Danish telephone numbers have eight digits, and they are usually given in pairs—for 75 58 85 19 one would say "seventy-five, fifty-eight, eighty-five, nineteen." Sometimes a phone number occurs as follows: +45 7558 8519. To reach an operator, dial 80 80 80 80 and ask for customer service (*kundeservice*). By dialing 80 60 40 50 (*Samtaleformidlingen*) it is possible to order international calls and pay for them collect. There is a fee for this service.

emergency calls	**alarm**—dial 112—free call from any phone
operator assistance	**telefonistassistance**—dial 80 80 80 80
directory (domestic numbers)	**oplysningen**—dial 118
directory (international numbers)	**oplysningen**—dial 113
to order international calls	**samtaleformidlingen**—dial 80 60 40 50
800 number	**frikaldsnummer**
collect call	**modtagerbetalt opkald**
* (star)	**stjerne**
# (pound)	**firkant**
country code	**landekode** (Denmark 45, U.S. 1)

* * * * * *

answering machine, voicemail	**telefonsvarer, duetsvar**
answering service	**telefonvagt** *n.: -en*
call	**ringe** *v.: -ede*
call forwarding	**viderestilling, medflyt**
call waiting	**banke-på-funktion**
cellular phone	**mobiltelefon** *n.: -en, pl. -er*
conference call	**konferencesamtale** *n.: -n, pl. -r*, **telefonmøde** *n.: -t, pl. -r*
customer service	**kundeservice** *n.: -n*
dial	**indtaste, taste** *v.: -ede*
extension	**lokalnummer, lokal**
international call	**udlandsopkald** *n.: -et, pl. same*
local call	**næropkald** *n.: -et, pl. same*
long distance call	**fjernopkald** *n.: -et, pl. same*
message	**talemeddelelse** *n.: -n, pl. -r*, **telefonbesked** *n.: -en, pl. -er*
operator	**telefonist** *n.: -en, pl. -er*
pager	**personsøger** *n.: -en, pl. -e*
pay phone, public phone	**telefonautomat** *n.: -en, pl. -er*, **telefonboks** *n.: -en, pl. -e*, **mønttelefon** *n.: -en, pl. -er*
phone card	**taletidskort** *n.: -et, pl. same*
redial	**gentag sidste opkald**
service fee	**betjeningsgebyr** *n.: -et, pl. -er*
spending limit	**beløbsgrænse** *n.: -n, pl. -r*
switchboard	**omstilling** *n.: -en*
telephone	**telefon** *n.: -en, pl. -er*
telephone book	**telefonbog** *n.: -en, pl. telefonbøger*
telephone call	**telefonopkald** *n.: -et, pl. same*, **telefonopringning** *n.: -en, pl. -er*
telephone number	**telefonnummer** *n.: -et, pl. telefonnumre*

white pages	**navneregister** *n.: -et* or *navneregistret,* *pl. navneregistre*
yellow pages	**fagregister** *n.: -et* or *fagregistret,* *pl. fagregistre*

May I borrow your phone?
Må jeg låne telefonen?

Hello.
Hallo.

May I speak to Jens Hansen?
Træffer jeg Jens Hansen?

Just a moment.
Lige et øjeblik.

I'm sorry, he is not here right now.
Han er her desværre ikke i øjeblikket.

May I leave a message?
Må jeg lægge en besked?

I'll call back later.
Jeg ringer tilbage senere.

Where would I find a pay phone?
Hvor finder jeg en telefonautomat?

Insert coin. Minimum two kr.
Indkast mønt. Minimum to kr.

Welcome to customer service.
Velkommen til kundeservice.

Please hold while you are transferred.
Vent venligst, mens De bliver omstillet.

This is the switchboard. How may I help you?
Det er omstillingen. Hvad kan jeg hjælpe med?

Cannot connect to this number.
Der er ingen forbindelse til det kaldte nummer.

The number has been disconnected.
Det kaldte nummer er udgået.

The number you called is not valid.
Det kaldte nummer er ugyldigt.

The number is busy.
Det kaldte nummer er optaget.

It costs one krone and twenty øre.
Det koster en krone og tyve.

Dial nine to leave a message.
Tryk ni, hvis De vil indtale en besked.

It costs 95 øre extra.
Det koster 95 øre ekstra.

For personal service dial two.
Ønsker De personlig betjening, tast to.

Dial three followed by the pound sign.
Tast tre, og afslut med firkant.

You are third in line.
De er nummer tre i køen.

You now have three choices. If you would like …,
dial one.
De har nu tre muligheder. Ønsker De … tast et.

Please leave a message after the beep.
Læg venligst en besked efter tonen.

Media

Newspapers and magazines in English are available in
the big cities, especially at railroad stations and airports,
but also at many kiosks. Radio programs are primarily
broadcast in Danish. An abundance of cable TV stations
are now broadcasting news and shows in English. Generally, Danish newspapers and news broadcasts offer solid
background information and in-depth reporting. Pay-per-
view service is available through *Canal Digital Kiosk* or
ViaSat Ticket.

advertisement	**reklame** *n.: -n, pl. -r*
article	**artikel** *n.: artiklen,*
	pl. artikler
boom box	**ghettoblaster** *n.: -en,*
	pl. -e
car radio	**bilradio** *n.: -en, pl. -er*
chief editor	**chefredaktør** *n.: -en,*
	pl. -er

column	**spalte** *n.: -n, pl. -r*
editor	**redaktør** *n.: -en, pl. -er*
editorial	**leder** *n.: -en, pl. -e*
letter to the editor	**læserbrev** *n.: -et, pl. -e*
listen to the radio	**høre radio** *v.: -te radio*
magazine	**blad** *n.: -et, pl. -e,*
	magasin *n.: -et, pl. -er*
newspaper	**avis** *n.: -en, pl. -er*
the news (radio)	**radioavisen**
the news (TV)	**nyhederne, tv-avisen**
pay-per-view	**Canal Digital Kiosk,**
	ViaSat Ticket
portable radio	**transistor** *n.: -en, pl. -er*
professional journal	**fagblad** *n.: -et, pl. -e*
radio	**radio** *n.: -en, pl. -er*
satellite	**parabolantenne** *n.: -n,*
	pl. -r
television	**tv** *n.: -'et, pl. -'er,*
	fjernsyn *n.: -et,*
	pl. same
watch television	**se fjernsyn** *v.: så, set*
	fjernsyn
weekly magazine	**ugeblad** *n.: -et, pl. -e*

Internet

If your hotel does not offer Internet access, a *netcafé* is a good option. They are available in many cities both for accessing the Internet and for playing computer games. They typically cost 25–30 kr. per hour and it may be necessary to make a reservation. Denmark is up-to-date on high-speed Internet access.

See page 293 for basic computer expressions.

E-mail

contacts, addresses	**adressekartotek** *n.: -et,*
	pl. -er
delete	**slet**
deleted items	**slettet post**
draft	**kladde** *n.: -n, pl. -r*
e-mail	**e-mail** *n.: -en,* **e-post**
	n.: -en

e-mail address	**e-mail-adresse** *n.: -n, pl. -r*
forward message	**videresend besked**
from	**fra**
inbox	**indbakke** *n.: -n, pl. -r*
new message	**ny meddelelse** *(meddelelse n.: -n, pl. -r)*
outbox	**udbakke** *n.: -n, pl. -r*
password	**adgangskode** *n.: -n, pl. -r*
reply	**svar til forfatter**
reply to all	**svar til alle**
send and receive	**send og hent**
sent items	**sendt post**
subject	**emne** *n.: -t, pl. -r*
user name	**brugernavn** *n.: -et, pl. -e*

Internet Café

connection	**forbindelse** *n.: -n, pl. -r*
deposit	**depositum** *n.: -met, pl. -mer*
display, monitor	**skærm** *n.: -en, pl. -e,* **monitor** *n.: -en, pl. -er*
display adapter, video card	**grafikkort** *n.: -et, pl. same*
Internet café	**netcafé** *n.: -en, pl. -er*
network card	**netkort** *n.: -et, pl. same*
special night program	**natarrangement** *n.: -et, pl. -er*

Remember to make a reservation.
   Husk at bestille tid.

Postal Service

The Danish postal service is very efficient. Generally, you can count on next-day delivery for first-class letters. Mail is delivered every day except on Sundays and religious holidays. No parcels are delivered on Saturdays. Delays may occur around Christmastime. A wide variety of tickets, for example concert tickets, are sold through the postal service (*Billetnet*), and vast numbers of bills get paid through giro transfer. Various types of packaging

materials are available at post offices. Airmail stationery is
not required. Parcels are automatically insured for a certain
amount, but additional insurance may be purchased.

Where would I find a mailbox?
Hvor er der en postkasse?

Where is the closest post office?
Hvor ligger det nærmeste posthus?

I would like to mail this letter.
Jeg vil gerne sende det her brev.

How much does it cost?
Hvor meget koster det?

address	**adresse** *n.: -n, pl. -r*
addressee	**modtager** *n.: -en, pl. -e*
airmail	**luftpost**
brown paper	**brunt papir** *(papir n.: -et)*
bubble mailer	**boblekonvolut** *n.: -ten, pl. -ter*
bubble wrap	**boblefolie** *n.: -n or -t, pl. -r*
COD (letter)	**postopkrævningsbrev** *n.: -et, pl. -e*
COD (parcel)	**postopkrævningspakke** *n.: -n, pl. -r*
content of parcel	**pakkens indhold** *(indhold n.: -et)*
envelope	**kuvert** *n.: -en, pl. -er,* **konvolut** *n.: -ten, pl. -ter*
extra fee	**tillæg** *n.: -get, pl. same,* **tillægsgebyr** *n.: -et, pl. -er*
first-class mail	**Prioritaire (A)** – blue sticker
for later pickup use mailbox at ...	**Senere afsendelse kan ske fra postkassen ved ...**
for next day delivery	**til omdeling næste dag**
fragile parcel	**forsigtigpakke** *n.: -n, pl. -r*

from	**fra**
insurance	**forsikring** *n.: -en*
insured letter	**værdibrev** *n.: -et, pl. -e*
insured parcel	**værdipakke** *n.: -n, pl. -r*
letter	**brev** *n.: -et, pl. -e*
Letters cannot contain money.	**Brevene må ikke indeholde penge.**
mailbox	**postkasse** *n.: -n, pl. -r*
mail carrier	**postbud** *n.: -et, pl. same*
Mail collected at …	**Postkassen tømmes kl. …**
maximum measurements	**Største mål, maksimummål**
minimum measurements	**Mindste mål, minimummål**
No postage necessary.	**Sendes ufrankeret. Modtager betaler portoen.**
oversized parcel	**volumenpakke** *n.: -n, pl. -r*
packing box	**postæske** *n.: -n, pl. -r*
parcel	**pakke** *n.: -n, pl. -r*
parcel post	**pakkepost** *n.: -en*
Please take a number.	**Tag venligst et nummer.**
postage	**porto** *n.: -en*
postal rate	**priser, takster**
postal service	**postvæsen** *n.: -et*
postcard	**postkort** *n.: -et, pl. same*
poster tubes	**rør** *n.: -et, pl. same*
post office	**posthus** *n.: -et, pl. -e, postkontor* *n.: -et, pl. -er*
receipt requested	**modtager kvittering påkrævet**
registered letter/parcel	**rekommanderet brev/pakke**
rush (letter)	**Post Exprés brev**
rush (parcel)	**eksprespakke** *n.: -n, pl. -r*
second-class mail	**Economique (B)** (green sticker)
send	**sende** *v.: -te*
sender	**afsender** *n.: -en, pl. -e*
Service	**Servicekasse** *n.: -n, pl. -r*
signature	**underskrift** *n.: -en, pl. -er*

Communications

stamp	**frimærke** *n.: -t, pl. -r* (postage)
	stemple *v.: -ede*; **stempel** *n.: stemplet, pl. stempler*
surface mail	**almindelig post**
to	**til**
weigh	**veje** *v.: -ede*
weight	**vægt** *n.: -en*
with stamp	**frankeret**
without stamp	**ufrankeret**

Shipping

Private shipping companies such as UPS and FedEx are also available in Denmark, especially for international shipments. They are listed in the yellow pages under *Internationale transporter*.

Weather

General Phrases and Vocabulary

How is the weather?
Hvordan er vejret?

It is cold.
Det er koldt.

It is warm.
Der er varmt.

What is the weather forecast?
Hvad siger vejrudsigten?

How cold (warm) is it outside?
Hvor koldt (varmt) er det ude?

It is 29 degrees.
Det er 29 grader.

It is two degrees below zero.
Det fryser to grader.

Supposedly it is going to be cold tomorrow.
Det skulle blive koldt i morgen.

They predict thunder tonight.
De lover tordenvejr i nat.

There is a chance of icy roads.
Der er risiko for isglatte veje.

There is not a cloud in the sky.
Himlen er helt skyfri.

The skies are partly clear.
Der er lidt blå himmel.

air	**luft** *n.: -en*
atmospheric pressure	**lufttryk** *n.: -ket*
average temperature	**gennemsnitstemperatur** *n.: -en, pl. -er*
barometer	**barometer** *n.: -et* or *barometret, pl. barometre*

below freezing	**under frysepunktet** *(frysepunkt n.: -et)*
chance of	**mulighed for**
changeable	**ustadig** *adj.*
clearing skies	**opklaring** *n.: -en*
clear skies	**klar himmel, skyfri himmel** *(himmel n.: -en* or *himlen, pl. himle)*
cloud	**sky** *n.: -en, pl. -er*
cloudy	**skyet, overskyet** *adj.*
cold	**kold** *adj.*
cool	**kølig** *adj.*
crosswind	**sidevind** *n.: -en, pl. -e*
degree	**grad** *n.: -en, pl. -er*
depression	**lavtryk** *n.: -ket, pl. same*
drizzle	**let regn** *(regn n.: -en)*
drought	**tørke** *n.: -n, pl. -r*
dry	**tør** *adj.*
five-day forecast	**femdøgnsprognose** *n.: -n, pl. -r*
flood	**oversvømmelse** *n.: -n, pl. -r*
fog	**tåge** *n.: -n*
foggy	**tåget, diset** *adj.*
frost	**frost** *n.: -en*
frosty mist	**rimtåge** *n.: -n*
full moon	**fuldmåne** *n.: -n*
hail	**hagl** *n.: -et, pl. same*
half-moon	**halvmåne** *n.: -en*
headwind	**modvind** *n.: -en*
heat stroke	**hedeslag** *n.: -et, pl. same*
heat wave	**hedebølge** *n.: -n, pl. -r*
high	**høj** *adj.*
high-pressure	**højtryk** *n.: -ket, pl. same*
high tide	**flod** *n.: -en*
humidity	**luftfugtighed** *n.: -en*
ice	**is** *n.: -en*
ice storm	**isslag** *n.: -et*
icy roads	**isglatte veje**
in spots	**pletvis, stedvis** *adj.*
lightning	**lyn** *n.: -et, pl. same*
light wind	**let vind** *(vind n.: -en)*
low	**lav** *adj.*

low tide	**ebbe** *n.: -n*
moderate wind	**jævn vind** *(vind n.: -en)*
moist	**fugtig** *adj.*
moon	**måne** *n.: -n, pl. -r*
new moon	**nymåne** *n.: -en*
northern lights	**nordlys** *n.: -et*
partly cloudy	**let skyet**
pollen count	**pollental** *n.: -let, pl. same*
precipitation	**nedbør** *n.: -en*
rain	**regn** *n.: -en*
rainy weather	**regnvejr** *n.: -et*
rough sea	**oprørt hav** *(hav n.: -et, pl. -e)*
scattered showers	**spredte byger** *(byge n.: -n, pl. -r)*
shower	**byge** *byge n.: -n, pl. -r*
sleet	**slud** *n.* (used with indef. art. **et = et slud**)
slippery	**glat** *adj.*
snow	**sne** *n.: -en*
snowdrift	**snedrive** *n.: -en, pl. -er*
snowstorm	**snestorm** *n.: -en, pl. -e*
star	**stjerne** *n.: -n, pl. -r*
sun	**sol** *n.: -en, pl. -e*
sunrise	**solopgang** *n.: -en, pl. -e*
sunset	**solnedgang** *n.: -en, pl. -e*
sunshine, sunny	**solskin** *n.: -net*
tailwind	**medvind** *n.: -en*
temperature	**temperatur** *n.: -en, pl. -er*
temperature during the day	**dagtemperatur** *n.: -en, pl. -er*
temperature at night	**nattemperatur** *n.: -en, pl. -er*
thermostat	**termostat** *n.: -en, pl. -er*
thunder	**torden** *n.: -en*
tide	**tidevand** *n.: -et*
warm	**varm** *adj.*
wave	**bølge** *n.: -n, pl. -r*
weather forecast	**vejrudsigt** *n.: -en, pl. -er*, **vejrmelding** *n.: -en, pl. -er*
wet	**våd** *adj.*
wind	**blæst** *n.: -en*, **vind** *n.: -en, pl. -e*
windy	**blæsende** *adj.*

Temperature Chart

To convert from Fahrenheit to Celsius, subtract 32 from
Fahrenheit figure, divide by nine, and multiply by five.
To convert from Celsius to Fahrenheit, multiply the Cel-
sius figure by nine, divide by five, and add 32.

Fahrenheit	Celsius
–4°	**–20°**
5°	**–15°**
14°	**–10°**
23°	**–5°**
32°	**0°**
41°	**5°**
50°	**10°**
59°	**15°**
68°	**20°**
77°	**25°**
86°	**30°**
95°	**35°**
98.6°	**37°**
104°	**40°**
212°	**100°**

Note! In the metric system, all decimal points are commas
and vice versa.

Pollen Count

pollen	**pollen** *n.: -et, pl. same*
pollen count	**pollental** *n.: -let, pl. same*
alder	**el** *n.: -len, pl. -le*
birch	**birk** *n.: -en, pl. -e*
elm	**elm** *n.: -en, pl. -e*
grass	**græs** *n.: -set, pl. -ser*
hazel	**hassel** *n.: -en or haslen,*
	pl. hasler
wormwood	**bynke** *n.: -n, pl. -r*

Time

General Vocabulary and Phrases

afternoon	**eftermiddag** *n.: -en, pl. -e*
ago; two days ago	**for … siden; for to dage siden**
day	**dag** *n.: -en, pl. -e*
day before yesterday	**i forgårs**
evening	**aften** *n.: -en, pl. -er*
every day	**hver dag**
hour	**time** *n.: -n, pl. -r*
in four years	**om fire år**
in two months	**om to måneder**
midnight	**midnat**
minute	**minut** *n.: -tet, pl. -ter*
month	**måned** *n.: -en, pl. -er*
month of May	**maj måned**
morning	**formiddag** *n.: -en, pl. -e,* **morgen** *n.: -en, pl. -er*
next week	**næste uge**
next year	**næste år**
night	**nat** *n.: -ten, pl. nætter*
noon	**klokken 12 middag**
on Saturday	**på lørdag**
on Saturdays	**om lørdagen**
second	**sekund** *n.: -et, pl. -er*
time	**tid** *n.: -en, pl. -er*
today	**i dag**
tomorrow	**i morgen**
tonight	**i aften, i nat**
twenty-four hours	**døgn** *n.: -et, pl. same*
week	**uge** *n.: -n, pl. -r*
weekday	**hverdag** *n.: -en, pl. -e*
year	**år** *n.: -et, pl. same*
yesterday	**i går**

Note! In Danish, seasons, months, days of the week, and holidays are not capitalized unless they start a sentence.

Time

Days of the Week

Monday	**mandag** *n.: -en, pl. -e*
Tuesday	**tirsdag** *n.: -en, pl. -e*
Wednesday	**onsdag** *n.: -en, pl. -e*
Thursday	**torsdag** *n.: -en, pl. -e*
Friday	**fredag** *n.: -en, pl. -e*
Saturday	**lørdag** *n.: -en, pl. -e*
Sunday	**søndag** *n.: -en, pl. -e*

day of the week	**ugedag** *n.: -en, pl. -e*
every day of the week	**alle ugens dage**
Sundays and religious holidays	**søn- og helligdage**
weekday (Monday through Saturday)	**hverdag** *n.: -en, pl. -e*

Months

month	**måned** *n.: -en, pl. -er*
January	**januar**
February	**februar**
March	**marts**
April	**april**
May	**maj**
June	**juni**
July	**juli**
August	**august**
September	**september**
October	**oktober**
November	**november**
December	**december**

Seasons

season	**årstid** *n.: -en, pl. -er*
spring	**forår** *n.: -et, pl. same*
summer	**sommer** *n.: -en, pl. somre*
fall	**efterår** *n.: -et, pl. same*
winter	**vinter** *n.: -en, pl. vintre*

in the spring	**i foråret**
in the summer	**om sommeren**

| in the fall | **i efteråret** |
| in the winter | **om vinteren** |

The Danes also divide the year according to weeks (week = *uge*). A Dane would typically say, *Jeg har ferie i uge 27 og 28* (I'll be on vacation week 27 and 28)—meaning the first two weeks in July.

Religious Holidays and Red-Letter Days

| religious holiday | **helligdag** *n.: -en, pl. -e* |
| red-letter day | **mærkedag** *n.: -en, pl. -e* |

❋ ❋ ❋ ❋ ❋ ❋

anniversary	**bryllupsdag** *n.: -en, pl. -e*
25th anniversary	**sølvbryllup** *n.: -pet, pl. -per*
50th anniversary	**guldbryllup** *n.: -pet, pl. -per*
baptism	**barnedåb** *n.: -en*
birthday	**fødselsdag** *n.: -en, pl. -e*
death	**dødsfald** *n.: -et, pl. same*
funeral	**begravelse** *n.: -n, pl. -r*
jubilee	**jubilæum** *n.: jubilæet, pl. jubilæer*
obituary	**dødsannonce** *n.: -n, pl. -r*
wedding	**bryllup** *n.: -pet, pl. -per*

❋ ❋ ❋ ❋ ❋ ❋

New Year's Eve	**nytårsaften**
New Year's Day	**nytårsdag**
leap year	**skudår**
Epiphany	**helligtrekonger**
Groundhog Day	**kyndelmisse**
Shrovetide (Feb.)	**fastelavn**
April 9th	**Danmarks besættelse** (German invasion 1940)
Palm Sunday	**palmesøndag**
Maundy Thursday	**skærtorsdag**
Good Friday	**langfredag**
Easter Day	**påskedag**
Whitsunday	**pinsedag**

May Day	**1. maj, første maj, majdag** (Labor Day)
May 5th	**Danmarks befrielsesdag** (Liberation Day 1945)
Mother's Day	**mors dag** (second Sunday in May)
Constitution Day	**grundlovsdag** (June 5— Constitution ratified June 5, 1849)
Father's Day	**fars dag** (June 5)
Midsummer Eve	**sankthansaften** (June 23)
Martinmas Eve	**mortensaften** (November 10)
Dec. 23rd	**lillejuleaften**
Christmas	**jul**
Christmas Eve	**juleaften** (the Danes celebrate the evening of the 24th instead of the 25th)
Christmas Day	**juledag**
Day after Christmas	**2. juledag**

What Time Is It?

The Danes do not use A.M. and P.M. Instead, 1 P.M. is 13.00, 2 P.M. is 14.00, etc. The Danes are punctual people; if you are expected for dinner at 18.30, you should come at 18.30.

What time is it?
> **Hvad er klokken? / Hvor mange er klokken?**

It is 10 A.M.
> **Den er ti. / Den er ti.**

It is 3 P.M.
> **Den er tre. / Den er femten.**

It is 2:10 P.M.
> **Den er ti minutter over to. / Den er 14.10. / Den er fjorten ti.**

It is 2:15 P.M.
> **Den er et kvarter over to. / Den er 14.15. / Den er fjorten femten.**

It is 2:20 P.M.
> **Den er tyve minutter over to. / Den er 14.20. / Den er fjorten tyve.**

It is 2:25 P.M.
> **Den er femogtyve minutter over to. / Den er fjorten femogtyve.**

It is 2:30 P.M.
> **Den er halv tre. / Den er fjorten tredive.**

It is 2:35 P.M.
> **Den er femogtyve minutter i tre. / Den er fjorten femogtredive.**

It is 2:40 P.M.
> **Den er tyve minutter i tre. / Den er fjorten fyrre.**

It is 2:45 P.M.
> **Den er et kvarter i tre. / Den er fjorten femogfyrre.**

It is 2:50 P.M.
> **Den er ti minutter i tre. / Den er fjorten halvtreds.**

It is 2:55 P.M.
> **Den er fem minutter i tre. / Den er fjorten femoghalvtreds.**

At What Time?

At what time?	**Hvad tid?**
When?	**Hvornår?**

What time are we eating?
> **Hvad tid skal vi spise?**

When will we be arriving?
> **Hvornår ankommer vi?**

When does the train depart?
> **Hvornår kører toget?**

When is Easter this year?
> **Hvornår falder påsken i år?**

What time does the film start?
> **Hvad tid starter filmen?**

at 6:30 P.M.	**klokken halv syv / klokken 18.30**
at 9:15 A.M.	**klokken kvart over ni / klokken 9.15**
at noon	**klokken tolv middag / klokken 12 middag**
ten o'clock sharp	**præcis klokken ti / præcis klokken 10**
around 10 A.M.	**ved titiden / cirka klokken 10**
be on time	**komme til tiden**
be late	**komme for sent**

Dates

date	**dato** *n.: -en, pl. -er*

The Danes reverse the date and month:
January 6, 2002 would be 06/01/02.
May 8, 2002 would be 08/05/02.

Today is March 29, 2002.
   I dag er det d. 29, marts 2002.

Sports and Recreation

The Danish landscape is rather flat with rolling hills and an extensive coastline. The western part of Jutland is very sandy and can be quite windblown, but its wonderful beaches are a great tourist attraction. The rest of Denmark predominantly consists of farmland, beautiful forests, streams, and lakes. The landscape, waterways, and beaches facilitate a wide variety of outdoor sports and recreation, and good indoor sports facilities are available for both team sports and individual use.

Nature Areas and Parks

bay	**bugt** *n.: -en, pl. -er*
beach	**strand** *n.: -en, pl. -e*
bike path	**cykelsti** *n.: -en, pl. -er*
bog	**mose** *n.: -n, pl. -r*
buried in sand	**tilsandet** *adj.*
cliff	**klint** *n.: -en, pl. -er*
coast	**kyst** *n.: -en, pl. -er*
conservation area	**fredet område** (*område n.: -t, pl. -r*)
creek	**bæk** *n.: -ken, pl. -ke*
dune	**klit** *n.: -ten, pl. -ter*
dune (drifting, migrating)	**vandreklit** *n.: -ten, pl. -ter*
dune plantation	**klitplantage** *n.: -n, pl. -r*
ebb	**ebbe** *n.: -n,* **lavvande**
eclipse	**eklipse** *n.: -n, pl. -r*
field	**mark** *n.: -en, pl. -r*
fjord	**fjord** *n.: -en, pl. -e*
flood	**flod** *n.: -en,* **højvande**
garden	**have** *n.: -n, pl. -r*
hill	**bakke** *n.: -n, pl. -r*
island	**ø** *n.: -en, pl. -er*
lake, pond	**sø** *n.: -en, pl. -er*
levee, dike	**dige** *n.: -t, pl. -r*
marsh	**marsk** *n.: -en*
meadow	**eng** *n.: -en, pl. -e*
moor	**hede** *n.: -n, pl. -r* (main vegetation: heather)
nature area	**naturområde** *n.: -t, pl. -r*
nature path	**natursti** *n.: -en, pl. -er*

ocean	**hav** *n.: -et, pl. -e*
park	**park** *n.: -en, pl. -er*
scenic route	**Marguerit-ruten** (see page 183)
stream, small river	**å** *n.: -en, pl. -er*
tidal area	**vadehav** *n.: -et*
tidewater	**tidevand** *n.: -et*
valley	**dal** *n.: -en, pl. -e*
waterfall	**vandfald** *n.: -et, pl. same*
wetlands	**vådområde** *n.: -et, pl. -er*
woods, forest	**skov** *n.: -en, pl. -e*

Dogs must be kept on a leash.
Hunde skal holdes i snor.

Keep off the grass.
Græsset må ikke betrædes.

Keep off the ice.
Isen er usikker.

Plants

annual	**sommerblomst** *n.: -en, pl. -er*, **etårig plante** *(plante n.: -n, pl. -r)*
barley	**byg** *n.: -gen*
beech	**bøg** *n.: -en, pl. -e*
berry	**bær** *n.: -ret, pl. same*
birch	**birk** *n.: -en, pl. -e*
bush, shrub	**busk** *n.: -en, pl. -e*
deciduous	**løvfældende** *adj.*
elm	**elm** *n.: -en, pl. -e*
evergreen	**stedsegrøn** *adj.*
fir	**fyr** *n.: -ren, pl. -re*
flower	**blomst** *n.: -en, pl. -er*
flower bulb	**blomsterløg** *n.: -et, pl. same*
garden flower	**haveblomst** *n.: -en, pl. -er*
grass	**græs** *n.: -set, pl. -ser*
heather	**lyng** *n.: -en*
mushroom	**svamp** *n.: -en, pl. -e*
oak	**eg** *n.: -en, pl. -e*
oats	**havre** *n.: -n*

perennial	**staude** *n.: -n, pl. -r,* **flerårig plante**
plant	**plante** *n.: -n, pl. -r*
rape (plant)	**raps** *n.: -en*
rye	**rug** *n.: -en*
spruce	**gran** *n.: -en, pl. -er*
tree	**træ** *n.: -et, pl. -er*
wheat	**hvede** *n.: -n*
wildflower	**vild blomst** *(blomst n.: -en, pl. -er)*

Birds, Animals, and Insects

animal	**dyr** *n.: -et, pl. same*
badger	**grævling** *n.: -en, pl. -er*
bee	**bi** *n.: -en, pl. -er*
bird	**fugl** *n.: -en, pl. -e*
butterfly	**sommerfugl** *n.: -en, pl. -e*
chicken	**kylling** *n.: -en, pl. -er*
cow	**ko** *n.: -en, pl. køer*
cuckoo	**gøg** *n.: -en, pl. -e*
deer	**rådyr** *n.: -et, pl. same*
duck	**and** *n.: -en, pl. ænder*
fly	**flue** *n.: -n, pl. -r*
fox	**ræv** *n.: -en, pl. -e*
frog	**frø** *n.: -en, pl. -er*
goat	**ged** *n.: -en, pl. -er*
goose	**gås** *n.: -en, pl. gæs*
grass snake	**snog** *n.: -en, pl. -e*
hare	**hare** *n.: -n, pl. -r*
hedgehog	**pindsvin** *n.: -et, pl. same*
hen	**høne** *n.: -n, pl. -r*
horse	**hest** *n.: -en, pl. -e*
insect	**insekt** *n.: -et, pl. -er*
lark	**lærke** *n.: -n, pl. -e*
magpie	**skade** *n.: -n, pl. -r*
mole	**muldvarpe** *n.: -n, pl. -r*
mosquito	**myg** *n.: -gen, pl. same*
mouse	**mus** *n.: -en, pl. same*
nightingale	**nattergal** *n.: -en, pl. -e*
pheasant	**fasan** *n.: -en, pl. -er*
pig	**gris** *n.: -en, pl. -e,* **svin** *n.: -et, pl. same*
quail	**agerhøne** *n.: -n, pl. agerhøns*

rat	**rotte** *n.: -n, pl. -r*
rooster	**hane** *n.: -n, pl. -r*
seal	**sæl** *n.: -en, pl. -er*
sheep	**får** *n.: -et, pl. same*
snail	**snegl** *n.: -en, pl. -e*
snake	**slange** *n.: -n, pl. -r*
sparrow	**spurv** *n.: -en, pl. -e*
squirrel	**egern** *n.: -et, pl. same*
starling	**stær** *n.: -en, pl. -e*
stork	**stork** *n.: -en, pl. -e*
swallow	**svale** *n.: -n, pl. -r*
swan	**svane** *n.: -n, pl. -r*
viper	**hugorm** *n.: -en, pl. -e*
whale	**hval** *n.: -en, pl. -er*

Beaches

When the weather is warm the Danish beaches are a sheer delight. You can pick a beach according to your personal taste and needs—big waves, sandy bottom, shallow water, etc. *Blå badestrande* (blue beaches) are the best; they are marked on the map with a blue band along the coast. The beaches along the west coast of Jutland are considered the best by most tourists, but there is often a strong undertow. It is not uncommon for people to drown there. Naturally, the water in the North Sea is also colder than the water in bays and fjords. Young children usually run naked on the beaches, and you should expect topless bathers; on some beaches you will find nudists as well. Sunscreen with SPF 8 will usually suffice. The beaches are also a great place to walk year round.

able to reach the bottom (to be)	**at kunne bunde** *(kunne v.: kunne, kunnet [pre. kan])*
bathing suit (men)	**badebukser** *n. (pl.)*
bathing suit (women)	**badedragt** *n.: -en, pl. -er*
beach	**strand** *n.: -en, pl. -e,* **badestrand**
bikini	**bikini** *n.: -en, pl. -er*
blue beach	**blå badestrand** *(badestrand n.: -en, pl. -e)*
bottom	**bund** *n.: -en, pl. -e*
crab	**krabbe** *n.: -n, pl. -r*

current	**strøm** *n.: -men, pl. -me*
drown	**drukne** *v.: -ede*
drowning accident	**drukneulykke** *n.: -n,*
	pl. -r
fish	**fisk** *n.: -en, pl. same*
jellyfish	**vandmand** *n.: -en,*
	pl. vandmænd
stinging jellyfish	**brandmand** *n.: -en,*
	pl. brandmænd
lifeguard	**livredder** *n.: -en, pl. -e*
life saving station	**redningsstation** *n.: -en,*
	pl. -er
mussel	**musling** *n.: -en, pl. -er*
naked	**nøgen** *adj.*
no swimming	**badning forbudt**
nudist	**nudist** *n.: -en, pl. -er*
offshore wind	**fralandsvind** *n.: -en*
onshore wind	**pålandsvind** *n.: -en*
oyster	**østers** *n.: -en, pl. same*
pebble	**sten** *n.: -en, pl. -e*
private beach	**privat badestrand**
public beach	**offentlig badestrand**
salt water	**saltvand** *n.: -et*
sand	**sand** *n.: -et*
sandbar	**revle** *n.: -n, pl. -r*
sandy bottom	**sandbund** *n.: -en*
seaweed	**tang** *n.: -en*
shallow	**lavvandet** *adj.*
SPF 15	**solfaktor 15**
sun	**sol** *n.: -en, pl. -e*
sunbathe	**tage solbad** *v.: tog, taget*
	solbad
sunburned	**solskoldet** *adj.*
sunglasses	**solbriller** *n. (pl.)*
sunscreen, suntan lotion	**solcreme** *n.: -n, pl. -r*
sunshade, parasol	**parasol** *n.: -len, pl. -ler*
swim	**svømme** *v.: -ede*
tanned	**solbrun** *adj.*
topless	**topløs** *adj.*
towel	**håndklæde** *n.: -t, pl. -r*
undertow	**understrøm** *n.: -men,*
	pl. -me
wade, paddle	**soppe** *v.: -ede*
wave, swell	**bølge** *n.: -n, pl. -r*

Excuse me, is it dangerous to swim here?
Undskyld, er det farligt at svømme her?

Excuse me, what does the red flag mean?
Undskyld, hvad betyder det røde flag?

It means that swimming here is dangerous.
Det betyder, at det er farligt at svømme her.

Swimming Pools

Denmark has lots of beautifully maintained indoor swimming pools—and some outdoor—with room to swim laps and dive from boards as tall as 10 meters. Many of them also have indoor water parks for younger children as well as saunas, steam baths, and tanning opportunities. At indoor pools, even young children are expected to wear bathing suits, and those with long hair should wear a cap. The pools are kept very clean. Shoes are not allowed beyond a certain point in the locker rooms, and you must shower thoroughly with soap and water, and without clothes, before entering the pool area. After a bathroom visit you must shower again before reentering the pool. People with plantar warts, infected cuts, athlete's foot or communicable diseases are expected to stay out. Guests who want to use deep areas may be asked to swim 200 meters to show proficiency.

athlete's foot	**fodsvamp** *n.: -en*
bathing suit	**badedragt** *n.: -en, pl. -er* (women)
bathing suit	**badebukser** *n. (pl.)* (men)
changing room, locker room	**omklædningsrum** *n.: -met, pl. same*
chlorine	**klor** *n.: -et or -en*
communicable disease	**smitsom sygdom** *(sygdom n.: -men, pl. -me)*
contagious	**smitsom** *adj.*
deep	**dyb** *adj.*
dive	**springe ud** *v.: sprang, sprunget ud*
dive; diving	**udspring** *n.: -et, pl. same*
diving board	**vippe** *n.: -n, pl. -r*

indoor	**indendørs** *adj.*
lifeguard	**livredder** *n.: -en, pl. -e*
locker	**værdiskab** *n.: -et, pl. -e*
men's locker room	**herreomklædning**
outdoor	**udendørs** *adj.*
outdoor pool	**friluftsbad** *n.: -et*
plantar wart	**fodvorte** *n.: -n, pl. -r*
sauna	**sauna** *n.: -en, pl. -er*
shallow	**lavvandet** *adj.*
shower	**brusebad** *n.: -et, pl. -e*
soap	**sæbe** *n.: -n*
solarium	**solarium** *n.: solariet, pl. solarier*
starting block	**startskammel** *n.: -en or startskamlen, pl. startskamler*
steam bath	**dampbad** *n.: -et, pl. -e*
swim	**svømme** *v.: -ede*
swimming pool	**svømmehal** *n.: -len, pl. -ler,* **svømmebassin** *n.: -et, pl. -er*
wash oneself	**vaske sig** *v.: -ede sig*
women's locker room	**dameomklædning**

Lockers are 2 kr.
Værdiskabe koster 2 kr.

Valuables stored at one's own risk.
Værdigenstande opbevares på eget ansvar.

Use pool at own risk.
Brug af svømmehal er på eget ansvar.

Wash thoroughly without clothes.
Vask dig grundigt uden badetøj på.

Wash after each bathroom visit.
Vask dig efter hvert toiletbesøg.

Wash entire body with soap, including hair.
Vask dig med sæbe over det hele—også håret.

Do it for your own and others' sake.
Gør det for din egen og andres skyld.

Must wash hair or wear bathing cap.
Hårvask eller badehætte påkrævet.

Children must be accompanied by an adult.
Børn kun adgang ledsaget af voksne.

Please sit or lie on towel while in sauna.
Benyt håndklæde som underlag ved saunabesøg.

Do not shave in sauna.
Barbering i sauna ikke tilladt.

Rinse thoroughly before entering sauna.
Sauna må kun bruges efter grundig skylning.

Do not wear swimsuits in sauna.
Saunaen må kun benyttes uden badetøj.

No diving.
Udspring forbudt.

Diving—only from boards and starting blocks.
Udspring—kun fra vipper og startskamler.

Bouncing on diving boards results in expulsion.
Trambolinspring på vipperne medfører bortvisning.

Do not swim under diving board.
Svøm ikke under vippen.

Only one person on diving board at a time.
En på vippen ad gangen.

No running, shouting, or pushing others into the water.
Ikke løbe, råbe eller skubbe andre i vandet.

No snorkels or flippers.
Brug af snorkel eller svømmefødder forbudt.

Fitness Centers

Fitness centers can be found as part of public sports facilities, in hotels, and as private clubs.

aerobic	**aerobic**
changing room, locker room	**omklædningsrum** *n.: -met, pl. same*
exercise	**motionere** *v.: -ede*
fitness center	**motionscenter, fitnesscenter** *(center n.: centret, pl. centre)*

free weight(s)	**håndvægt** *n.: -en, pl. -e*
massage	**massage** *n.: -n, pl. -r*
men	**herrer**
nautilus equipment	**styrketræningsudstyr**
rowing machine	**romaskine** *n.: -n, pl. -r*
solarium	**solarium** *n.: solariet,* *pl. solarier*
spinning	**spinning**
stairmaster	**stepmaskine** *n.: -n, pl. -r,* **trappemaskine** *n.: -n,* *pl. -r*
stationary bicycle	**motionscykel** *n.: -en or* *motionscyklen,* *pl. motionscykler*
treadmill	**løbebånd** *n.: -et, pl. same*
weightlifting	**styrketræning** *n.: -en*
women	**damer**

Wipe off machines after use.
Maskinerne skal tørres af efter brug.

Please use towel while working out.
Brug venligst håndklæde, mens du træner.

Soccer

Soccer is, of course, to Denmark what baseball and football are to the United States—a national sport. It is played on many different levels—the national team, the *Superliga* (the top league), many club levels, on the beaches, in parks, streets, and backyards. You can find at least one soccer field in almost any Danish village. It is played both indoors and outdoors. National games are played in *Idrætsparken*—also just called *Parken*—in Copenhagen. If you want to flatter a Danish soccer fan, mention that you are aware that Denmark beat Germany in 1992 to win the European Championship and that you have heard of Peter Schmeichel, Denmark's all-time best goalkeeper. Denmark is a regular participant in both *EM* (the European Cup) and *VM* (the World Cup).

blow the whistle	**fløjte** *v.: -ede*
corner kick	**hjørnespark** *n.: -et,* *pl. same*

crossbar	**overligger** *n.: -en, pl. -e*
field player	**markspiller** *n.: -en, pl. -e*
free kick	**frispark** *n.: -et, pl. same*
get thrown out	**blive vist ud**
	v.: blev, blevet ...,
	få en udvisning
	v.: fik, fået ...
goal	**mål** *n.: -et, pl. same*
goalkeeper	**målmand** *n.: -en,*
	pl. målmænd
goal kick	**målspark** *n.: -et, pl. same*
halftime, half	**halvleg** *n.: -en, pl. -e*
hand ball	**hånd på bolden**
header	**hovedstød** *n.: -et, pl. same*
hit	**ramme** *v.: -te*
kick	**sparke** *v.: -ede*
lose	**tabe** *v.: -te*
loss	**nederlag** *n.: -et, pl. same*
miss (a shot)	**brænde** *v.: -te*
miss (the goal)	**skyde ved siden af**
	v.: skød, skudt ved
	siden af
national team	**landshold** *n.: -et, pl. same*
penalty kick	**straffespark** *n.: -et,*
	pl. same
post	**stolpe** *n.: -n, pl. -r*
red card	**rødt kort** *(kort n.: -et,*
	pl. same)
referee	**dommer** *n.: -en, pl. -e*
regulation time	**almindelig spilletid**
save	**redde** *v.: -ede*
score	**score** *v.: -ede,* **lave mål**
	v.: -ede mål
	stilling *n.: -en, pl. -er*
shoot	**skyde** *v.: skød, skudt*
shoot-out	**straffesparkskonkurrence**
	n.: -n, pl. -r
soccer (the sport)	**fodbold** *n.*
soccer ball	**fodbold** *n.: -en, pl. -e*
soccer field	**fodboldbane** *n.: -n, pl. -r*
soccer match	**fodboldkamp** *n.: -en, pl. -e*
soccer player	**fodboldspiller** *n.: -en, pl. -e*
spectator	**tilskuer** *n.: -en, pl. -e*

stoppage time	**forlænget spilletid**
	(spilletid n.: -en)
throw-in	**indkast** *n.: -et, pl. same*
tie	**spille uafgjort** *v.: -ede*
	uafgjort
win	**vinde** *v.: vandt, vundet*
win, victory	**sejr** *n.: -en, pl. -e*
yellow card	**gult kort** *(kort n.: -et,*
	pl. same)

Team Handball

Although not very known by Americans, team handball is almost as popular in Europe as soccer. It was invented in Denmark as a way of keeping soccer players in shape during the winter. Now it is a game in itself, played both indoors and outdoors. It is an Olympic game as well, and the Danish women's team has won the gold twice. Like soccer, it is played professionally and on many club levels. The court is about the size of a basketball court, and seven players can throw, catch, and dribble the ball with their hands. The goals are much smaller than soccer goals, and shots must be taken from at least six meters away. The vocabulary used in team handball is basically the same as for soccer.

corner throw	**hjørnekast** *n.: -et,*
	pl. same
free throw	**frikast** *n.: -et, pl. same*
goal throw	**målkast** *n.: -et, pl. same*
handball (the ball)	**håndbold** *n.: -en, pl. -e*
penalty throw	**straffekast** *n.: -et,*
	pl. same
team handball (the sport)	**håndbold** *n.*

Water Sports

Denmark is the perfect place for water enthusiasts. Beaches and charming coastal towns with marinas are plentiful. On a beautiful, breezy summer day, white sails adorn the Danish waters, surfers assess the wind, and fishing rods, canoes, kayaks, diving equipment, and water skis leave the closets. Trips, lessons, and rental equipment are widely available for tourists. The Danish equivalent of a boating license/sailing qualification card is called *duelighedsbevis i sejlads for fritidssejlere*, and the permit required to drive a speedboat is called *speed-bådskørekort*. When renting a boat, the individual rental place will assess your abilities and decide whether to honor a foreign license.

bascule drawbridge	**vippebro** *n.: -en, pl. -er*
boat rentals	**bådudlejning**
boating license	**duelighedsbevis i sejlads for fritidssejlere, speedbådskørekort**
bridge will open at ...	**bro åbner kl. ...** (signs will indicate when a bascule drawbridge will open)
buoy	**afmærkningsbøje** *n.: -n, pl. -r*
buoyed channel	**afmærket rende/løb** (*rende n.: -n, pl. -r/løb n.: -et, pl. same*)
canoe	**kano** *n.: -en, pl. -er*
chart	**søkort** *n.: -et, pl. same*
direction of wind	**vindretning** *n.: -en*
dive	**dykke** *v.: -ede*
diving certificate	**dykkercertifikat** *n.: -et, pl. -er*
diving equipment	**dykkerudstyr** *n.: -et*
fish	**fiske** *v.: -ede*
harbor dues	**havnepenge** *n. (pl.)*
harbor guidebook	**havneguide** *n.: -n, pl. -r*
harbor master	**havnefoged** *n.: -en, pl. -er*
kayak	**kajak** *n.: -ken, pl. -ker*
marine forecast	**farvandsudsigt** *n.: -en, pl. -er*
pleasure boat	**lystbåd** *n.: -en, pl. -e*
power boat	**motorbåd** *n.: -en, pl. -e*
sail	**sejle** *v.: -ede*
sailing	**sejlads** *n.: -en*
sailing gear	**sejludstyr** *n.: -et*
sailmaker	**sejlmager** *n.: -en, pl. -e*
surf	**surfe** *v.: -ede*

surfboard	**surfbræt** *n.: -tet, pl. -ter*
victualling port	**provianteringshavn** *n.: -en, pl. -e*
water-ski	**stå på vandski** *v.: stod, stået på vandski*
wetsuit	**våddragt** *n.: -en, pl. -er*
wind speed	**vindstyrke** *n.: -en*
yachting	**lystsejlads** *n.: -en*
yachting harbor, marina	**lystbådehavn** *n.: -en, pl. -e*

Fishing

In order to fish in saltwater, people 17–67 years of age must have a fishing permit issued by *Fiskeriministeriet* (Department of Fisheries). Permits are available from tourist information centers and certain vacation-area kiosks. You need to provide a name, address, and social security number. The receipt and proper identification must be carried while fishing. To fish in freshwater an additional permit must be purchased at the individual fishing facility or the local fishing store. The most commonly caught fish are listed below.

angler	**lystfisker** *n.: -en, pl. -e*
bait	**madding** *n.: -en,* **agn** *n.: -en*
catch and release	**tvungen genudsætning** *(genudsætning n.: -en)*
deep-sea fishing	**dybvandsfiskeri** *n.: -et*
fish	**fiske** *v.: -ede*
fishing boat	**fiskekutter** *n.: -en, pl. -e*
fishing harbor	**fiskerihavn** *n.: -en, pl. -e*
fishing permit	**fisketegn** *n.: -et, pl. same*
fishing rod	**fiskestang** *n.: -en, pl. fiskestænger*
hook	**krog** *n.: -en, pl. -e*
minimum size limit	**mindstemål** *n.: -et, pl. same*

* * * * * *

cod	**torsk** *n.: -en, pl. same*
dab	**ising** *n.: -en, pl. -er*

eel	**ål** *n.: -en, pl. same*
mackerel	**makrel** *n.: -len, pl. -ler*
perch	**aborre** *n.: -n, pl. -r*
pike	**gedde** *n.: -n, pl. -r*
plaice	**rødspætte** *n.: -n, pl. -r*
trout (sea, river, rainbow)	**ørred (havørred, bækørred, regnbueørred)** *n.: -en, pl. -er*
turbot	**pighvar** *n.: -ren, pl. -rer*

Hunting

Hunting season runs from September 1 to January 31, but more specific dates apply to individual species. In order to hunt in Denmark you must send a copy of your present hunting permit to:

Skov -og Naturstyrelsen
Haraldsgade 53
2100 København Ø
Tel: +45 39 47 21 59

For a fee of approximately 500 kr. you will be issued a Danish hunting permit. Allow ample time for processing.

hunter	**jæger** *n.: -en, pl. -e*
hunting	**jagt** *n.: -en, pl. -er*
hunting permit	**jagttegn** *n.: -et, pl. same*
hunting season	**jagtsæson** *n.: -en, pl. -er*
rifle	**riffel** *n.: -en or riflen, pl. rifler*, **gevær** *n.: -et, pl. -er*

✱ ✱ ✱ ✱ ✱ ✱

deer	**rådyr** *n.: -et, pl. same*
duck	**and** *n.: -en, pl. ænder*
fox	**ræv** *n.: -en, pl. -e*
hare	**hare** *n.: -n, pl. -r*
pheasant	**fasan** *n.: -en, pl. -er*
quail	**agerhøne** *n.: -n, pl. agerhøns*

Golf

Denmark now has more than 130 beautiful golf courses—many of them located in the woods and fields of former farms. Call the individual club for availability and green fees (usually around 250 kr.). The clubs typically offer an 18-hole course and a par-3 course—also called *øvebane* (practice course). The practice course is usually open to any player, but to play on the 18-hole course you need an official handicap. Some clubs allow you to play with a handicap of 54, others require 48 or 36—a few even lower. Most of the English golf terms are used by Danish golfers as well.

clubhouse	**klubhus** *n.: -et, pl. -e*
glove	**handske** *n.: -n, pl. -r*
golf ball	**golfbold** *n.: -en, pl. -e*
golf cart	**golfvognl** *n.: -en, pl. -e*
golf club	**golfklub** *n.: -ben, pl. -ber* (the kind you belong to)
	golfkølle *n.: -n, pl. -r* (the kind you hit the ball with)
golf course	**golfbane** *n.: -n, pl. -r*
handicap card	**handicapbevis** *n.: -et, pl. -er*, **handicapkort** *n.: -et, pl. same*
hole	**hul** *n.: -let, pl. -ler*
iron	**jern** *n.: -et, pl. same*
tee off	**slå ud** *v.: slog, slået ud*
wood	**kølle** *n.: -n, pl. -r*

It's your honor.
  Du har honnøren.

Other Sports

Many other sports are popular and available to tourists in Denmark, both as participants and spectators.

archery	**bueskydning**
badminton	**badminton**
basketball	**basketball**

beach volleyball	**beach-volley**
bicycle race	**cykelløb**
bowling	**bowling**
boxing	**boksning**
bungee jumping	**elastikspring**
car racing	**bilvæddeløb**
climbing indoors	**vægklatring**
climbing wall	**klatrevæg**
court, field, track	**bane**
cycling	**cykelsport**
dog racing	**hundevæddeløb**
fencing	**fægtning**
gliding	**svæveflyvning**
horse race	**hestevæddeløb**
horseback riding	**ridning**
ice-skating	**skøjteløb**
in-line skates	**inline rulleskøjter**
martial arts	**kampsport**
miniature golf	**minigolf**
model airplanes	**modelflyvning**
parachuting	**faldskærmsudspring**
racquet	**ketsjer**
rock climbing	**klippeklatring**
tennis	**tennis**
tilting at the ring	**ringridning**
trotting track	**travbane**
volleyball	**volleyball**
wrestling	**brydning**

Sightseeing and Entertainment

The opportunities for sightseeing and entertainment are many, varied and often similar to those in the United States. Tourist guides, brochures, and maps are available at tourist information centers, in bookstores, etc., and they are usually translated into English. Therefore the following word list is meant only to provide a few pointers. Remember to reserve seats—for movies, too. You can order movie tickets over the phone, and the seats are reserved. Denmark has become known for hosting great outdoor music festivals, the two biggest being *Midtfyns Festival* and *Roskilde Festival*. Copenhagen hosts a whole week of jazz every summer, and "green concerts" (*Grønne koncerter*) are held in a number of locations. A brewery tour is worth considering, too.

Buying Tickets

adult ticket	**voksenbillet** *n.: -ten, pl. -ter*
audience	**publikum** *n.: -et, pl. -er*
available seat	**ledig plads** (*plads n.: -en, pl. -er*)
balcony	**balkon** *n.: -en, pl. -er*
box office	**billetkontor** *n.: -et, pl. -er*
child ticket	**børnebillet** *n.: -ten, pl. -ter*
closed	**lukket** (*lukke v.: -ede*)
evening performance	**aftenforestilling** *n.: -en, pl. -er*
first row	**første række** (*række n.: -n, pl. -r*)
guided tour	**rundvisning** *n.: -en, pl. -er*
hours	**åbningstider** (*tid n.: -en, pl. -er*) (See Time.)
matinee	**matiné** *n.: -en, pl. -er*, **eftermiddagsforestilling** *n.: -en, pl. -er*
orchestra seat	**orkesterplads** *n.: -en, pl. -er*
seat	**siddeplads** *n.: -en, pl. -er*
sold out	**udsolgt**
ticket	**billet** *n.: -ten, pl. -ter*

History

Stone Age	**stenalderen** *n.*
Bronze Age	**bronzealderen** *n.*
Iron Age	**jernalderen** *n.*
Viking Period	**vikingetiden** *n.*
Middle Ages	**middelalderen** *n.*
bunker	**bunker** *n.: -en, pl. -e* or *-s* (from WWII)
burial mound	**gravhøj** *n.: -en, pl. -e*
castle	**borg** *n.: -en, pl. -e*
drawbridge	**vindebro** *n.: -en, pl. -er*
manor house	**herregård** *n.: -en, pl. -e*
moat	**voldgrav** *n.: -en, pl. -e*
museum of natural history	**naturhistorisk museum** (*museum n.: museet, pl. museer*)
palace	**slot** *n.: -tet, pl. -te*
runic stone	**runesten** *n.: -en, pl. -e*
Viking	**viking** *n.: -en, pl. -er*

Visual Arts

art	**kunst** *n.: -en*
art exhibit	**kunstudstilling** *n.: -en, pl. -er*
artist	**kunstner** (male) *n.: -en, pl. -e*, **kunstnerinde** (female) *n.: -n, pl. -r*
art museum	**kunstmuseum** *n.: kunstmuseet, pl. kunstmuseer*
auction	**auktion** *n.: -en, pl. -er*
draw	**tegne** *v.: -ede*
etching	**ætsning** *n.: -en, pl. -er*
exhibit	**udstilling** *n.: -en, pl. -er*
gallery	**galleri** *n.: -et, pl. -er*
lithograph	**litografi** *n.: -et, pl. -er*
museum	**museum** *n.: museet, pl. museer*
oil painting	**oliemaleri** *n.: -et, pl. -er*
paint	**male** *v.: -ede*

photography exhibit	**fotoudstilling** *n.: -en, pl. -er*
sculpture	**skulptur** *n.: -en, pl. -er*
statue	**statue** *n.: -n, pl. -r*
vernissage	**fernisering** *n.: -en, pl. -er*
visual arts	**billedkunst** *n.: -en*
watercolor	**akvarel** *n.: -len, pl. -ler*

Movies

Ratings:
T.O. 15 (Tilladt over 15)   Allowed over 15
FR.U. 7 (Frarådes under 7) Not recommended for
children under 7

❋ ❋ ❋ ❋ ❋

action movie	**spændingsfilm** *n.: -en, pl. same*
cartoon	**tegnefilm** *n.: -en, pl. same*
children's movie	**børnefilm** *n.: -en, pl. same*
comedy	**komedie** *n.: -n, pl. -r*
costume	**kostume** *n.: -t, pl. -r*
documentary	**dokumentarfilm** *n.: -en, pl. same*
dogma movie	**dogmefilm** *n.: -en, pl. same*
DVD	**DVD** *n.: -'en, pl. -'er*
film	**film** *n.: -en, pl. same*
movie theater	**biograf** *n.: -en, pl. -er*
new release	**premiere film**
pay-per-view	**Canal Digital Kiosk, ViaSat Ticket**
playing time	**spilletid** *n.: -en, pl. -er,* **varighed** *n.: -en*
preview	**forfilm** *n.: -en, pl. same*
rent a movie	**leje en film** *v.: -ede en film*
single feature	**helaftensfilm** *n.: -en, pl. same*
subtitle	**undertekst** *n.: -en, pl. -er*
videotape	**videobånd** *n.: -et, pl. same,* **videofilm** *n.: -en, pl. same*

Theater and Dance

actor/actress	**skuespiller** (male) *n.: -en, pl. -e*, **skuespillerinde** (female) *n.: -n, pl. -r*
ballet	**ballet** *n.: -ten, pl. -ter*
ballet dancer	**balletdanser** (male) *n.: -en, pl. -e*, **balletdanserinde** (female) *n.: -n, pl. -r*
box	**loge** *n.: -n, pl. -r*
cabaret show	**kabaretforestilling** *n.: -en, pl. -er*
children's theater	**børneteater** *n.: -et* or *børneteatret, pl. børneteatre*
choreography	**koreografi** *n.: -en, pl. -er*
costume	**kostume** *n.: -t, pl. -r*
dance	**dans** *n.: -en*
gala performance	**gallaforestilling** *n.: -en, pl. -er*
intermission	**pause** *n.: -n, pl. -r*
marionette theater	**dukketeater** *n.: -et* or *dukketeatret, pl. dukketeatre*
musical	**operette** *n.: -n, pl. -r*, **musical** *n.: -en, pl. -er* or *-s*
opera	**opera** *n.: -en, pl. -er*
opera singer	**operasanger** (male) *n.: -en, pl. -e*, **operasangerinde** (female) *n.: -n, pl. -r*
play	**skuespil** *n.: -let, pl. same*
playwright	**dramatiker** *n.: -en, pl. -e*, **skuespilforfatter** *n.: -en, pl. -e*
rehearsal	**generalprøve** *n.: -n, pl. -r*
revolving stage	**drejescene** *n.: -n, pl. -r*
set piece	**kulisse** *n.: -n, pl. -r*
theater	**teater** *n.: -et* or *teatret, pl. teatre*
theater performance	**teaterforestilling** *n.: -en, pl. -er*

theater play	**teaterstykke** n.: -t, pl. -r
The Royal Theater	**Det Kongelige Teater**
understudy	**understudy** n.
ventriloquist	**bugtaler** n.: -en, pl. -e

Music

acoustic	**akustisk** adj.
acoustics	**akustik** n.: -ken
backstage	**bag scenen** (scene n.: -n, pl. -r)
band	**band** n.: -et, pl. -s
chamber music	**kammermusik** (musik n.: -ken)
choir	**kor** n.: -et, pl. same
classical music	**klassisk musik**
composer	**komponist** n.: -en, pl. -er
concert	**koncert** n.: -en, pl. -er
conductor	**dirigent** n.: -en, pl. -er
ear plug	**øreprop** n.: -pen, pl. -per
encore	**ekstranummer** n.: -et or ekstranumret, pl. ekstranumre
music	**musik** n.: -ken
music festival	**musikfestival** n.: -en, pl. -er
opening band	**opvarmningsgruppe** n.: -n, pl. -r
orchestra	**orkester** n.: -et or orkestret, pl. orkestre
play	**spille** v.: -ede
sing	**synge** v.: sang, sunget

Instruments

bow instrument	**strygeinstrument** n.: -et, pl. -er
percussion instrument	**slaginstrument** n.: -et, pl. -er
stringed instrument	**strengeinstrument** n.: -et, pl. -er
wind instrument	**blæseinstrument** n.: -et, pl. -er

✱ ✱ ✱ ✱ ✱ ✱

Sightseeing and Entertainment

accordion	**harmonika** *n.: -en, pl. -er*
base	**bas** *n.: -sen, pl. -ser*
cello	**cello** *n.: -en, pl. -er*
clarinet	**klarinet** *n.: -ten, pl. -ter*
drum	**tromme** *n.: -n, pl. -r*
flute	**fløjte** *n.: -n, pl. -r*
guitar	**guitar** *n.: -en, pl. -er*
harp	**harpe** *n.: -n, pl. -r*
piano	**klaver** *n.: -et, pl. -er*
saxophone	**saxofon** *n.: -en, pl. -er*
trombone	**trombone** *n.: -n, pl. -r*
trumpet	**trompet** *n.: -en, pl. -er*
viola	**bratsch** *n.: -en, pl. -er*
violin	**violin** *n.: -en, pl. -er*

Literature

author	**forfatter** (male) *n.: -en, pl. -e*, **forfatterinde** (female) *n.: -n, pl. -r*
book	**bog** *n.: -en, pl. bøger*
book review	**boganmeldelse** *n.: -n, pl. -r*
borrow	**låne** *v.: -te*
checkout	**udlån** *n.: -et*
comic strip	**tegneserie** *n.: -n, pl. -r*
dictionary	**ordbog** *n.: -en, pl. ordbøger*
fiction	**skønlitteratur** *n.: -en*
hardcover	**med stift bind**
librarian	**bibliotekar** *n.: -en, pl. -er*
library	**bibliotek** *n.: -et, pl. -er*
literature	**litteratur** *n.: -en*
non-fiction	**faglitteratur** *n.: -en*
novel	**roman** *n.: -en, pl. -er*
paperback	**billigbog** *n.: -en, pl. billigbøger*
poem	**digt** *n.: -et, pl. -e*
reference book	**håndbog** *n.: -en, pl. håndbøger*
return date	**afleveringsdato** *n.: -en, pl. -er*
short story	**novelle** *n.: -n, pl. -r*

Bars and Dancing

bar	**bar** *n.: -en, pl. -er*
beer	**øl** *n.: -len, pl. -ler; -let* *(collective noun)*
bouncer	**udsmider** *n.: -en, pl. -e*
café	**café** *n.: -en, pl. -er*
club soda	**danskvand** *n.: -en,* *pl. same*
cover charge	**entré** *n.: -en*
dance	**danse** *v.: -ede*
dance restaurant	**danserestaurant** *n.: -en,* *pl. -er,* **dansested** *n.: -et, pl. -er*
discotheque, disco	**diskotek** *n.: -et, pl. -er*
drink	**drikke** *v.: drak, drukket*
drink, shot	**genstand** *n.: -en, pl. -e*
soda	**sodavand** *n.: -en, pl. same*

Adult Entertainment

blue movie	**pornofilm** *n.: -en,* *pl. same*
escort service	**eskortbureau** *n.: -et,* *pl. -er*
porn shop	**pornoforretning** *n.: -en,* *pl. -er*
prostitute	**prostitueret kvinde,** **luder** or **ludder** *n.: -en, pl. -e (slang)*
striptease	**striptease** *n.: -en*

Parks

amusement park	**forlystelsespark** *n.: -en,* *pl. -er,* **sommerland** *n.: -et*
aquarium	**akvarium** *n.: akvariet,* *pl. akvarier*
bumper car	**radiobil** *n.: -en, pl. -er*
Ferris wheel	**pariserhjul** *n.: -et,* *pl. same*
merry-go-round	**karrusel** *n.: -len, pl. -ler*

planetarium	**planetarium** *n.:* *planetariet,* *pl. planetarier*
roller coaster	**rutschebane** *n.: -n, pl. -r*
video arcade	**videoarkade** *n.: -n, pl. -r*
water park	**badeland** *n.: -et*
water slide	**vandrutschebane** *n.: -n,* *pl. -r*

Circus

acrobat	**akrobat** *n.: -en, pl. -er*
arena	**arena** *n.: -en, pl. -er*
circus	**cirkus** *n.: -et, pl. -er*
clown	**klovn** *n.: -en, pl. -e*
fairgrounds	**markedsplads** *n.: -en,* *pl. -er*
ringmaster	**sprechstallmeister** *n.: -en, pl. -e*
tent	**telt** *n.: -et, pl. -e*
tightrope walker	**linedanser** *n.: -en, pl. -e*

Zoo

anteater	**myresluger** *n.: -en, pl. -e*
antelope	**antilope** *n.: -n, pl. -r*
bear	**bjørn** *n.: -en, pl. -e*
camel	**kamel** *n.: -en, pl. -er*
crocodile	**krokodille** *n.: -n, pl. -r*
dromedary	**dromedar** *n.: -en, pl. -er*
elephant	**elefant** *n.: -en, pl. -er*
endangered species	**truet dyreart** (*dyreart* *n.: -en, pl. -er*)
flamingo	**flamingo** *n.: -en, pl. -er*
giraffe	**giraf** *n.: -fen, pl. -fer*
hippopotamus	**flodhest** *n.: -en, pl. -e*
kangaroo	**kænguru** *n.: -en, pl. -er*
koala	**koala** *n.: -en, pl. -er*
leopard	**leopard** *n.: -en, pl. -er*
lion	**løve** *n.: -n, pl. -r*
monkey	**abe** *n.: -n, pl. -r*
ostrich	**struds** *n.: -en, pl. -er*
panda	**panda** *n.: -en, pl. -er*

pelican	**pelikan** *n.: -en, pl. -er*
penguin	**pingvin** *n.: -en, pl. -er*
polar bear	**isbjørn** *n.: -en, pl. -e*
rhinoceros	**næsehorn** *n.: -et, pl. same*
snake	**slange** *n.: -n, pl. -r*
seal	**sæl** *n.: -en, pl. -er*
sea lion	**søløve** *n.: -n, pl. -r*
tapir	**tapir** *n.: -en, pl. -er*
tiger	**tiger** *n.: -en, pl. -e or tigre*
wolf	**ulv** *n.: -en, pl. -e*
zebra	**zebra** *n.: -en, pl. -er*
zoo	**zoologisk have**
zookeeper	**dyrepasser** *n.: -en, pl. -e*

Games and Toys

ball	**bold** *n.: -en, pl. -e*
balloon	**ballon** *n.: -en, pl. -er*
bead	**perle** *n.: -n, pl. -r*
bicycle	**cykel** *n.: -en or cyklen, pl. cykler*
block	**klods** *n.: -en, pl. -er*
board game	**brætspil** *n.: -let, pl. same*
car	**bil** *n.: -en, pl. -er*
chess	**skak** *n.: -ken*
colored pencil	**farveblyant** *n.: -en, pl. -er*
coloring book	**malerbog** *n.: -en, pl. malerbøger*
computer game	**computerspil** *n.: -let, pl. same*
crayon	**farve** *n.: -n, pl. -r*
croquet	**kroket** *n.: -en or -et*
crossword puzzle	**krydsogtværs** *n.: -en, pl. -er*
doll	**dukke** *n.: -n, pl. -r*
drawing pad	**tegneblok** *n.: -ken, pl. -ke*
game	**spil** *n.: -let, pl. same*
hide-and-seek	**skjul**
jump rope	**sjippetov** *n.: -et, pl. -e*
kite	**drage** *n.: -n, pl. -r*
lego	**legoklods** *n.: -en, pl. -er*
marker	**tusch** *n.: -en*

miniature golf	**minigolf** *n.: -en*
model airplane	**modelflyver** *n.: -en, pl. -e*
monopoly	**matador**
musical mobile	**musikuro** *n.: -en, pl. -er*
paper doll	**påklædningsdukke** *n.: -n, pl. -r*
Parcheesi	**ludo** *n.: -et*
playground	**legeplads** *n.: -en, pl. -er*
puzzle	**puslespil** *n.: -let, pl. same*
rocking horse	**gyngehest** *n.: -en, pl. -e*
sandbox	**sandkasse** *n.: -n, pl. -r*
seesaw	**vippe** *n.: -n, pl. -r*
sled	**kælk** *n.: -en, pl. -e*
tag	**tik**
teddy bear	**bamse** *n.: -n, pl. -r*
toys	**legetøj** *n. (pl.)*
tricycle	**trehjulet cykel**
truck	**lastbil** *n.: -en, pl. -er*

Crafts

embroider	**brodere** *v.: -ede*
crochet	**hækle** *v.: -ede*
do macrame	**knytte** *v.: -ede*
do needlepoint	**sy stramaj** *v.: -ede stramaj*
knit	**strikke** *v.: -ede*
sew (on sewing machine)	**sy (på symaskine)** *v.: -ede*
sewing machine	**symaskine** *n.: -n, pl. -r*
tie-dyeing	**viklebatik** *n.: -ken*

Health

The Danes enjoy nationalized health and dental care, and prescription medicine is subsidized. As a tourist, you will have access to medical and dental care, but you will have to cover the costs and make arrangements with your insurance upon your return. Emergency medicine is excellent and readily available. For non-emergency treatment, the first step is to see a family practitioner who may refer you to a specialist. A normal consultation costs about US$40. Lab work and drugs would be additional. Prescription medicine is best brought from home, and by U.S. standards the availability of over-the-counter medicine is rather limited. Over-the-counter drugs are available at pharmacies and to a very small extent at grocery stores. It is recommended to bring a container from home, so the pharmacist can try to match the active ingredients as closely as possible. Medicine that causes drowsiness is marked with a red triangle. Hygiene is generally very high in Denmark, food poisoning is very rare, and it is safe to drink tap water unless otherwise stated. Visit an optician to buy contact lens accessories.

General Vocabulary and Phrases

admission history	**indlæggelsesjournal** *n.: -en, pl. -er*
admissions	**modtagelse** *n.: -n*
ambulance	**ambulance** *n.: -n, pl. -r*
doctor	**læge** *n.: -n, pl. -r*
emergency room	**skadestue** *n.: -n, pl. -r*
family practitioner	**praktiserende læge**
first aid	**førstehjælp** *n.: -en*
hospital	**sygehus** *n.: -et, pl. -e,* **hospital** *n.: -et, pl. -er*
illness	**sygdom** *n.: -men, pl. -me*
intensive care	**intensivafdeling** *n.: -en, pl. -er*
nurse	**sygeplejerske** *n.: -n, pl. -r*
outpatient clinic	**ambulatorium** *n.: ambulatoriet, pl. ambulatorier*
over-the-counter medicine	**håndkøbsmedicin** *n.: -en*

paramedic	**falckredder** *n.: -en, pl. -e*
patient record	**journal** *n.: -en, pl. -er*
pharmacy	**apotek** *n.: -et, pl. -er*
physical exam	**lægeundersøgelse** *n.: -n, pl. -r*
prescription	**recept** *n.: -en, pl. -er*
rounds	**stuegang** *n.. -en*
stretcher	**båre** *n.: -n, pl. -r*
to be admitted to a hospital	**at blive indlagt på et hospital**
treat	**behandle** *v.: -ede*
treatment	**behandling** *n.: -en, pl. -er*

✳ ✳ ✳ ✳ ✳ ✳

Where is the nearest hospital?
Hvor ligger det nærmeste hospital?

I need a doctor, please.
Jeg har brug for en læge.

Call an ambulance!
Tilkald en ambulance!

I feel sick.
Jeg føler mig syg.

I am nauseous.
Jeg har kvalme.

Where is the nearest pharmacy?
Hvor ligger det nærmeste apotek?

Do you have medical insurance?
Har De sygesikring?

Yoy will have to pay for treatment yourself.
De skal selv betale for behandlingen.

Where does it hurt?
Hvor gør det ondt?

What's wrong?
Hvad er der i vejen?

What caused it?
Hvad er årsagen?

When did you last have a tetanus shot?
Hvornår er De sidst blevet vaccineret mod stivkrampe?

I have a headache.
Jeg har hovedpine.

I think my leg is broken.
Jeg tror, mit ben er brækket.

I have a pain in my chest.
Jeg har ondt i brystet.

I suffer from diabetes.
Jeg lider af sukkersyge.

I have high blood pressure.
Jeg har højt blodtryk.

My ... hurts.
Jeg har ondt i min ... ("min" if the following noun is common gender, singular)
Jeg har ondt i mit ... ("mit" if the following noun is neuter gender, singular)
Jeg har ondt i mine ... ("mine" if the following noun is plural)

The Body

adenoids	**polypper** n. (pl.)
adrenal gland	**binyre** n.: -n, pl. -r
ankle	**ankel** n.: -en or anklen, pl. ankler
appendix	**blindtarm** n.: -en, pl. -e
arm	**arm** n.: -en, pl. -e
artery	**arterie** n.: -n, pl. -r, **pulsåre** n.: -n, pl. -r
back	**ryg** n.: -gen, pl. -ge
bladder	**blære** n.: -n, pl. -r
blood	**blod** n.: -et
bone	**knogle** n.: -n, pl. -r
bowel movement	**afføring** n.: -en
breast	**bryst** n.: -et, pl. -er
buttock	**balle** n.: -n, pl. -r
cartilage	**brusk** n.: -en, pl. -e
cerebral hemorrhage	**hjerneblødning** n.: -en, pl. -er
cervix	**livmoderhals** n.: -en, pl. -e
cheek	**kind** n.: -en, pl. -er

chest	**bryst** *n.: -et*
chin	**hage** *n.: -n, pl. -r*
ear	**øre** *n.: -t, pl. -r*
eardrum	**trommehinde** *n.: -n, pl. -r*
elbow	**albue** *n.: -n, pl. -r*
eye	**øje** *n.: -t, pl. øjne*
face	**ansigt** *n.: -et, pl. -er*
fallopian tube	**æggeleder** *n.: -en, pl. -e*
finger	**finger** *n.: -en, pl. fingre*
foot	**fod** *n.: -en, pl. fødder*
forehead	**pande** *n.: -n, pl. -r*
front tooth	**fortand** *n.: -en,* *pl. fortænder*
gland	**kirtel** *n.: -en or kirtlen,* *pl. kirtler*
hair	**hår** *n.: -et*
hand	**hånd** *n.: -en, pl. hænder*
head	**hoved** *n.: -et, pl. -er*
heart	**hjerte** *n.: -t, pl. -r*
heart valve	**hjerteklap** *n.: -pen,* *pl. -per*
heel	**hæl** *n.: -en, pl. -e*
hip	**hofte** *n.: -n, pl. -r*
immune system	**immunforsvar** *n.: -et,* *pl. same*
intestine	**tarm** *n.: -en, pl. -e*
kidney	**nyre** *n.: -n, pl. -r*
knee	**knæ** *n.: -et, pl. same*
leg	**ben** *n.: -et, pl. same*
ligament	**ledbånd** *n.: -et, pl. same,* **ligament** *n.: -et, pl. -er*
lip	**læbe** *n.: -n, pl. -r*
liver	**lever** *n.: -en, pl. -e*
lower back	**lænd** *n.: -en, pl. -er*
lung	**lunge** *n.: -n, pl. -r*
lymph node	**lymfekirtel** *n.: -en or* *lymfekirtlen, pl.* *lymfekirtler*
molar	**kindtand** *n.: -en,* *pl. kindtænder*
mouth	**mund** *n.: -en, pl. -e*
muscle	**muskel** *n.: -en or* *musklen, pl. muskler*

nail	**negl** *n.: -en, pl. -e*
neck	**hals** *n.: -en, pl. -e*
nerve	**nerve** *n.: -n, pl. -r*
nervous breakdown	**nervesammenbrud** *n.: -et, pl. same*
nose	**næse** *n.: -n, pl. -r*
ovary	**æggestok** *n.: -ken, pl. -ke*
penis	**penis** *n.: -en, pl. -er,* **lem** *n.: -met*
prostate	**prostata** *n.: -en, pl. -er*
pulse	**puls** *n.: -en, pl. -e*
rib	**ribben** *n.: -et, pl. same*
shoulder	**skulder** *n.: -en, pl. skuldre*
skin	**skind** *n.: -et,* **hud** *n.: -en*
spine	**rygrad** *n.: -en, pl. -e*
spleen	**milt** *n.: -en, pl. -e*
stomach	**mave** *n.: -n, pl. -r*
tailbone	**haleben** *n.: -et, pl. same*
tendon	**sene** *n.: -n, pl. -r*
thigh	**lår** *n.: -et, pl. same*
throat	**hals** *n.: -en, pl. -e*
thumb	**tommelfinger** *n.: -en, pl. tommelfingre*
tissue	**væv** *n.: -et, pl. same*
toe	**tå** *n.: -en, pl. tæer*
tongue	**tunge** *n.: -n, pl. -r*
tonsils	**mandler** *n. (pl.)*
tooth	**tand** *n.: -en, pl. tænder*
urine	**urin** *n.: -en*
uterus	**livmoder** *n.: -en, pl. -e*
vagina	**skede** *n.: -n, pl. -r,* **vagina** *n.: -en*
vein	**blodåre** *n.: -n, pl. -r,* **vene** *n.: -n, pl. -r*
wrist	**håndled** *n.: -det, pl. same*

Common Medical Conditions

What is the problem?
  Hvad er problemet?

I have (a/an) ...
  Jeg har (en/et) ...

abrasion	**hudafskrabning** *n.: -en, pl. -er*
acne	**filipens** *n.: -en, pl. -er,* **akne** *n.: -n*
AIDS	**AIDS**
allergies (to have allergies)	**allergi** *n.: -en, pl. -er* **(at lide af allergi)**
allergic (to be allergic to)	**allergisk** *adj.* **(at være allergisk/overfølsom over for)**
amnesia	**hukommelsestab** *n.: -et*
anemia	**blodmangel** *n.: -en* or *blodmanglen,* **anæmi** *n.: -en, pl. -er*
appendicitis	**blindtarmsbetændelse** *n.: -n*
asthma	**astma** *n.: -en*
benign	**godartet** *adj.*
bladder dysfunction	**vandladningsbesvær** *n.: -et*
bladder infection	**blærebetændelse** *n.: -n*
bleed	**bløde** *v.: -te*
blood clot	**blodprop** *n.: -pen, pl. -per*
boil	**byld** *n.: -en, pl. -er*
bronchitis	**bronkitis** *n.: -en, pl. -er*
bruise	**blåt mærke** *(mærke n.: -t, pl. -r)*
bunion	**ligtorn** *n.: -en, pl. -e*
cancer	**kræft** *n.: -en,* **cancer** *n.: -en, pl. -e*
cataract	**grå stær, katarakt**
chicken pox	**skoldkopper** *n.(pl.)*
childhood disease	**børnesygdom** *n.: -men, pl. -me*
cold	**forkølelse** *n.: -n, pl. -r*
cold sore	**forkølelsessår** *n.: -et, pl. same*
colic	**kolik** *n.: -ken*
compound fracture	**åbent benbrud** *(benbrud n.: -det, pl. same)*
concussion	**hjernerystelse** *n.: -n, pl. -r*
conjunctivitis	**øjenbetændelse** *n.: -n*

constipation	**forstoppelse** *n.: -en*
contagious disease	**smitsom sygdom** *(sygdom n.: -men, pl. -me)*
cough	**hoste** *n.: -n*
cramps	**krampe** *n: -n, pl. -r*
cut	**flænge** *n.: -n, pl. -r*
dehydration	**dehydrering** *n.: -en, pl. -er*
dental abscess	**tandbyld** *n.: -en, pl. -er*
diabetes	**sukkersyge** *n.: -en*
dialysis	**dialyse** *n.: -n, pl. -r*
diaper rash	**hudløs numse, "rød hale"**
diarrhea	**diaré** *n.: -en, pl. -er*
dislocate	**få af led** *v.: fik, fået af led*
faint	**besvime** *v.: -ede*
fatigue	**træthed** *n.: -en*
ear infection	**mellemørebetændelse** *n.: -n*
epilepsy	**epilepsi** *n.: -en*
fever	**feber** *n.: -en*
flu	**influenza** *n.: -en, pl. -er*
food poisoning	**madforgiftning** *n.: -en, pl. -er*
fracture	**knoglebrud** *n.: -det, pl. same* **brække** *v.: -ede*
hay fever	**høfeber** *n.: -en*
headache	**hovedpine** *n.: -n*
heart attack	**hjertetilfælde** *n.: -t, pl. same*
heatstroke	**hedeslag** *n.: -et, pl. same*
hemorrhoid(s)	**hæmoride** *n.: -n, pl. -r*
hernia	**brok** *n.: -ken or -ket, pl. same*
high blood pressure	**for højt blodtryk** *(blodtryk n.: -ket)*
hypothermia	**hypotermi** *n.: -en*
impetigo	**børnesår** *n.: -et, pl. same*
infection	**infektion** *n.: -en, pl. -er,* **betændelse** *n.: -n*
inflammation	**inflammation** *n.: -en, pl. -er*
ingrown nail	**nedgroet negl** *(negl n.: -en, pl. -e)*

internal bleeding	**indre blødning** (*blødning n.: -en, pl. -er*)
itch	**kløe** *n.: -n*
kidney stone	**nyresten** *n.: -en, pl. same*
left	**venstre** *adj.*
low blood pressure	**for lavt blodtryk** (*blodtryk n.: -ket*)
Lyme disease	**Lyme sygdom** (*sygdom n.: -men, pl. -me*)
malignant	**ondartet** *adj.*
measles	**mæslinger** *n.* (*only pl.*)
meningitis	**meningitis** *n.: -en*
menopause	**overgangsalder** *n.: -en*
metastasis	**metastase** *n.: -n, pl. -r*
migraine	**migræne** *n.: -n, pl. -r*
miscarriage	**spontan abort** (*abort n.: -en, pl. -er*)
mononucleosis	**mononukleose** *n.: -n* (also called **kyssesyge**)
motion sickness	**køresyge** *n.: -n* (car), **søsyge** *n.: -n* (sea)
nausea	**kvalme** *n.: -n*, **luftsyge** *n.: -n* (air)
nosebleed	**næseblod** *n.: -et*
pain	**smerte** *n.: -n, pl. -r*
period	**menstruation** *n.: -en*
pinworm	**børneorm** *n.* (*pl.*)
pneumonia	**lungebetændelse** *n.: -n*
preexistent condition	**forudgående tilstand** (*tilstand n.: -en, pl. -e*)
pregnancy	**graviditet** *n.: -en, pl. -er*
rash	**udslæt** *n.: -tet*
rheumatism	**gigt** *n.: -en*
right	**højre** *adj.*
rubella, German measles	**røde hunde** *n.* (*always pl.*)
scar	**ar** *n.: -ret, pl. same*
seizure	**krampeanfald** *n.: -et, pl. same*
septicemia	**blodforgiftning** *n.: -en, pl. -er*
sexually transmitted disease	**kønssygdom** *n.: -men, pl. -me*
side effect	**bivirkning** *n.: -en, pl. -er*

sinus infection	**bihulebetændelse** *n.: -n* and/or **pandehulebetændelse** *n.: -n*
skull fracture	**kraniebrud** *n.: -det, pl. same*
sore	**sår** *n.: -et, pl. same*
sprain	**forstrække** *v.: forstrakte, forstrakt,* **forstuve** *v.: -ede*
stiff neck	**stiv nakke** *(nakke n.: -n, pl. -r)*
stomachache	**mavepine** *n.: -n*
stomach ulcer	**mavesår** *n.: -et, pl. same*
stuffy nose	**snue** *n.: -n*
sty	**bygkorn** *n.: -et, pl. same*
suffer from	**lide af** *v.: led, lidt af*
sunstroke	**solstik** *n.*
swelling	**hævelse** *n.: -n*
symptom	**symptom** *n.: -et, pl. -er*
tetanus	**stivkrampe** *n.: -n* (tetanus shot **stivkrampevaccination**)
temperature, fever	**feber** *n.: -en*
toothache	**tandpine** *n.: -n*
tumor	**tumor** *n.: -en, pl. -er,* **svulst** *n.: -en, pl. -er*
twist	**forvride** *v.: forvred, forvredet*
unconscious	**bevidstløs** *adj.*
vaginal discharge	**udflåd** *n.: -et*
vaginitis	**skedebetændelse** *n.: -n*
vomit	**kaste op** *v.: -ede op*
vomiting	**opkastning** *n.: -en, pl. -er*
whooping cough	**kighoste** *n.: -n*
yeast infection	**svampeinfektion** *n.: -en, pl. -er*

Common Medical and Dental Procedures

abortion	**provokeret abort** *(abort n.: -en, pl. -er)* – under 18 parental consent is required

acupuncture	**akupunktur** *n.: -en*
adrenocortial hormone	**binyrebarkhormon** *n.: -et, pl. -er*
ambulatory	**ambulant** *adj.*
antidote	**modgift** *n.: -en*
bandage	**bandage** *n.: -n, pl. -r,* **forbinding** *n.: -en, pl. -er*
Band-Aid	**hæfteplaster** *n.: hæfteplastret, pl. hæfteplastre*
birth control pill	**p-pille** *n.: -n, pl. -r*
blood pressure (high/low)	**blodtryk (højt/lavt)** *n.: -ket*
blood test	**blodprøve** *n.: -n, pl. -r*
blood-thinning	**blodfortyndende** *adj.*
blood transfusion	**blodtransfusion** *n.: -en, pl. -er*
blood type	**blodtype** *n.: -n, pl. -r*
capsule (gelatin)	**kapsel (gelatine)** *n.: -en* or *kapslen, pl. kapsler*
cast	**gips** *n.: -en*
cavity (in tooth)	**hul** *n.: -let, pl. -ler*
cesarean	**kejsersnit** *n.: -tet, pl. same*
chemotherapy	**kemoterapi** *n.: -en*
condom	**kondom** *n.: -et, pl. -er,* **præservativ** *n.: -et, pl. -er*
contact(s)	**kontaktlinse** *n.: -n, pl. -r*
contraception	**prævention** *n.: -en*
crutch(es)	**krykke** *n.: -n, pl. -r*
D & C	**udskrabning** *n.: -en, pl. -er*
disinfectant	**desinficeringsmiddel** *n.: -et* or *desinficeringsmidlet, pl. desinficeringsmidler*
electrocardiogram	**elektrokardiogram** *n.: -met, pl. -mer*
filling (in tooth)	**plombe** *n.: -n, pl. -r*
general anesthesia	**fuld bedøvelse** *(bedøvelse n.: -en)*
glasses	**brille** *n.: -n, pl. -r (usually plural)*

hydrogen peroxide	**brintoverilte** *n.: -n*
injection, shot	**indsprøjtning** *n.: -en, pl. -er*
insulin	**insulin** *n.: -en* or *-et*
IV	**drop** *n.: -pet*
local anesthesia	**lokalbedøvelse** *(bedøvelse n.: -en)*
medicine	**medicin** *n.: -en*
pacemaker	**pacemaker** *n.: -en, pl. -e*
painkillers	**smertestillende medicin**
pill	**pille** *n.: -n, pl. -r*
radiation treatment	**strålebehandling** *n.: -en, pl. -er*
rehabilitation	**genoptræning** *n.: -en*
respirator	**respirator** *n.: -en, pl. -er*
resuscitate	**genoplive** *v.: -ede*
R-negative	**rhesusnegativ** *adj.*
R-positive	**rhesuspositiv** *adj.*
root canal treatment	**rodbehandling** *n.: -en, pl. -er*
scanning	**scanning** or **skanning** *n.: -en, pl. -er*
sedative	**beroligende middel** *(middel n.: midlet, pl. midler)*, **nervepille** *n.: -n, pl. -r*
sedimentation test	**blodsænkning** *n.: -en, pl. -er*
sterilize	**sterilisere** *v.: -ede*
surgery	**operation** *n.: -en, pl. -er*
suture	**sting** *n.: -et, pl. same*
thermometer	**termometer** *n.: -et* or *termometret, pl. termometre*
tweezers	**pincet** *n.: -ten, pl. -ter*
ultrasound	**ultralyd** *n.: -en*
vaginal cream	**vaginalcreme** *n.: -n, pl. -r*
vaginal suppository	**vagitorie** *n.: -t, pl. -r*
X ray	**røntgenbillede** *n.: -t, pl. -r*
x-ray	**røntgenfotografere** *v.: -ede*

Medical Professionals

acupuncturist	**akupunktør** *n.: -en, pl. -er*
anesthesiologist	**narkoselæge** *n.: -n, pl. -r,* **anæstesiolog** *n.: -en, pl. -er*
chiropractor	**kiropraktor** *n.: -en, pl. -er*
dentist	**tandlæge** *n.: -n, pl. -r*
dermatologist	**dermatolog** *n.: -en, pl. -er,* **hudlæge** *n.: -n, pl. -r*
ear, nose and throat doctor	**hals- og ørelæge** *n.: -n, pl. -r*
family practitioner	**praktiserende læge** *(læge n.: -n, pl. -r)*
gynecologist	**gynækolog** *n.: -en, pl. -er*
massage therapist	**massør** (male) *n.: -en, pl. -er,* **massøse** (female) *n.: -n, pl. -r*
midwife	**jordemoder** *n.: -en, pl. jordemødre*
nurse	**sygeplejerske** *n.: -n, pl. -r*
ophthalmologist	**øjenlæge** *n.: -n, pl. -r*
orthopedist	**ortopæd** *n.: -en, pl. -er*
pediatrician	**børnelæge** *n.: -n, pl. -r*
physical therapist	**fysioterapeut** *n.: -en, pl. -er*
physician	**læge** *n.: -n, pl. -r,* **doktor** *n.: -en, pl. -er*
physician on call	**vagtlæge** *n.: -n, pl. -r*
podiatrist	**fodterapeut** *n.: -en, pl. -er*
psychiatrist	**psykiater** *n.: -en, pl. -e*
psychologist	**psykolog** *n.: -en, pl. -er*
surgeon	**kirurg** *n.: -en, pl. -er*

At the Pharmacy

Evening and night service: ....
Aften- og weekendvagt: ....

I am allergic to …
Jeg er allergisk over for …

Shall I swallow or chew this medicine?
Skal medicinen synkes eller tygges?

How many times a day shall I take it?
Hvor mange gange om dagen skal jeg tage medicinen?

Three times a day.
Tre gange daglig.

Does this medicine have side effects?
Har medicinen bivirkninger?

Will it make me dizzy?
Bliver jeg svimmel af medicinen?

Will it make me drowsy?
Bliver jeg døsig af medicinen?

It may cause drowsiness.
Den kan virke sløvende.

Should I take this pill with water?
Skal jeg drikke vand til?

allergy-friendly	**allergivenlig**
chewable tablet	**tyggetablet** *n.: -ten, pl. -ter*
children's	**junior**
date	**dato** *n.: -en, pl. -er*
dose	**dosering** *n.: -en, pl. -er*
dry skin	**tør hud**
effervescent tablet	**brusetablet** *n.: -ten, pl. -ter*
expiration date	**anv. før …** (date)
for	**indikation** *n.: -en, pl. -er*
instruction sheet	**indlægsseddel** *n.: -en* or *indlægssedlen, pl. indlægssedler*
label	**mærkat** *n.: -et, pl. -r,* **etiket** *n.: -ten, pl. -ter*
liquid	**flydende** *adj.*
name	**navn** *n.: -et, pl. -e*
pill	**pille** *n.: -n, pl. -r*
pregnancy test	**graviditetstest** *n.: -en, pl. -er*

quick relief	**hurtig lindring**
suppository	**stikpille** *n.: -n, pl. -r*
tablet	**tablet** *n.: -ten, pl. -ter*

Do not use if pregnant.
Bør ikke anvendes af gravide.

Do not use if nursing.
Bør ikke anvendes ved amning.

Do not use for children under 15.
Bør ikke anvendes til børn under 15.

Keep out of reach of children.
Opbevares utilgængeligt for børn.

Store in a dry place.
Bør opbevares tørt.

Do not use with blood-thinning drugs.
Bør ikke tages sammen med blodfortyndende midler.

Overdose may cause fatal poisoning.
Overdosering kan medføre livstruende forgiftning.

reduces fever	**febernedsættende**
reduces pain	**smertestillende**
Adults: 1–2 tablets	**Voksne: 1–2 tabletter**
1–4 times a day	**1–4 gange daglig**

Dissolve 1 tablet in ½ glass of water.
1 tablet opløses i ½ glas vand.

Common Over-the-Counter Medicines

Acinil	reduces production of stomach acid
Alkasid	neutralizes stomach acid
B₅-Panthex	relieves diaper rash (mild rash)
Balancid	neutralizes stomach acid
Basiron	relieves acne (5% benzoylperoxid)
Benadryl	antihistamine
Brintoverilte	hydrogen peroxide
Canesten	relieves yeast infections
Dexofan	relieves dry cough

Hexokain	relieves sore throat
Ibumetin	relieves swelling
Imodium	relieves severe diarrhea
Inotyol	relieves diaper rash (severe rash)
Ipecac	to induce vomiting (only available at emergency rooms)
Ipren	relieves swelling
Kodymagnyl	relieves pain and reduces fever
Kuracid	reduces production of stomach acid
Laktolose	relieves constipation
Magnesia	relieves constipation
Marzine	to prevent motion sickness
Mucomyst	relieves wet cough
Otrivin	nasal spray
Pamol	relieves pain and reduces fever
Panodil	relieves pain and reduces fever (available as children's medicine)
Paraghurt	relieves and prevents diarrhea
Strepsil	relieves sore throat
Treo	relieves headaches
Zymelin	nasal spray
Zyrtez	antihistamine

Business Expressions

Most international business between Americans and Danes will doubtless be conducted in English, but the following list should provide a few key concepts. (See also sections on Communications and Time.)

General Vocabulary

business card	**visitkort** *n.: -et, pl. same*
number	**nummer (nr.)** *n.: -et* or *numret, pl. numre*
phone number	**telefonnummer (tlf. nr.)** (See page 226 for phone expressions.)
fax number	**faxnummer** *n.: -et* or *faxnumret, pl. faxnumre*
e-mail address	**e-mail-adresse, e-post-adresse** *(adresse n.: -n, pl. -r)*
tax ID number	**CVR-nr.**
social security number	**personnummer, CPR-nr.** (for example 220620-1587— birthday + four digits)

You can reach me at 75 58 85 19.
  De/du kan få fat i mig på telefon 75 58 85 19.

I have a message for you.
  Jeg har en besked til Dem/dig.

When does the meeting start?
  Hvornår begynder mødet?

It starts at 3 P.M. in room number 105.
  Det starter kl. 15 i lokale 105.

Please remit within 30 days.
  Betalingsfrist 30 dage.

advisor	**rådgiver** *n.: -en, pl. -e*
agenda	**dagsorden** *n.: -en, pl. -er*

annual audit	**årlig revision** *(revision n.: -en)*
article(s) of association	**vedtægt** *n.: -en, pl. -er*
auditors' report	**revisionsberetning** *n.: -en, pl. -er*
board of directors	**bestyrelse** *n.: -n, pl. -r*
bond	**obligation** *n.: -en, pl. -er*
boss	**chef** *n.: -en, pl. -er,* **boss** *n.: -en, pl. -er*
budget	**budgettere** *v.: -ede*
budget planning	**budgetplanlægning** *n.: -en*
business account	**forretningskonto, erhvervskonto** *(konto n.: -en, pl. -er* or *konti)*
business administration	**virksomhedsledelse** *n.: -en, pl. -er*
business associate	**forretningskollega** *n.: -en, pl. -er* or *kolleger*
business connection	**forretningsforbindelse** *n.: -n, pl. -r*
business consultant	**virksomhedskonsulent** *n.: -en, pl. -er*
business cost	**driftsomkostning** *n.: -en, pl. -er*
business ethics	**forretningsmoral** *n.: -en*
business letter	**forretningsbrev** *n.: -et, pl. -e*
businessman	**forretningsmand** *n.: -en, pl. forretningsmænd*
business trip	**forretningsrejse** *n.: -n, pl. -r*
businesswoman	**forretningskvinde** *n.: -n, pl. -r*
buy at par	**købe til parikurs**
cash discount	**kontantrabat** *n.: -ten*
cash flow	**likviditet** *n.: -en, pl. -er*
cash payment	**kontant betaling** *(betaling n.: -en)*
certified public accountant (CPA)	**statsautoriseret revisor** *(revisor n.: -en, pl. -er)*
chairman of a meeting	**ordstyrer** *n.: -en, pl. -e*

chairman of the board	**bestyrelsesformand** *n.: -en,* *pl. bestyrelsesformænd*
chief executive director (CEO)	**ordførende direktør** *(direktør n.: -en,* *pl. -er)*
commercial	**kommerciel** *adj.*
committee	**udvalg** *n.: -et, pl. same*
company	**firma** *n.: -et, pl. -er*
conference	**konference** *n.: -n, pl. -r*
consumer	**forbruger** *n.: -en, pl. -e*
contract	**kontrakt** *n.: -en, pl. -er*
controlling interest, majority of shares	**aktiemajoritet** *n.: -en,* *pl. -er*
corporate tax	**selskabsskat** *n.: -ten,* *pl. -ter*
customer	**kunde** *n.: -en, pl. -r*
customized	**skræddersyet** *adj.*
deficit	**underskud** *n.: -det,* *pl. same*
discount, discount for large quantity	**rabat, mængderabat** *n.: -ten*
due date	**forfaldsdato** *n.: -en,* *pl. -er*
during business hours	**i kontortiden,** **i forretningstiden,** **i åbningstiden**
employee	**medarbejder** *n.: -en,* *pl. -e*
employee benefit(s)	**personalegode** *n.: -t,* *pl. -r*
employer	**arbejdsgiver** *n.: -en,* *pl. -e*
employer's liability, vicarious liability	**principalansvar** *n.: -et*
enclose	**vedlægge** *v.: vedlagde,* *vedlagt,* **sende som** **bilag** *v.: -te som bilag*
endorse	**endossere** *v.: -ede*
exchange rate	**vekselkurs** *n.: -en, pl. -er*
expand	**udvide** *v.: -ede*
expense, expenditure	**udgift** *n.: -en, pl. -er*
external	**ekstern** *adj.*

file for bankruptcy	**indgive konkurserklæring** *v.: indgav, indgivet konkurserk.*
fluctuating exchange rate	**flydende valutakurs**
fluctuating prices	**flydende priser** *(pris n.: -en, pl. -er)*
fluctuation in price	**prissvingning** *n.: -en, pl. -er,* **konjunkturbevægelse** *n.: -n, pl. -r*
fluctuation of rates	**kurssvingning** *n.: -en, pl. -er*
framework agreement	**rammeaftale** *n.: -n, pl. -r*
go bankrupt	**gå konkurs, gå fallit** *(gå v.: gik, gået)*
income	**indtægt** *n.: -en, pl. -er,* **indkomst** *n.: -en, pl. -er*
income tax	**indkomstskat** *n.: -ten, pl. -ter*
internal	**intern** *adj.*
invalid	**ugyldig** *adj.*
invalid check, bounced check	**afvist check, dækningsløs check, gummicheck, ugyldig check**
invest; investment	**investere** *v.: -ede;* **investering** *n.: -en, pl. -er*
invoice	**faktura** *n.: -en, pl. -er;* **fakturere** *v.: -ede*
issue of shares	**aktieemission** *n.: -en, pl. -er*
joint liability	**solidarisk ansvar, solidarisk hæfte**
leasing agreement	**leasingaftale** *n.: -n, pl. -r*
limited liability company	**selskab med begrænset ansvar**
loss	**tab** *n.: -et, pl. same*
management	**ledelse** *n.: -n, pl. -r*
managing director	**administrerende direktør** *(direktør n.: -en, pl. -er)*

Business Expressions

meeting	**møde** *n.: -t, pl. -r*
meeting room	**mødelokale** *n.: -t, pl. -r*
memorandum of association	**stiftelsesoverenskomst** *n.: -en, pl. -r*
merger	**fusion** *n.: -en, pl. -er*
minutes	**møderreferat** *n.: -et, pl. -er*
moonlighting	**sort arbejde**
mortgage loan	**pantelån, prioritetslån** *n.: -et, pl. same*
negotiate	**forhandle** *v.: -ede*
net profit after taxes	**nettooverskud efter skat**
net profit before taxes	**nettooverskud før skat**
notary public	**notar** *n.: -en, pl. -er*
outstanding amounts	**udestående beløb** *(beløb n.: -et, pl. same)*
owner	**ejer** *n.: -en, pl. -e,* **indehaver** *n.: -en, pl. -e*
partnership	**kompagniskab** *n.: -et, pl. -er*
patent	**patent** *n.: -et, pl. -er*
pay; payment	**betale** *v.: -te;* **betaling** *n.: -en, pl. -er*
personally liable (to be)	**hæfte personligt** *v.: -ede personligt*
planning stage	**planlægningsfase** *n.: -n, pl. -r*
power of attorney	**fuldmagt** *n.: -en, pl. -er*
product development	**produktudvikling** *n.: -en*
profits	**overskud** *n.: -det,* **fortjeneste** *n.: -en*
proposal	**forslag** *n.: -et, pl. same*
public liability company	**børsnoteret aktieselskab (A/S)** *(aktieselskab n.: -et, pl. -er)*
public relations department	**PR-afdeling** *n.: -en, pl. -er*
public stocks	**børsnoterede aktier** *(aktie n.: -n, pl. -r)*
purchase price	**købspris** *n.: -en, pl. -er*
qualified acceptance	**accept med forbehold**
recruitment	**rekruttering** *n.: -en, pl. -er*

report	**rapport** *n.: -en, pl. -er*
resource	**ressource** *n.: -n, pl. -r*
retail	**detailhandel** *n.: -en*
right of preemption	**forkøbsret** *n.: -ten*
sales department	**salgsafdeling** *n.: -en, pl. -er*
sales figures	**salgstal** *n.: -let, pl. same*
sales manager	**salgschef** *n.: -en, pl. -er,* **salgsdirektør** *n.: -en, pl. -er*
sales planning	**salgsplanlægning, markedsføringsplanlægning** *n.: -en*
schedule, plan	**planlægge** *v.: planlagde, planlagt*
secured, preferred creditor	**begunstiget kreditor** *(kreditor n.: -en, pl. -er)*
securities	**værdipapirer** *(værdipapir n.: -et, pl. -er)*
self-employed	**selvstændig** *adj.,* **selverhvervende** *adj.*
share capital	**aktiekapital** *n.: -en, pl. -er*
shareholder	**aktionær** *n.: -en, pl. -er*
shareholders' agreement	**aktionæroverenskomst** *n.: -en, pl. -er*
sign	**skrive under på, underskrive** *(skrive v.: skrev, skrevet)*
signature	**underskrift** *n.: -en, pl. -er*
single currency	**fællesmønt** *n.: -en*
single market	**indre marked** *(marked n.: -et, pl. -er)*
skill	**kompetence** *n.: -n, pl. -r,* **færdighed** *n.: -n, pl. -r*
skill development	**kompetenceudvikling** *n.: -en*
standard business practice	**almindelig forretningskutyme** *(kutyme n.: -n)*

Business Expressions

stock	**aktie** *n.: -n, pl. -r*
stockbroker	**børsmægler** *n.: -en, pl. -e*
stock market	**aktiemarked, børsmarked** *n.: -et, pl. -er*
subcontractor	**underleverandør** *n.: -en, pl. -er*
target group	**målgruppe** *n.: -n, pl. -r*
tax	**skat** *n.: -ten, pl. -ter*
tax-free	**skattefri** *adj.*
tax on consumption	**forbrugsskat** *n.: -ten, pl. -ter*
taxpayer	**skatteyder** *n.: -en, pl. -e*
tax shelter	**skattely** *n.: -et, pl. same*
tax year	**skatteår** *n.: -et, pl. same*
term(s) of a contract	**kontraktbetingelse** *n.: -n, pl. -r*
terms(s) of payment	**betalingsbetingelse** *n.: -n, pl. -r*
third party	**tredjemand** *n.: -en, pl. tredjemænd*
trade agreement	**handelsaftale** *n.: -n, pl. -r*
unlimited company	**selskab med personlig hæftelse**
unsecured creditor	**simpel kreditor**
VAT, sales tax	**moms** *n.: -en,* **merværdiafgift** *n.: -en, pl. -er*
violation of a contract	**kontraktbrud** *n.: -det, pl. same,* **misligholdelse af en kontrakt**
vote by proxy	**stemme ved stedfortræder** *(stemme v.: -te)*
wholesale	**engroshandel** *n.: -en*
work permit	**arbejdstilladelse** *n.: -n, pl. -r*

Computers

See page 230 for e-mail expressions.

attached file	**vedhæftet fil** *(fil n.: -en, pl. -er)*
compatible	**kompatibel** *adj.*
computer	**computer** *n.: -en, pl. -e*
delete	**slette** *v.: -ede*
document	**dokument** *n.: -et, pl. -er*
e-commerce	**e-handel** *n.: -en*
e-mail	**e-mail** *n.: -en,* **e-post** *n.: -en*
file	**fil** *n.: -en, pl. -er*
floppy disk	**diskette** *n.: -n, pl. -r*
folder	**mappe** *n.: -n, pl. -r*
ink cartridge	**blækpatron** *n.: -en, pl. -er*
keyboard	**tastatur** *n.: -et, pl. -er*
laptop computer	**bærbar computer** *(computer n.: -en, pl. -e)*
monitor	**skærm** *n.: -en, pl. -e*
network	**netværk** *n.: -et, pl. -er* or *same*
off-line	**off-line**
on-line	**on-line**
printer	**printer** *n.: -en, pl. -e*
print	**udskrive** *v.: udskrev, udskrevet*
save	**gemme** *v.: -te*
update	**opdatere** *v.: -ede*
upgrade	**opgradere** *v.: -ede*
word processing	**tekstbehandling** *n.: -en*

Danish Society

Government and Law

The Kingdom of Denmark (*Kongeriget Danmark*) is a constitutional monarchy currently headed by Queen Margrethe II (*Hendes Majestæt Dronning Margrethe II*). The constitution (*Grundloven*) dates back to June 5, 1849. Denmark has a single-chamber representative government, supplemented by referendums. The voting age is 18. Parliament (*Folketinget*) has 179 members (175 from Denmark, two from the Faeroe Islands, and two from Greenland). Representation is proportional based on the number of votes; however, a political party must receive a minimum of two percent of the votes to gain a seat. The largest political parties are *Venstre* (Denmark's Liberal Party) and *Socialdemokratiet* (The Social Democratic Party). Tourists are invited to visit *Christiansborg* to see the politicians at work. The Danish judicial system is primarily based on statute rather then common law. Compared to America, criminal sentences tend to be light, and Denmark does not employ the death penalty; however, punishment for traffic violations and drunk driving are generally harsher than in the United States. Denmark is a founding member of NATO (with compulsory military service) and a member of the European Union.

administration	**regering** *n.: -en, pl. -er*
age of consent	**seksuelle lavalder** *(lavalder n.: -en)*
age of criminal responsibility	**kriminelle lavalder** *(lavalder n.: -en)*
Amalienborg	**Amalienborg** (the royal palace in Copenhagen)
authority	**myndighed** *n.: -en, pl. -er*
common law	**sædvaneret** *n.: -ten*
community service	**samfundstjeneste** *n.: -n*
compulsory military service	**værnepligt** *n.: -en*
conscientious objector	**militærnægter** *n.: -en, pl. -e*
constitution	**grundlov** *n.: -en*
crown prince	**kronprins** *n.: -en, pl. -er* (Kronprins Frederik)

death penalty	**dødsstraf** *n.: -fen, pl. -fe*
election	**valg** *n.: -et, pl. same*
election campaign	**valgkampagne** *n.: -n, pl. -r*, **valgkamp** *n.: -en, pl. -e*
fine	**bøde** *n.: -n, pl. -r*
(the) government	**det offentlige**
heir to the throne	**tronfølger** *n.: -en, pl. -e*, **tronarving** *n.: -en, pl. -er*
judicial system	**retssystem** *n.: -et, pl. -er*
king	**konge** *n.: -n, pl. -r*
kingdom	**kongerige** *n.: -t, pl. -r*
legal age	**myndighedsalder** *n.: -en*
member of parliament	**folketingsmedlem** *n.: -met, pl. -mer*
palace, castle	**slot** *n.: -tet, pl. -e*
Parliament	**Folketinget**
parliamentary election	**folketingsvalg** *n.: -et, pl. same*
prince	**prins** *n.: -en, pl. -er*
princess	**prinsesse** *n.: -n, pl. -r*
prison sentence	**fængselsstraf** *n.: -fen, pl. -fe*
public vote, referendum	**folkeafstemning** *n.: -en, pl. -er*
queen	**dronning** *n.: -en, pl. -er*
sentence	**straf** *n.: -fen, pl. -fe* (punishment); **dom** *n.: -men, pl. -me* (ruling)
statute law	**positiv lov**
Supreme Court	**Højesteret**
verdict	**dom** *n.: -men, pl. -me*
vote	**stemme** *v.: -te*; *n.: -n, pl. -r*

Economy

The Danish economy is generally healthy and stable. Denmark joined the European Community in 1972 and is still—with four restrictions—a member of the European Union. On September 28, 2000, the Danes rejected the single currency (the Euro), but the Danish krone is pegged to it. The labor unions have been strong for decades, so people enjoy reliable benefits, high wages, a relatively safe work environment, paid maternity/paternity leave, and by American standards short hours and generous vacation time. Many enjoy flexible schedules, and people generally retire in their early sixties. Strikes are not unusual, and once in a while a general strike brings the country to a halt.

economy	**økonomi** *n.: -en*
general strike	**generalstrejke** *n.: -n, pl. -r*
labor union	**fagforening** *n.: -en, pl. -er*
minimum wage	**mindsteløn** *n.: -nen*
restriction	**forbehold** *n.: -et, pl. same*
retire	**gå på pension** *v.: gik, gået på pension*; **blive pensioneret** *v.: blev, blevet pensioneret*
single currency	**fællesmønt** *n.: -en*
single market	**indre marked** *(marked n.: -et, pl. -er)*
strike	**strejke** *n.: -n, pl. -r*
The European Union	**Den Europæiske Union**
treaty	**traktat** *n.: -en, pl. -er*
work environment	**arbejdsmiljø** *n.: -et, pl. -er*
workplace	**arbejdsplads** *n.: -en, pl. -er*

Education

Denmark's educational system is similar to that of the U.S. The percentage of working parents is very high, so many children spend their early years in daycare. They usually start kindergarten at age six. First through ninth grade is mandatory. The majority of children attend public schools, but private schools are gaining ground. Higher education is free and financial aid is available to cover living expenses. Rather than pursuing higher education, many teenagers attend vocational schools and enter a trade through an apprenticeship. Denmark is also known for its folk high schools (*højskoler*). Here teenagers and adults can spend anywhere from one week to several months pursuing specific subjects and gaining a deeper understanding of societal and philosophical issues. Teenagers can complete eighth through tenth grade at such a school. Many Danes attend evening classes, and a lot of career-related training takes place during and outside work hours.

apprenticeship	**lærlingeuddannelse** *n.: -en, pl. -er*
class, grade	**klasse** *n.: -n, pl. -r*
classroom	**klasseværelse** *n.: -t, pl. -r*
daycare	**dagpleje** *n.: -n*
education	**uddannelse** *n.: -n, pl. -r*
evening school	**aftenskole** *n.: -n, pl. -r*
folk high school	**folkehøjskole** *n.: -n, pl. -r*
get a good education	**få en god uddannelse** *v.: fik, fået en god uddannelse*
grade school	**folkeskolen**
high school	**gymnasium** *n.: gymnasiet, pl. gymnasier;* **HF (Højere forberedelseseksamen)**
kindergarten	**børnehaveklasse** *n.: -n, pl. -r*
learn	**lære** *v.: -te*
pedagogue	**pædagog** *n.: -en, pl. -er*
preschool	**børnehave** *n.: -n, pl. -r*
school	**skole** *n.: -n, pl. -r*
student	**elev** *n.: -en, pl. -er*
teach	**undervise** *v.: -te*
teacher	**lærer** *n.: -en, pl. -e*
university	**universitet** *n.: -et, pl. -er*
vocational school	**teknisk skole**

What do you teach?
Hvad underviser du i?

I teach biology and English.
Jeg underviser i biologi og engelsk.

What grade are you in?
Hvilken klasse går du i?

I am in fourth grade.
Jeg går i 4. klasse.

Welfare State

The Danes believe strongly in every human being's right to a decent standard of living, and to support that belief they have developed one of the strongest welfare systems in the world. The price they pay is high taxes, but in return they get free health and dental care, subsidized prescription medicine, free education, subsidized child care, great public sports facilities and parks, social security payments, subsidized housing, nursing homes, etc. Likewise, government policy has created a very reasonable workweek, generous amounts of paid vacation, good sick pay and unemployment benefits, paid maternity/paternity leave, etc. Since 1973, Denmark has allowed legal abortion for women 18 years of age and older (under 18 require parental consent). Generally, the Danish welfare system works very well, but the allocation of often limited resources is a constant issue.

cash benefits	**kontanthjælp** *n.: -en*
free	**gratis** *adj.*
housing benefits	**boligtilskud** *n.: -det, pl. same*
legal abortion	**fri abort** *(abort n.: -en, pl. -er)*
maternity/paternity leave	**barselsorlov** *n.: -en*
nursing home	**plejehjem** *n.: -met, pl. same*
public assistance	**hjælp fra det offentlige**
sick pay	**sygepenge** *n. (pl.)*
social security	**folkepension** *n.: -en*
subsidy	**tilskud** *n.: -det, pl. same*, **statsstøtte** *n.: -n*
tax	**skat** *n.: -ten, pl. -ter*
unemployment benefits	**arbejdsløsheds-understøttelse** *n.: -n*
vacation	**ferie** *n.: -n, pl. -r*
welfare state	**velfærdsstat** *n.: -en, pl. -er*
workweek	**arbejdsuge** *n.: -n, pl. -r*

Religion

Other than the monarch, who must be a member of *Den Danske Folkekirke* (The Danish Lutheran Evangelical Church), all people living in Denmark enjoy complete religious freedom. *Den danske Folkekirke* is run by the state and financed through taxes paid by those citizens who choose to be members. At the moment, membership is dwindling, and there is a call for rejuvenation; nevertheless, about 85 percent of the Danish population were members in the year 2000. Atheists and people of other religious persuasions made up the remaining 15 percent. The Danes are strongly committed to preserving their beautiful churches, and although most Danes cannot be described as deeply religious, they see the church and the Christian philosophy as a framework for life—christenings, confirmations, weddings, and funerals take place within church walls, and through the welfare state and foreign aid they care for their fellow man. In 1998, 78.8 percent of all newborns were christened; in 1999, 48.1 percent of all weddings took place in church; in 1999, 79.9 percent of those 14 and 15 years of age were confirmed; and in 1999, 92.2 percent of those who died were buried through the church.

Morning and evening church bells ring throughout Denmark, and many churches are well worth visiting for their beauty, atmosphere, and historical value. Any tourist is welcome to worship. *Den danske Folkekirke* offers services on Sunday mornings and on religious holidays. See the list of holidays on page 241. Schedules for other houses of worship, such as synagogues or mosques, should be checked individually.

General Phrases and Vocabulary

Where is the closest church / mosque / synagogue / temple?
   Hvor ligger den nærmeste kirke / moske / synagoge / tempel?

What time is the service?
   Hvad tid er der gudstjeneste?

Is there a service tomorrow morning?
Er der gudstjeneste i morgen formiddag?

atheist / Atheism	**ateist** n.: -en, pl. -er / **ateisme**
Buddhist / Buddhism	**buddhist** n.: -en, pl. -er / **buddhisme**
Catholic / Catholicism	**katolik** n.: -ken, pl. -ker / **katolicisme**
Christian / Christianity	**kristen** n.: -en, pl. kristne / **kristendom**
Hindu / Hinduism	**hindu** n.: -en, pl. -er / **hinduisme**
Jew / Judaism	**jøde** n.: -n, pl. -r / **jødedom**
Mormon / Mormonism	**mormon** n.: -en, pl. -er / **mormonisme**
Muslim / Islam	**muslim** n.: -en, pl. -er / **islam**

✽ ✽ ✽ ✽ ✽ ✽

altar	**alter** n.: -et or altret, pl. altre
altar candle	**alterlys** n.: -et, pl. same
altar cloth	**alterdug** n.: -en, pl. -e
altarpiece	**altertavle** n.: -n, pl. -r
baptism	**dåb** n.: -en
baptismal font	**døbefont** n.: -en, pl. -e or -er
believe	**tro** v.: -ede
Bible	**Bibelen**
birth certificate	**fødselsattest** n.: -en, pl. -er
bury	**begrave** v.: -ede
cathedral	**domkirke** n.: -n, pl. -r
cemetery, graveyard	**kirkegård** n.: -en, pl. -e
certificate of baptism	**dåbsattest** n.: -en, pl. -er
choir	**kor** n.: -et, pl. same (group of singers)
	kor n.: -et, pl. same (part of church building)
christen	**døbe** v.: -te
Christian	**kristen** adj.

Christianity	**kristendom** *n.: -men*
church	**kirke** *n.: -n, pl. -r*
church bell	**kirkeklokke** *n.: -n, pl. -r*
church box	**kirkebøsse** *n.: -n, pl. -r*
church register	**kirkebog** *n.: -en,* *pl. kirkebøger*
church service	**gudstjeneste** *n.: -n, pl. -r*
church tower	**kirketårn** *n.: -et, pl. -e*
church wedding	**kirkebryllup** *n.: -pet,* *pl. -per*
coffin	**kiste** *n.: -n, pl. -r*
collection	**indsamling** *n.: -en, pl. -er*
Communion cup	**alterkalk** *n.: -en, pl. -e*
Communion wine	**altervin** *n.: -en*
concluding/final prayer	**udgangsbøn** *n.: -nen*
confession	**skriftemål** *n.: -et*
confession of faith	**trosbekendelse** *n.: -en,* *pl. -er*
confirm; get confirmed	**konfirmere** *v.: -ede*; **blive** **konfirmeret** *v.: blev,* *blevet konfirmeret*
confirmation	**konfirmation** *n.: -en,* *pl. -er*
congregation	**menighed** *n.: -en, pl. -er*
cremate	**brænde** *v.: -te*
cremation	**ligbrænding** *n.: -en*
crucifix	**krucifiks** *n.: -et, pl. -er*
Earth	**jorden**
fresco	**kalkmaleri** *n.: -et, pl. -er*
funeral	**begravelse** *n.: -n, pl. -r,* **bisættelse** *n.: -n, pl. -r*
funeral wreath	**krans** *n.: -en, pl. -e*
get married	**blive viet/gift** *v.: blev,* *blevet viet/gift*
go to church	**gå i kirke** *v.: gik, gået i* *kirke*
God	**Gud** *(gud n.: -en, pl. -er)*
godmother	**gudmoder** *n.: -en,* *pl. gudmødre*
grave	**grav** *n.: -en, pl. -e*
graveside ceremony	**jordpåkastelse** *n.: -n*
hearse	**rustvogn** *n.: -en, pl. -e*
Heaven	**himlen**

Hell	**helvede**
Holy Communion	**altergang** *n.: -en*
Holy Ghost	**Helligånden**
hymn	**salme** *n.: -n, pl. -r*
hymnal book	**salmebog** *n.: -en, pl. salmebøger*
introductory prayer	**indgangsbøn** *n.: -nen*
Lord's Prayer	**fadervor**
marriage certificate	**vielsesattest** *n.: -en, pl. -er*
minister	**præst** *n.: -en, pl. -er*
nave	**skib** *n.: -et, pl. -e*
organ	**orgel** *n.: -et or orglet, pl. orgler*
organ player	**organist** *n.: -en, pl. -er*
Our Lord	**Vorherre**
parish	**sogn** *n.: -et, pl. -e*
parish clerk	**degn** *n.: -en, pl. -e,* **kirketjener** *n.: -en, pl. -e*
pew	**kirkestol** *n.: -en, pl. -e*
porch	**våbenhus** *n.: -et, pl. -e*
pulpit	**prædikestol** *n.: -en, pl. -e*
religious	**religiøs** *adj.*
round church	**rundkirke** *n.: -n, pl. -r* (found on the island of Bornholm)
sermon	**prædiken** *n.: -en, pl. -er*
sexton	**graver** *n.: -en, pl. -e*
Son	**Sønnen**
sponsor	**fadder** *n.: -en, pl. -e*
spray	**bårebuket** *n.: -ten, pl. -ter*
stand sponsor to	**stå fadder til** *v.: stod, stået fadder til*
Trinity	**treenigheden**
vicarage	**præstegård** *n.: -en, pl. -e* (farm), **præstebolig** *n.: -en, pl. -er* (house)
village church	**landsbykirke** *n.: -n, pl. -r*
wafer	**oblat** *n.: -en, pl. -er*

Miscellaneous

Cardinal Numbers

cardinal numbers	**mængdetal**
one	**en/et** (depending on the gender of the noun)
two	**to**
three	**tre**
four	**fire**
five	**fem**
six	**seks**
seven	**syv**
eight	**otte**
nine	**ni**
ten	**ti**
eleven	**elleve**
twelve	**tolv**
thirteen	**tretten**
fourteen	**fjorten**
fifteen	**femten**
sixteen	**seksten**
seventeen	**sytten**
eighteen	**atten**
nineteen	**nitten**
twenty	**tyve**
twenty-one	**enogtyve**
twenty-two	**toogtyve**
thirty	**tredive**
forty	**fyrre**
fifty	**halvtreds**
sixty	**tres**
seventy	**halvfjerds**
eighty	**firs**
ninety	**halvfems**
one hundred	**hundrede, et hundrede**
one thousand	**tusind, et tusind**
one million	**en million**
one billion	**en milliard**
one trillion	**en billion**
20,000	**20.000 / tyve tusind**
55,500.30 kr.	**55.560,30 kr. / femoghalvtreds tusind fem hundrede og tres kroner og tredive øre**

Miscellaneous

Ordinal Numbers

ordinal numbers — **ordenstal**

first	**første**
second	**anden**
third	**tredje**
fourth	**fjerde**
fifth	**femte**
sixth	**sjette**
seventh	**syvende**
eighth	**ottende**
ninth	**niende**
tenth	**tiende**
eleventh	**ellevte, elvte**
twelfth	**tolvte**
thirteenth	**trettende**
fourteenth	**fjortende**
fifteenth	**femtende**
sixteenth	**sekstende**
seventeenth	**syttende**
eighteenth	**attende**
nineteenth	**nittende**
twentieth	**tyvende**
thirtieth	**tredivte, tredvte**
fortieth	**fyrretyvende**
fiftieth	**halvtredsindstyvende**
sixtieth	**tresindstyvende**
seventieth	**halvfjerdsindstyvende**
eightieth	**firsindstyvende**
ninetieth	**halvfemsindstyvende**
hundredth	**nummer hundrede**

Basic Math

Operations

add (addition)
   lægge sammen *v.: lagde, lagt sammen*, **addere**
      v.: -ede (**addition**)

subtract (subtraction)
   trække fra *v.: trak, trukket fra*, **subtrahere** *v.: -ede*
      (**subtraktion**)

multiply (multiplication)
gange *v.: -ede*, **multiplicere** *v.: -ede* (**multiplikation**)

divide (division)
dele *v.: -te*, **dividere** *v.: -ede* (**division**)

equal
være lig med *v.: var, været lig med (pre. er lig med)*

Symbols

United States	Denmark
+	+
−	−
x or *	· or *
÷ or /	: or /

Shapes

circle	**cirkel** *n.: -en* or *cirklen, pl. cirkler*
diameter	**diameter** *n.: -en, pl. diametre*
line	**linie, linje** *n.: -n, pl. -r*
pentagon	**femkant** *n.: -en, pl. -er*
radius	**radius** *n.: -en* or *radien, pl. -er* or *radier*
rectangle	**rektangel** *n.: -et* or *rektanglet, pl. rektangler*
square	**firkant** *n.: -en, pl. -er*
triangle	**trekant** *n.: -en, pl. -er*

Metric System

1 kilometer (km) = 1000 meters (m)
1 meter (m) = 10 decimeters (dm) = 100 centimeters (cm)
1 decimeter (dm) = 10 centimeters (cm)
1 centimeter (cm) = 10 millimeters (mm)

1 liter (l) = 10 deciliter (dl) = 100 centiliters (cl)
1 deciliter (dl) = 10 centiliters (cl) = 100 milliliters (ml)
1 centiliter (cl) = 10 milliliters (ml)

Miscellaneous

1 kilogram (kg) = 1000 gram (g)
1 gram (g) = 10 milligram

Conversions

Length – Længde

1 millimeter = 0.0394 inches	1 inch = 2.54 cm
1 centimeter = 0.3937 inches	1 foot = 0.3048 m
1 meter = 1.0936 yard	1 yard = 0.9144 m
1 kilometer = 0.6214 mile	1 mile = 1.6093 km

Area – Areal

1 cm^2 = 0.1550 inch^2	1 inch^2 = 6.4516 cm^2
1 m^2 = 1.1960 yards^2	1 foot^2 = 0.0929 m^2
1 hectare = 2.4711 acres	1 yard^2 = 0.8361 m^2
1 km^2 = 0.3861 mile^2	1 acre = 4046.9 m^2
1 mile^2 = 2.59 km^2	

Volume – Rumfang

1 cm^3 = 0.0610 inch^3	1 inch^3 = 16.387 cm^3
1 dm^3 = 0.0353 foot^3	1 foot^3 = 0.0283 m^3
1 m^3 = 1.3080 yard^3	1 fluid ounce = 29.574 ml
1 cl = 0.338 fluid ounce	1 pint = 0.473 l
1 dl = 0.21 pint	1 quart = 0.946 l
1 liter = 1.0527 quarts	1 gallon = 3.7854 l

Weight – Vægt

1 gram = 0.0353 ounces	1 ounce = 28.35 g
1 kilogram = 2.2046 pounds	1 pound = 0.453 kg
1 metric ton = 1.102 short ton	1 short ton = 0.907 metric ton
	1 long ton = 1.016 metric ton

Temperature

To convert from Fahrenheit to Celsius, subtract 32 from Fahrenheit figure, divide by 9, and multiply by 5.

To convert from Celsius to Fahrenheit, multiply the Celsius figure by nine, divide by 5, and add 32.

Common Abbreviations

adr.	adresse	address
afs.	afsender	sender
R	(rekommanderet) anbefalet	registered (mail)
ang.	angående	regarding
ca.	cirka	circa
d.	den	the (dates)
d.d.	dags dato	today's date
dkr.	danske kroner	Danish kroner
dvs.	det vil sige	that is
dr.	doktor	doctor
ekskl.	eksklusive	exclusive of
f.eks., fx	for eksempel	for example
fhv.	forhenværende	former
fr.	fru/frøken	Mrs./Miss
frk.	frøken	Miss
hr.	herre	Mr.
inkl.	inklusive	inclusive of
Kbh.	København	Copenhagen
kl.	klokken	at … (time) – kl. 15.
kr.	kroner	kroner
maks.	maksimum	maximum
mdr.	måneder	months
mht.	med hensyn til	regarding
mia.	milliard	billion
mio.	million	million
modt.	modtager	addressee
nr.	nummer	number
obs.	observér	note
o.l.	og lignende	and the like
osv.	og så videre	etc.
pct.	procent	percent
pga.	på grund af	because of
st.	stuen	ground floor
stk.	per styk	apiece
str.	størrelse	size
s.u.	svar udbedes	please RSVP
tlf.	telefon	telephone
att.	til	attention
th.	til højre	to the right

tv.	til venstre	to the left
vha.	ved hjælp af	by means of
vær.	værelse	room
årh.	århundrede	century
årl.	årligt	annually

Geographical Names

Where are you from?
Hvor er du/De fra?

I am from …
Jeg er fra …

Denmark	**Danmark**
Faeroe Islands	**Færøerne**
Greenland	**Grønland**
Fynen	**Fyn**
Jutland	**Jylland**
Zealand	**Sjælland**
the North Sea	**Nordsøen**
the Baltic Sea	**Østersøen**
the Great Belt	**Storebælt**

* * * * * *

Africa	**Afrika**
Antarctica	**Antarktis**
Asia	**Asien**
Australia	**Australien**
Europe	**Europa**
North America	**Nordamerika**
South America	**Sydamerika**

* * * * * *

Austria	**Østrig**
Belgium	**Belgien**
Bulgaria	**Bulgarien**
Canada	**Canada**
China	**Kina**
Czech Republic	**Tjekkiet**
Egypt	**Egypten**
Finland	**Finland**
France	**Frankrig**

Germany	**Tyskland**
Great Britain	**Storbritannien**
Greece	**Grækenland**
Hungary	**Ungarn**
Ireland	**Irland**
Israel	**Israel**
Italy	**Italien**
Japan	**Japan**
Luxembourg	**Luxembourg**
Netherlands	**Holland, Nederlandene**
Norway	**Norge**
Poland	**Polen**
Portugal	**Portugal**
Romania	**Rumænien**
Saudi Arabia	**Saudi-Arabien**
Scotland	**Skotland**
Spain	**Spanien**
Sweden	**Sverige**
Switzerland	**Schweiz**
Turkey	**Tyrkiet**
United States	**USA**

Scandinavian Interest Titles

Danish-English/English-Danish Practical Dictionary
32,000 entries • 601 pages • 4⅜ x 7 • 0-87052-823-8 •
$16.95pb • (198)

Finnish-English/English-Finnish Concise Dictionary
12,000 entries • 411 pages • 3½ x 4¾ • 0-87052-813-8 •
$11.95pb • (142)

Finnish-English/English-Finnish
Dictionary & Phrasebook
3,000 entries • 200 pages • 3¾ x 7½ • 0-7818-0956-8 •
$11.95pb • (314)

Norwegian-English/English-Norwegian
Concise Dictionary
10,000 entries • 599 pages • 4 x 6 • 0-7818-0199-0 •
$14.95pb • (202)

Norwegian-English/English-Norwegian
Dictionary & Phrasebook
3,500 entries • 275 pages • 3¾ x 7½ • 0-7818-0955-X •
$11.95pb • (415)

Swedish-English/English-Swedish
Standard Dictionary
70,000 entries • 804 pages • 5½ x 8½ • 0-7818-0379-9 •
$19.95pb • (242)

Swedish-English/English-Swedish
Dictionary & Phrasebook
3,000 entries • 135 pages • 3½ x 7½ • 0-7818-0903-7 •
$11.95pb • (228)

All prices subject to change without prior notice. **To purchase Hippocrene Books** contact your local bookstore, call (718) 454-2366, visit www.hippocrenebooks.com, or write to: Hippocrene Books, 171 Madison Avenue, New York, NY 10016. Please enclose check or money order, adding $5.00 shipping (UPS) for the first book and $.50 for each additional book.